REAL WORLD
LATIN AMERICA

Edited by the *Dollars & Sense* Collective and the
North American Congress on Latin America (NACLA)

dollars&sense

Real World Latin America

Edited by Daniel Fireside, Pablo Morales, Alejandro Reuss,
Christy Thornton & Chris Tilly

ISBN: 978-1-878585-73-8

Published by:
Dollars & Sense
Economic Affairs Bureau
29 Winter Street
Boston, MA 02108
(617) 447-2177
www.dollarsandsense.org

Production: Christy Thornton

Printed in the United States

CONTENTS

INTRODUCTION

This book is intended primarily for students taking classes (mostly at U.S. colleges and universities) in Latin American studies or history, the economic development or political economy of Latin America, or other disciplines dealing with the region today. Latin America is a major world region, and it is important for U.S. students to gain at least a basic understanding of its countries' diverse histories, contemporary politics, and relationships to the United States.

Some Latin American countries are, of course, among the United States' geographically closest neighbors. Many are tied closely to the United States economically. Mexico and Brazil rank among the top 15 countries in total trade with the United States, and Mexico is in the top 10 in total U.S. direct investment. Latin Americans also form a growing proportion of the U.S. population. Over 17 million people born in Latin America—and over 45 million people of "Hispanic" backgrounds—live in the United States. U.S. leaders, in addition, have often regarded Latin America as the United States' "sphere of influence" or "backyard," fueling repeated conflict and lasting friction with Latin American governments and peoples.

THE DIVERSITY OF THE REGION

For the purposes of this book, "Latin America" refers to Mexico, Central America, South America, and the numerous islands of the Caribbean. While the dimensions of the region may vary from one definition to another—some exclude the Caribbean altogether, others include only Spanish- and Portuguese-speaking countries, and so on—by any definition it is a large and incredibly diverse region.

Latin America stretches over 6,000 miles from Tijuana, Mexico, on the border with the United States, to Punta Arenas, Chile, at the southern extreme of South America. It includes 33 independent states, as well as 16 inhabited dependencies of other countries (including territories controlled by France, the Netherlands, the

United Kingdom, and the United States).

In addition to Spanish and Portuguese, French, English, and Dutch are widely spoken in some Latin American countries, results of the region's colonial past (and in some places, present). Latin America is also home to speakers of hundreds of indigenous languages. Some of the region's indigenous languages and language groups—including Aymara (Bolivia), Guaraní (Paraguay), the Mayan languages (Guatemala, Mexico), Nahuatl (Mexico), and the Quechuan languages (Argentina, Bolivia, Ecuador, Peru)—as well as creole languages, such as Haitian Creole and Jamaican Patois, have speakers numbering in the millions.

Latin America is ethnically diverse. Its population includes descendants of colonists from Spain, Portugal, and other European countries, more recent immigrants from various parts of the world and their descendants, indigenous peoples whose ancestors have lived on these continents for millennia, and descendants of people kidnapped in Africa and brought as slaves to the Americas. It includes people whose heritage, of course, traces to two or more of these groups.

The region includes both extensive rural areas and some of the most populous urban areas in the world. Four metropolitan areas in Latin America—Buenos Aires, Mexico City, Rio de Janeiro, and São Paulo—are home to more than 10 million inhabitants each. Overall, more than 75% of Latin America's people live in urban areas. The region, however, also includes more than a few countries, mainly in Central America and the Caribbean, that are still majority rural.

For students new to Latin American studies or history, a good lesson to draw from this book is that Latin America is far too large and complex to sum up with a single simple image. *Real World Latin America* attempts to capture as much of this diversity as possible within the bounds of one relatively thin volume. While the largest and most politically influential countries, like Mexico, Brazil, and Venezuela, get the most coverage, the book also features articles focusing on more than a dozen different nations.

INEQUALITY AND CONFLICT

Social differences in Latin America, as in other parts of the world (the United States included) do not simply involve people of diverse backgrounds and ways of life coexisting side-by-side. Dramatic inequalities of status, wealth, and power, both within and between countries, have shaped the region historically and continue to shape it today.

Latin America includes countries with per capita incomes as high as $14,000 per year and as low as $1,800. The extremes are much further apart, of course, if we compare the wealthiest and poorest individuals, rather than national averages. Using the standard measure of income inequality (the Gini coefficient),

15 Latin American countries ranked 100th of worse out of 126 countries ranked in the 2007–08 *United Nations Development Report*. The wage of the average Guatemalan agricultural worker is about 40 cents per hour. At the other end of the spectrum, about 300,000 people in the region have net wealth (excluding primary residence) of more than $1 million, and about 7,000 have net wealth of over $30 million.

Nor do Latin America's different "racial" or ethnic groups coexist on the basis of rough equality. Across Latin America, as in the United States, one finds mainly people of European backgrounds at the top of social hierarchies of status, wealth, and power, with people of indigenous or African heritage more likely to be at the bottom. According to a World Bank report on countries with large indigenous populations (Bolivia, Ecuador, Guatemala, Mexico, Peru), for example, indigenous people were 10% to 30% more likely to live in poverty. The average monthly income for indigenous people in Mexico was about one fourth that of non-indigenous people.

One also finds men at the top of most social hierarchies. While women increasingly participate in the paid labor force, they often do so in lower-paid and lower-status occupations. In Chile, for example, the average hourly wage for women is about one fourth lower than the average wage for men, despite the fact that wage-earning women in Chile average more years of education than their male counterparts. Women have made some inroads into influential government positions in the region—three Latin American countries (Argentina, Costa Rica, and Cuba) actually rank among the top 10 in the world in terms of the age of women in parliament, in each case between 35% and 40%—but women in positions of power are still everywhere outnumbered by men. The parliaments of 22 Latin American countries have less than 20% women (so does the U.S. Congress, with 17%).

THE HISTORICAL CONTEXT

The articles in this book were all originally published within the last five years. They have been chosen because they remain up-to-date and provide a good snapshot of contemporary Latin America. While many of the articles include historical background on the specific issues and events they describe, together they also touch on several recent, key historical transformations in the region:

- A transition toward elected civilian government, following a period during which military dictatorships dominated the region.
- The rise of "neoliberal" (or "free market") economic policies and the embrace by many of the region's governments of "free trade" and foreign investment, followed by a widespread backlash against these policies.

- The recent electoral victories for "leftist" parties in a number of important Latin American countries, along with the advent of new kinds of movements for social change.
- Shifts in the primary justification for U.S. intervention in the region, from fighting Communism to the "war on drugs" and fighting terrorism.
- Large-scale migration both within Latin America and between Latin America and the United States, and the rise of both anti-immigrant and immigrants-rights movements in the United States.

The ideological distance between the two ends of the political spectrum (between major parties or movements on the far "right" and far "left") is much greater in Latin America than in the United States. Most Latin America's governments defend capitalist economic relations—the private ownership of factories, mines, farms, and other production goods, employment of wage labor, and production for exchange in markets. Even some governing "socialist" parties are content to leave this basic economic structure intact, while enacting some reforms to alleviate the extremes of inequality and poverty. At least two current Latin American governments, those of Cuba and Venezuela, however, espouse what they call a revolutionary brand of socialism. (This is also true of opposition movements in other Latin American countries.) Political views on other issues, such as gender and sexuality, likewise range over a broad spectrum. The Latin American political scene includes "traditionalists" who condemn abortion (illegal in most Latin American countries, with few exceptions), divorce, and homosexuality, but it also includes feminists and proponents of gay liberation. **Chapter 1** introduces the politics of Latin America's left and right with respect to these and other issues.

Between the 1960s and 1990s, about 15 Latin American countries suffered periods of military dictatorship. (The U.S. government supported many of these regimes due to their anti-Communism and friendliness to U.S. corporations.) Dictatorships banned political parties and labor unions, violently put down public protests, made widespread use of torture, and "disappeared" (kidnapped and murdered) political dissidents. In some countries, dictatorships pursued "counter-insurgency" warfare—the suppression of armed rebel movements—almost always involving massacres and other human rights violations against noncombatants, and in some countries (especially Guatemala) going over into genocidal violence against indigenous people. The region was a human rights disaster. Even since the advent of elected civilian government in many Latin American countries during the 1980s and 1990s, the armed forces have often remained politically powerful, sometimes holding an effective veto over the elected government (in what is euphemistically called "limited" or "protected" democracy). While the human rights situation has improved in many, though not all, of the region's countries, political violence and human rights violations remain unacceptably widespread. **Chapter 2** focuses on the politics of armed forces (both public and private) and human rights.

The 1970s and 1980s also saw a dramatic shift in economic policy across Latin America. From the Great Depression of the 1930s to the beginning of this transition, many Latin American countries, while remaining within the general confines of the capitalist system, had embraced relatively high degrees of government economic intervention, mostly with the aim of promoting industrialization. A number of factors—the perceived failures of this approach; the opposition of business owners to labor unions, public employment, and government social welfare protections that sometimes came along with it; and the opposition of multinational corporations and the governments of powerful countries (especially the United States) to policies limiting the opportunities for foreign investment and profit—led to the rise of neoliberal economic policies. **Chapter 3** describes the politics of neoliberalism and so-called free trade, along with other aspects of Latin America's relationship to the global economy.

The recent backlash against neoliberalism has included both grassroots protest movements (e.g., the Zapatista rebellion in Chiapas, Mexico) and the coming to power of political parties, such as in Argentina, Bolivia, Ecuador, and Venezuela, opposing neoliberalism and proposing alternative policies. These parties share a broad view that neoliberal policies have enriched a wealthy few at the expense of workers and the poor, and that they have allowed multinational corporations to exploit the workers and plunder the natural wealth of these countries. (In Brazil and Chile, parties traditionally opposed to neoliberal policies have also come to power, but left these policies largely intact.) **Chapter 4** describes recent alternative economic policies from the heights of the state—including government ownership, redistributive policies, and poverty-alleviation efforts—as well as new forms of economic organization (such as workers cooperatives, farmers' fair-trade and organic-production projects, etc.) from the grassroots.

As noted earlier, various forms of social subordination are widespread in Latin America, as in other parts of the world. The people suffering this subordination, however, have not accepted it passively. There are powerful movements for social change in Latin America. Struggles over land have a long history in the region. The movement of the landless in Brazil stands out as a contemporary example. Both rural and urban workers have organized unions or gone on strike, often facing employer and government repression, both for improved wages and working conditions and as part of broader social movements. Movements of subordinated "racial" or ethnic groups, likewise, have a long history in the region. Today, for example, there are prominent indigenous rights movements in Bolivia, Mexico, and other countries. In recent years, feminist and gay / lesbian / transgender movements have become increasingly vocal in some Latin American countries. Environmental movements, too, are on the rise. **Chapter 5** focuses on such movements across Latin America.

Since 1965, the United States has received large numbers of immigrants, Latin America has become the number-one region of origin, and immigration has reemerged as a top issue in U.S. politics. Anti-immigrant movements and politicians have called (sometimes successfully) for the elimination of government benefits and public services to immigrants, the construction of a wall along the U.S.-Mexico border, raids at workplaces where immigrants work, and mass deportation of undocumented immigrants. Some U.S. policy makers call for a "guest worker" program, in some cases including a "path to citizenship," usually along with heightened border enforcement. Immigrants themselves, meanwhile, have built a vocal rights movement in recent years. And although many U.S. readers are likely to think of immigration to the United States first when they think about migration issues, most Latin American migration in recent decades has actually taken place within Latin America, from rural to urban areas within a single country or across borders within the region. **Chapter 6** includes articles on both Latin American migration to the United States and intra–Latin American migration.

The politics of land, natural resources, and the environment in Latin America belie common stereotypes about both the region and environmental politics. Environmental protection, contrary to some views, is not a "luxury good" that people in poor countries can ill-afford and do not want. Struggles over the control of land and other natural resources have a lengthy history in the region, long predating "modern" environmentalism, and they continue in today's struggles over water rights, pollution, and other environmental issues. Nor do the region's environmental movements find support only among affluent, highly educated urbanites. Environmental issues powerfully intersect with the struggles of small farmers, indigenous people, and others who do not fit stereotyped images of environmentalists. **Chapter 7** focuses on environmental and natural-resource struggles in the region.

The United States has a long history of conflict with its Latin American neighbors. Repeated U.S. interventions in the region (including military invasions, support for armed invasions or insurrections by allied armed groups, support for military coups and regimes, aid for counter-insurgency warfare, financing of favored parties in elections, etc.) bear witness to U.S. policy makers' view of Latin America as the United States' "backyard." During the Cold War, especially after the Cuban revolution of 1959, U.S. leaders largely justified such interventions by claiming they were fighting the spread of Communism (or Soviet and Cuban influence). After the fall of the U.S.S.R., the drug war and (especially since 2001) anti-terrorism have become the main justifications, though recent interventions have employed similar tactics (and, according to some critics, mask the same aims) as earlier interventions. **Chapter 8** focuses on these aspects of U.S.–Latin American relations.

A POINT OF VIEW

The contents of this book are drawn from two publications, *NACLA Report on the Americas* (published by the North American Congress on Latin America) and *Dollars & Sense* magazine. Both focus on contemporary political and economic affairs. *NACLA Report* deals specifically with Latin America and U.S.–Latin America relations. *D&S* focuses on U.S. and international economic issues, and has a long history of outstanding coverage of Latin America, especially on the region's land and labor issues, position in the world economy, and economic relations with the United States.

Like all commentary or analysis on social issues, the contributions collected in this volume come from a particular point of view. *NACLA Report* and *D&S* are both unapologetically "left" publications, sharing a point of view inspired by solidarity with the struggles of poor people, workers, racial and ethnic minorities, women, and others who face economic or social subordination, as well as with the people of countries (generally, the lower-income countries) dominated politically and economically by great powers like the United States, or by international institutions that are in turn controlled by such powers.

While *NACLA Report* and *D&S* openly declare their allegiances, they do not limit themselves to sloganeering or sacrifice careful and well-reasoned argument based on an honest and thorough analysis of the facts. The contents should be useful to any student who is interested in serious debate on the burning issues of the day, whether they share these allegiances or not.

CHAPTER 1
THE POLITICS OF
LEFT AND RIGHT

BREAKING WITH THE PAST: A CONVERSATION WITH MARGARITA LÓPEZ MAYA

BY FRED ROSEN
NACLA Report, May/June 2007*

One of Venezuela's most prominent left intellectuals, Margarita López Maya is a historian at the Center for Development Studies at the Central University of Venezuela. She has written extensively on popular protest in Latin America, the region's new political actors, and Venezuela's current socio-political transition. Her most recent book, Del viernes negro al referendo revocatorio *(Alfadil, 2005), is a study of recent Venezuelan history. On the occasion of NACLA's 40th anniversary, she spoke with NACLA's Fred Rosen.*

A few months ago you told BBC News that you saw President Hugo Chávez as a "powerful and extremely contradictory political figure." You praised his determination to deepen democracy and bring full participation and social equality to Venezuela, but you worried about his "desire to be the one who is essential in the process" and his "desire to perpetuate himself in power." How do you see that contradiction playing itself out in Venezuela?

The principal project of Chávez's Bolivarian movement has been to construct a new set of social relations, and he has tried to fulfill the goals of that project. By implementing new policies—above all, social policies—he has promoted the leading, participatory role of the great impoverished majorities of Venezuela. This has strengthened his standing, especially among the poor.

Today in Latin America there are other projects of this type, for example in Bolivia. The Bolivian process may even be stronger and perhaps more concrete than the one in Venezuela. This is because a leader of the indigenous community, Evo Morales, has come to power together with a social movement that is much more organized than the mobilized population that supports Chávez. Morales must answer to a very strong, autonomous social movement, but in Venezuela, there is nothing comparable to which Chávez is accountable. Venezuela has a politically mobilized population, but it is a population that has been mobilized by Chávez himself.

* Denotes date of initial publication.

Chávez's political movement—Bolivarianism or Chavismo—presents itself as the most extreme part of the new Latin American left. This is particularly true of its discourse. It has maintained a very confrontational, very aggressive discourse since Chávez first ran for president in 1998, and it has tended to become even more radical since then.

Chávez has successfully mobilized the poor and excluded to fight for first-class citizenship, and among the great majority of Venezuelans, who had never been able to participate in politics and society, many now feel like full citizens. These mobilizations have created very conflictive processes, and the country is now experiencing a very powerful polarization. Over the past few months it has tended to deepen as Chávez has proposed a new break with the past, essentially the destruction of the very state he himself brought into being with the Constitution of 1999.

Is this "break with the past" embodied in his calls for a "socialism of the 21st century"?

Yes. Chávez was elected in 1998 with the promise of creating a participatory state in which ordinary citizens would play a leading role. He is now proposing to transform the state that he himself began creating when he took office in order to move the country toward this still-undefined "socialism of the 21st century." He has requested and been granted extraordinary powers from the National Assembly to decree a package of new laws that would permit him to take the legislative initiative.

This grant of special powers, called an "enabling law," gives him the power to legislate in 11 areas over the next year and a half. In addition, he has named a presidential commission to propose constitutional reforms. And beyond that, he has announced his desire to move toward a single "united party of Venezuelan socialism." With these three moves, it seems to me that we are heading toward something new, but up to now it hasn't been clear to anybody what that something new will be. We only know it involves moving beyond the Constitution of 1999.

When you say that nobody is clear about where the process is heading, do you really mean nobody? How about the people closest to Chávez or even Chávez himself?

I think that to understand where the process may be heading, especially in light of Chávez's impressive electoral victory in December, we can make use of a concept that has been developed by Ernesto Laclau in his book *On Populist Reason*. I think Laclau's concept of the "empty signifier" has a great deal of explanatory power.

"Socialism of the 21st century" is an empty signifier. It's a program that represents a large number of unsatisfied demands, all of which have been linked—chained to one another—ending up in Chávez's populist discourse.

It's an empty signifier because everybody defines it as they like. In the last election, the people voted massively for the president—one person because socialism of the 21st century will give her a new house, another because socialism of the 21st century will continue the successful and popular social missions, another because she believes in the emancipatory potential of socialism, another because she really likes Cuba. They all define the concept as they understand it. And in reality, as Laclau says, the more popular the concept becomes, the emptier it is of meaning, because it incorporates all the aspirations that people have.

But now that Chávez has won the last election by such a large margin, I believe the concept will begin to take on concrete meaning. The president is beginning to tell us something about the contents of his socialism of the 21st century.

What has he been saying? What do those contents look like?

Well, so far, as we listen to what Chávez has declared, there has been very little clarification of the economic model that goes along with Bolivarianism. In fact, the economic model has been unclear since he took office. But what's clear is that we will see changes in the political sphere and in relations of power.

We have been presented with very concrete political proposals that were discussed during the electoral campaign and that have been gathered together and confirmed as a political program. This includes a proposal for the indefinite reelection of the president. There is also a proposal to eliminate proportional representation, which would eliminate the rights of minority parties to representation in the National Assembly. Another proposal Chávez has announced is the continued creation and strengthening of "popular power," which has its base in the structures of the communal councils that are being organized throughout the country, especially in poor communities.

At this time, these communal councils don't legally depend on any federal structures other than the presidency of the republic. They register with the presidency and receive their funding directly from it. Everything seems to indicate that Chávez wants to strengthen popular power and turn it into a "sixth power" of the state, along with the presidency, the legislature, the judiciary, citizens' power, and electoral power.

This power, it seems to me, is meant to limit the power of the legislature, in the sense of replacing the type of representation that characterizes the National Assembly with the power of people who come directly from the communities and the communal councils that are directly accountable to the president.

These are some concrete manifestations of Chávez's socialism of the 21st century. I think it signals a break with liberal democracy, subordinating legislative and judicial power to the presidency.

Let me give you another example. The Constitution of 1999 created a consultative body called the Council of State to discuss and reconcile questions regarding the constitutional structure of the state and matters of public policy. It is coordinated by the vice president, and composed of five people appointed by the president, plus one appointed by the National Assembly, one by the Supreme Court, and a governor appointed by agreement among the state governors. Chávez did not use this constitutional resource when it came time to propose reforms to the Constitution, but rather preferred to name all the members of the new Presidential Commission for Constitutional Reform by himself, handpicking those who would represent the National Assembly and the Supreme Court without their input.

This clearly represents the intended subordination of the other powers to the presidency. We don't know how the constitutional reform will work itself out legally, but we are seeing this subordination in practice.

And another example: In the recently passed enabling law, Chávez went to the National Assembly to request the power to legislate in 10 areas for a year and a half, and within a week the Assembly abdicated its right to deliberate and ceded to the president everything he asked for plus a few more things he had forgotten about. He had forgotten about hydrocarbons, so the legislature threw it into the package.

So up to now, the content of Chávez's socialism of the 21st century can only be seen in political terms—an attempt to bolster his authority by changing the structures of the state.

Why did the National Assembly abdicate its powers so quickly and so completely? Was it out of an ideological commitment to reconstructing the state, or was it out of personal loyalty to Chávez?

There is a great deal of ideology here, but since Chávez didn't publicly consult anyone beforehand, it's difficult to know what the ideological choices and positions were. Also, we must remember that since most of the opposition boycotted the last legislative elections, the National Assembly is 100% Chavista.

Now, the only motive for passing the enabling law for a year and a half, when you have a National Assembly that is 100% Chavista, is that you want to avoid discussion, because the only drawback to bringing these laws to the Assembly is that it would take more time with legislators debating the details.

Most of the members of the Assembly are there—and they know it—because during the primary stage of the last elections, their candidacies were known to have been approved by Chávez. And in the last legislative elections, voters overwhelmingly supported the president. Chávez has immense popular support, but it's a very personal support. And that's what's worrying. Chávez, instead of delegating responsibilities and building institutional support for his political platform, cultivates this support for his personal leadership.

This business of changing the Constitution to allow for indefinite reelection has to do with this cultivation of his personal rule, and reflects the political conception of the "maximum leader." So far, this is all we know about Chávez's socialism of the 21st century.

So there are no connections between these political changes and pending changes in economic and social relations?

In economic terms, Chávez has called for the nationalization of telecommunications and electricity and the broadening of what is called the social economy: cooperatives, "endogenous development centers," small enterprises, and so on. But nationalizations are nothing new in Venezuela, and they are explicitly permitted in the Constitution of 1999. In fact, the nationalization of the phone company, CANTV, is really a renationalization. The same can be said of the different structures that characterize the social economy; they are already considered in the 1999 Constitution. Besides that, as I said earlier, Chávez's proposed economic model has been unclear since he took office, and remains so.

As for social relations, the attraction of Chávez since he was elected in 1998 has been his attempt to create a deepening of democracy based on participation. Almost all of his administration's social policies involve organization and participation. You say, "We need a Cuban doctor here," and the government will facilitate it once you organize a health committee. You say, "We want to own the property on which we built the house we have lived in for 30 years," and the government will give you ownership once you fulfill certain requirements, such as organizing an urban land committee through a citizen assembly. You have the right—and the encouragement—to do all that now. The legal processes are still very slow, but the organizing has met with a great deal of success.

There is no indication that "socialism of the 21st century" will transform any of this, except perhaps that it will try to weave all the new social organizations into the communal councils and have them link not to the local government but directly to the presidency. It looks like an attempt to create a vertical, centralized structure that will weaken traditional local and regional levels of government.

In the popular sectors there is a great deal of enthusiasm for these new rights and abilities to organize, and in general the process has contributed to the strengthening of the social fabric in poor neighborhoods. The missions and the organizing and mobilization facilitated by the communal councils have brought a great deal of hope to poor communities—a hope that people can better their lives and participate in the process of doing so. This is one of the greatest strengths of Chavismo—made possible, of course, by the high oil rents collected by the state treasury.

And is this strength the basis of his personal popularity?

Yes, he has come through for the poor. Poverty indicators have improved, and there's a general sense that the quality of life for the poor has gotten better. And large numbers of people feel included in Venezuelan society for the first time. Popular expectations have risen under Chávez, along with his popularity. Rising hopes and expectations may be reflected in the low rate of abstention in the last presidential election. More people apparently think they have a stake in the country.

Measures of inequality, however, have remained unchanged, which is disquieting if we think ahead to the next drop in the price of oil.

The oil bonanza, by the way, has improved the lives of the middle class as well. If you go to the fashionable parts of the east side of Caracas, you'll see lots of new imported cars and crowded high-priced restaurants. It's like life in the boom years of the 1970s, under Carlos Andrés Pérez, which is also disquieting. We may simply be living off our oil rents.

What's the role of the military in all this?

Well, from the beginning, the Chavista movement, especially the MVR [Chávez's party, the Fifth Republic Movement], has considered itself to be a popular-military alliance. It's true that over the years the MVR has softened its military tone and adopted a more civilian profile, but Chávez has continued to make use of the military in various civic projects, like the missions, especially the state-subsidized grocery stores called Mercal. This was critical during the opposition's oil strike a few years ago when soldiers took on a large number of civilian tasks and kept the economy from coming to a standstill.

Chávez stays close to many of his military *compañeros*. He likes to rely on people with military training because they are accustomed to giving and following orders.

Chávez has become a key player in international politics. His calls for Latin American integration, his access to plentiful oil revenues, and his standing up to the United States have made him a hero in some parts of the world. How do

you see his role in Latin America?

Just as Venezuela is politically polarized, so is the world, and Chávez does well in polarized situations. He has created a self-image as a little David up against a big Goliath, but it's hard to say how much success he has had, or how much influence he has had in other countries.

His pugnacious discourse seems to have had great effect in already polarized countries like Bolivia and Ecuador, but less so in Peru, which has recently come out of a period of authoritarianism and whose voters last year were more in the mood for peace and compromise.

And even in Venezuela itself, polls have shown that people don't like the confrontational language he uses with the United States, especially since over 60% of Venezuela's oil revenues come from sales to U.S. markets. Nevertheless, there is general support for his alliances and for his drive toward Latin American independence and integration.

In general, he has been very careful to maintain amicable relations with other leaders in the region, even with Álvaro Uribe, the conservative president of Colombia. Center-left presidents like Brazil's Lula and Argentina's Kirchner tend to keep their distance from his confrontational rhetoric, but clearly appreciate him for widening the space for permissible dissent. Maybe that's his key international role, to keep widening the boundaries for dissent.

And it works both ways. He knows he needs to keep the more moderate left, especially in Brazil, on his side. He knows that without his close alliance with Lula's Brazil, he loses weight in the international arena.

Economic integration is an important theme for Latin America right now, and Chávez has used his oil money to good political advantage, helping Argentina out of its financial crisis, for example, by purchasing a major part of its debt, and offering favorable oil deals to countries throughout the Americas. He has been very good at rekindling the Latin American "imaginary" and raising the region's self-esteem. He has also been a key force in pushing for more regional cooperation by raising credible proposals for integrating the region's economies.

Finally, can you tell us whether there has been any opposition to what you have called the "cultivation of personal rule" within the broad Chavista movement?

So far there has been a lot of grumbling but no organized political expressions of dissent within the Chavista political culture.

When Chávez spoke of the necessity of a single united party on the left, for example, the smaller parties of the Chavista coalition reacted cautiously. It was clear they did not like the prospect of getting incorporated into one big party.

Chávez's party, the MVR, has always been his own personal instrument, and as such, voiced no objections, but the smaller parties would like to play a role in shaping the debates and did not immediately respond.

The president responded to their hesitation by saying that he didn't have time to wait for an answer, that the need for action was urgent, and that by the time the next electoral process began, the smaller parties would have to decide whether they were in or out of the new united party—and therefore in or out of his government. Otherwise, criticisms have come from previously pro-Chávez intellectuals on the left, like myself. This has been difficult, but I can't go along with this growing authoritarianism. The situation is very dangerous. Chávez has developed a vertical relationship with the people. He is hated by the opposition but venerated and adored by his followers. Many people respond to our criticisms by saying, "How can you say that? We love our president."

On the other hand, many Chavista militants have told us not to stop talking.

CUBAN DEVELOPMENT
IN THE BOLIVARIAN MATRIX

BY PEDRO MONREAL
NACLA Report, January/February 2006

Last summer, the Havana airport buzzed with traffic. Caracas had become the most connected city to Havana, with Venezuela quickly becoming one of the top senders of travelers to the island. Most of the Venezuelans arriving at the airport came to the island seeking medical attention; in the opposite direction, thousands of Cuban doctors were leaving for Venezuela. The scene signaled a new pattern of Cuba's participation in the global economy.

Cuba's main airport had quickly gone from being the port of entry for Europe and Canada's sand-and-sun enthusiasts to becoming the country's veritable hospital waiting room. Several tourist establishments began housing medical patients from Venezuela and other Latin American and Caribbean countries, while thousands of young Cubans were finding new jobs in the health care sector. The traditional tourist industry still remained the primary source of exchange, but it was increasingly evident that Cuba's "professional services"—mostly in health care—might soon become the island's top export activity.

This marks an important shift from just 15 years before. In 1990, the island was an exporter of sugar, minerals, other primary resources and semi-processed goods, as it had been for most of the century. But by the latter half of the 1990s, a large part of the island's economy rested on export services in tourism. Now the Cuban economy is undergoing yet another transformation, favoring export services with the intensive use of the island's wealth of human capital. Among many potential explanations for this last shift, two undoubtedly stand out: a half-century of successful programs geared at the creation of human capital; and the mutually beneficial agreements between Cuba and Venezuela—which I call "the Bolivarian Matrix."

Though it has yet to cover the totality of the two countries' economic integration, the Bolivarian Alternative for the Americas (ALBA) is conceived as a much larger process of alternative integration for Latin America and the Caribbean, toward which it could continue to evolve. To this end, the ALBA has taken notable strides with specific, complementary advancements through the PetroCaribe and PetroSur energy agreements, the TeleSur television channel, as well as programs for extending medical assistance to the poor citizens of a growing list of countries.[1] The Bolivarian Matrix has already made significant changes in Cuba's international insertion, with tangible results in economic growth as well as a gamut of other economic indicators—national disposable income, balance of trade, balance of payments, foreign exchange reserves, and others.

Indeed, despite record energy prices, the impact of various hurricanes, a prolonged drought, and the tightening economic blockade by the U.S. government, the Cuban economy's recovery is in full swing. Official Cuban figures, which generously calculate the impact of social services, project a 9% growth rate for 2005. And using the more conservative metrics applied by the United Nations' Economic Commission on Latin America and the Caribbean (CEPAL), the growth rate would still be a healthy 5%.[2]

However, the economic recovery must be understood keeping in mind at least three notes of caution. First, the recovery has not—at least, not yet—completely overcome the hurdles created by the crisis of the early 1990s: The population's relative consumption levels remain depressed, while the state of the country's productive sectors is still deplorable. Second, the current recovery is a starting point, but is not in itself sufficient for steering the country toward the path of economic development and massive socioeconomic transformation that it needs. And last, economic reactivations—like any growth process in an underdeveloped country—are always subject to the vicissitudes of external dynamics and actors.

Despite these weaknesses, the upturn in the economic cycle registered in 2004 and especially in 2005 has had immediate impacts. The recovery's recent acceleration—in good part courtesy of the Bolivarian Matrix—has allowed for the expansion of a series of social programs, particularly in the areas of education, health, housing, employment, and social security. Many of these programs existed as part of the government's "heterodox policies of social expenditures under conditions of restricted finances" (the phrase preferred by Cuban planning ministry officials) enacted during the most acute moments of economic crisis since the collapse of Communism in Europe. Nonetheless, it is beyond question that the Bolivarian Matrix has been the single most important factor leading to the Cuban government's recently flourishing social programs.

Broadly speaking, the Bolivarian Matrix is Cuba's current vehicle for a "pro-development" pattern of international insertion. In past decades, the island's foreign economic relations were largely based on the understanding that direct international involvement in world capitalist markets was a fundamentally precarious endeavor. In certain periods, as during the "Five-Year Plans" of the 1970s and 1980s, Cuba was relatively successful at maneuvering the international context in a way that facilitated its development. But with the collapse of the Soviet Union and accelerated globalization of the 1990s, direct international engagement became no longer an option, but a necessity.

What kind of long-term pro-development strategies, then, would suit Cuba's particular form of underdevelopment? Cuba is in many ways a typical export economy—highly specialized in producing commodities for foreign markets, leaving only a tiny portion of production to be directed at internal markets. (Beach tourism can be considered a kind of commodity that fits this pattern.) Such excessive specialization impedes the diversification of production, sapping the country of its ability to supply its own capital goods—the machinery or tools, for example, or other things used to make more valuable, exportable products. Without a productive sector of capital goods, internal savings don't automatically become investments, making the country structurally incapable of completing the production process on its own. Under these conditions, exports play a crucial "investment function."

In the last 30 years the central component of Cuba's pattern for international insertion was through import substitution industrialization (ISI), reducing dependence on imports by replacing them with locally produced goods. Substituting imports helps diversify a nation's productive base, including its production of capital goods, while export substitution—a much more recent development for Cuba—allows the replacement of traditional commodities with more profitable, value-added exports. Due to the structural incapacity of producing the capital goods it needs, the development strategies of a country like Cuba should include programs of both import and export substitution. Both can be complementary, despite tensions that often emerge as they essentially compete for the same limited investment resources.

Cuba has adapted its ISI model to distinct historical periods in trying to create a "pro-development" international environment. During the Five-Year Plans—mainly between 1975 and 1990—Cuba's entry into the international economy was largely driven by the benefits it enjoyed from its membership in the Council of Mutual Economic Assistance (Comecon), the economic organization of Communist states. Although Cuba continued its economic relations with global capitalist markets, the vast majority of its economic ties were politically and economically determined by the preferential arrangements garnered from its Comecon membership. Comecon's combination of trade deals, preferential prices, credits, technical assistance, and the massive transfers of resources from the European bloc, created a hugely favorable context for Cuba's development.

After the Soviet collapse, ISI remained the central plank of Cuba's development, but having lost the assistance of Europe's Communist states, the country's pattern of international insertion was obviously forced to change. Cuba made a vast and quick push into the global economy, mostly by incorporating a few sectors of the economy into global value chains—value-adding activities at different stages of the supply chain. Emphasis was placed on products and services that intensively used the island's natural resources: sugar, mining, and tourism. Access to family remittances from abroad, foreign direct investment, and commercial credits were other important mechanisms for Cuba's direct move into the global economy.

This shift kept the economy afloat, even producing a slight turnaround from the very depressed levels of the early 1990s. But its long-term meaning for development is less clear. Perhaps the most significant contribution was that it caused a partial recovery and modernization of some ISI activities. Remittances and tourism, for example, helped create internal hard currency markets that, in turn, led to greater demand for national industry.

By 2002 to 2003, however, it became increasingly clear that direct engagement in the global economy was not generating an ISI process large enough to function as the centerpiece of a development strategy. Under these circumstances, export substitution presumably offered an alternative, but which new exports could drive this change? Despite Cuba's vast pool of human capital, new exports (with few exceptions, such as the pharmaceutical industry) had failed to materialize.[3]

By 2004–05 a new transformation in Cuba's model of international economic insertion had begun to emerge. In this pattern there is a dual movement, whose components coexist for the moment in almost equal proportions: direct insertion into the global economy and the Bolivarian Matrix. The first component has basically economic determinants, or a "pro-business" strategy not automatically conducive to Cuba's national development. The latter has essentially "pro-development," political determinants, stemming from the substantial, and somewhat abrupt, recent expansion of the bilateral Comprehensive Cooperation Agreement signed in 2000 by Cuba and Venezuela. To be sure, Cuba also has agreements with other countries (China, for instance), but they are much more limited in scope and scale than the deal with Venezuela.

The Bolivarian Matrix provides both countries the best opportunity in recent years for an international context conducive to the design and application of development strategies. Obviously, schemes of direct insertion into the global economy are also based on political considerations. But what is different about the Bolivarian Matrix are the ideological assumptions, the social interests, and the quality of institutions upon which these political determinations are based.

The agreement has established mechanisms for collaboration in approximately two dozen sectors and has provided Cuba with advantages in significant areas: energy provision with preferential rates, generous credits for imports, loan concessions for investments, the creation of joint enterprises, the establishment of an expansive program for the export of Cuban medical services, and the creation of protected markets for some Cuban exports, such as medical equipment and software, among others.

The Bolivarian Matrix offers Cuba a chance to move from a primary export economy toward successive development-centered options. Its most positive effect in the short term is to strengthen external demand, thereby compensating for Cuba's structural incapacities. It does so by generating immediate and stronger economic growth, allowing a greater portion of economic surpluses to be invested for the future.

More specifically, the Bolivarian Matrix expands the "investment function" of exports in the economy by spurring the growth of more valuable exports—primarily, health care services. It also reduces the costs of several imports, such as the preferential rates and deferred payments on energy that Venezuela provides. Cuba is also able to reduce the relative weight of exogenous factors by gaining a margin of leverage that it can use in determining export prices—through negotiations on the price of medical services, for instance. Agreements establishing medium- and long-term stabilization also mitigate the normal oscillations of foreign trade.

In sum, by favoring the substitution of exports, the Bolivarian Matrix has increased national investment and improved Cuba's ability to set the terms of trade—both critical factors for short-term economic growth and development. What's more, Cuba has achieved these to a greater extent than would have been possible through only a direct insertion into the global economy.

Precisely evaluating the performance of the Bolivarian Matrix from 2004 to 2005 remains difficult because public data are not yet available. Nonetheless, it seems indisputable that the Bolivarian Matrix has provided Cuba the first opportunity in the last 15 years to undertake a sustainable process of ISI. During the country's direct insertion into the global economy in the 1990s, export substitution was possible—though not necessarily optimal—while a solid base for ISI never materialized. The long-term measure of the Bolivarian Matrix's contribution turns on its ability to help Cuba overcome the structural limitations of an export economy by encouraging an ISI process based on the internal production of capital goods and the concomitant expansion of organizational and technological capacities.

Within the dual framework, the two main mechanisms driving Cuban development—ISI and export substitution—have different possibilities. Export substitution can occur in both components of international insertion, but the Bolivarian Matrix favors a greater role for investments in this process, encouraging a broader spectrum of new exports. A solid and vigorous ISI strategy, on the other hand, is only viable for Cuba within the context of the Bolivarian Matrix.

Moving forward, Cuba must decide on the emphasis it will put on export substitution, as well as on the methods it will use to carry it out. In the short term, Cuba will likely continue focusing on exporting service professionals—again, mostly in health care—but there is a lack of emerging new exports in industry, an area in which Cuba counts on a deep reservoir of human capital. Also, when one considers the emphasis placed on service-based export substitution, on the one hand, and the internal expansion of social services, on the other, it might seem that Cuba is headed in a worrisome direction—toward an over-development and dysfunctional dependence on the "tertiary," or service, sector. Such a scenario is not inevitable, but active policy interventions would be needed to avoid it.

A significant challenge will be creating a productive sector of capital goods that takes advantage of the "internal" economies of scale resulting from the integration of the Cuban and Venezuelan markets. Coordinated industrial policies would be extremely beneficial to these processes. For example, the cooperation of productive branches of capital goods between countries allows them to bank on their complementarities while assuring that their domestic needs are met. Another challenge will be creating new value-adding industrial processes for a relatively broad spectrum of products within the Bolivarian Matrix, as well as incorporating certain industrial activities into global value chains. Again, by taking advantage of complementarities, global value chain activities can be localized. Cuba will also find it difficult to significantly reduce its import coefficient (i.e., the share of its domestic economy that's dependent on imports), and to increase investment multipliers (the change in national income caused by each unit of investment), which helps boost both employment and income generation.

Three concrete problems must also be tackled. First, Cuba needs to address shortcomings in the domestic production of foodstuffs, a crucial aspect if it is to reduce the import coefficient. Second, the growth of internal markets will require an increase in personal incomes, which is key in creating the demand dynamics needed for industrial upgrading and the construction of a productive sector of capital goods. And last, Cuba must stimulate innovation in sectors that already count on significant amounts of internal demand—namely, production, processing, and food distribution.

The prospects for development in Cuba are not self-evident. The advantages of the Bolivarian Matrix are clearly substantial, even at this early stage, but they still fall below their ultimate potential. A second stage may help correct some of Cuba's current imbalances—the disproportionate emphasis on services, for instance— while at the same time thwart potential pitfalls like the deindustrialization and over-tertiarization of the economy. But this will only be possible if a robust plan of reindustrialization—one capable of producing new exports and, above all, capital goods—assumes the forefront of a development strategy. Only then will the country be better equipped to successfully confront whatever the international arena throws its way.

Translated from the Spanish by NACLA.

NOTES

1. Strictly speaking, evaluating the prospects of the ALBA—which exceeds the scope of this article—should include scenarios that contemplate its stagnation and even its disappearance. Nonetheless, this article assumes the Bolivarian Matrix will continue providing Cuba a favorable context for its international insertion, for at least the next 10 years.
2. CEPAL, "Cuba: evolución económica durante 2004 y perspectivas para 2005," Document LC/MEX/L.664 (Mexico City, 2005).
3. Pedro Monreal and Julio Carranza, *Dilemas de la globalización en el Caribe: hacía una nueva agenda de desarrollo en Cuba* (Mexico City: Siglo XXI Editores, 2004).

THE JAMAICAN MOMENT: NEW PATHS FOR THE CARIBBEAN?

BY BRIAN MEEKS
NACLA Report, May/June 2006

It is evident that Latin American politics has made a decisive shift to the left. The startling presidential triumph of Evo Morales in Bolivia is only the latest in a series of electoral victories that has seen the rise and consolidation of left-leaning governments in several South American countries and, soon, possibly Mexico. This tendency is certainly not monolithic. The administration of Luiz Inácio Lula da Silva in Brazil, for instance, with its significant compromises with global capital, occupies an entirely different space from that of Hugo Chávez with his aggressive use of Venezuelan oil revenues to loosen Latin American and Caribbean reliance on traditional avenues of finance. Equally, Néstor Kirchner's attempts to chart a relatively autonomous path out of debt for Argentina is substantially different from the policies inherited by Michelle Bachelet in Chile, where social democracy continues to embrace "globalization" with some—albeit, ambiguous—success.

Similar tendencies have not so far been manifest in the Caribbean. Aside from the singular example of socialist Cuba and the stymied attempt at populist mobilization in Haiti under Jean-Bertrand Aristide, Caribbean governments since the collapse of the Grenadian Revolution in 1983 have largely avoided radical, transformational politics. From the Bahamas in the north, through Jamaica to Trinidad and Guyana in the south, there has been widespread adherence to the Washington Consensus and to neoliberal policies of structural adjustment.

In the Jamaican context the apparent stasis of the Caribbean's broader economic, social and political moment can be described as "hegemonic dissolution."[1] The term describes a situation where the old hegemonic alliance is unable to rule in the accustomed way, with alternative and competitive modes of hegemony from below equally unable to decisively place their stamp on the new and fluid situation. It also entails a disconnection between significant sections of the population and the formal order, toward which they no longer feel any loyalty, and which they perceive to have disrespected them repeatedly and to be unable to provide many with the modicum of a decent livelihood. Jamaica provides a compelling case for examining this trend, because the problems and possible ways forward—however tentative—have materialized most clearly.

As the Caribbean has become more firmly entrenched in the reformulated networks of global capital that have come to be termed "globalization," emphasis on primary exports has shifted toward economies based on services, tourism, and the remittance of income from emigrants working in the North. Beyond the legal economy, an entire sub-economy of gray and illegal activities, including drug transshipment, money laundering, extortion, and even kidnapping has mushroomed. The exact size of this sector is difficult to measure; however, based on the Jamaican experience, the popular demonstrations that have followed the arrest of purported gang leaders suggest that entire communities are dependent on the illegal economy for survival.

To assume, however, that the effects of globalization on the small states of the Caribbean have been uniformly negative would be a grave error. Some of the smallest states in the region—and particularly those still tied to their respective colonial powers—have certainly prospered, at least in terms of macroeconomic indicators. Thus, for instance, the tourism and offshore banking economies of the Cayman Islands and the British Virgin Islands have grown exponentially in the last three decades, while many of their larger neighbors have languished with little growth. Trinidad and Tobago has also experienced remarkable growth amid rising prices for its oil and the development of its extensive natural gas reserves. Barbados, after a brief recession in the early 1990s, implemented a "social partners" arrangement—basically, a tripartite pact between government, the private sector, and labor—that is partially accountable for the resumption of robust growth, placing Barbados in 2004 ahead of all its neighbors and 30th in the world on the UN Development Program's Human Development Index.[2]

The existence of a number of relative success stories within the region—as problematic as the notion of success may be—is certainly one reason why radical trends have vegetated in the past two decades, but there are also many other factors at work.

The paralyzing legacy of the abrupt end to the Grenadian Revolution, with the killing of Prime Minister Maurice Bishop, remains a formidable obstacle. When soldiers of his own People's Revolutionary Army executed Bishop in 1983, the Caribbean left suffered a mortal blow. The sudden collapse of Grenada's Revolution and subsequent U.S. invasion was not an instance of electoral defeat, as eventually happened in Nicaragua, or a purely military defeat in which the rump of the insurgency regroups and engages again under different circumstances. In Grenada, the instance of fellow revolutionaries killing the popular leader of the movement vilified the notion of radical change altogether and placed it outside the realm of viable options.

The end of the Cold War had multiple effects in the region. The fall of the Soviet Union and "really existing socialism" in Eastern Europe put an end to the notion of "socialist orientation" as an alternative path of development for Third World states. More specifically, the dramatic shrinkage of the Cuban economy as it entered the "special period" in the 1990s sent the decisive signal that Cuba's "basic needs" socialism was no longer on the agenda.[3]

In Jamaica, the decisive turn of Michael Manley and the People's National Party (PNP)—from a policy of resistance to one of engagement with global capital in the mid-1980s—closed the door to alternatives, as the two dominant parties resumed the consensual pattern of rule that had existed before Manley's initial rise to power.[4]

The massive migration of Caribbean citizens—mostly to the United States and Canada but also, depending on colonial connections, to Britain, France, and Holland—had multiple consequences. The social and political tensions that would have arisen from the presence of large numbers of well-educated but unemployed young people were partially alleviated. And to the extent that these migrants were able to get jobs in the North and send remittances home, emigration helped relieve some of their families' immediate material problems. However, as Prachi Mishra suggests in a recent International Monetary Fund (IMF) study, the scale of migration flows has deprived the region of a significant proportion of its skilled workers. Between 1965 and 2000, Caribbean countries lost an average of 70% of their college-trained workforce to developed countries. Individual cases are even more illustrative: Guyana lost 89% and Jamaica, 85%.[5] Further, as Mishra concludes, remittances, seen by many analysts as an economic lifeline, have not compensated for the loss in productivity resulting from the mass exodus of well-trained citizens. More critically, none of the statistics measure the loss of "social capital" in the sense of absent parents, teachers, community leaders, and role models. On balance, then, migration has eased some social tensions, while laying the basis for longer-term alienation and dissatisfaction. Indeed, a generation of youth now enters adulthood without the typical nurturing provided by a community, only connected to family by the narrow material nexus of "the moneygram."

Beyond the existence of some models of relative success and the absence of a vibrant politics of radical resistance, there is, however, a wider, more textured picture. Trinidad and Tobago's economic buoyancy has been accompanied by social and ethnic tensions reflected in a seemingly out-of-control crime rate. Guyana, on the South American continent, is certainly the richest "Caribbean" country on the basis of its known natural resources, but remains mired in a racial standoff between dominant Indian and African communities that has stalled any concerted policy of development. Crime and violence in Guyana, too, seem to have taken off on a steep trajectory with no clear end in sight. The emergence of ruthless drug-related gangs is pan-Caribbean in its nature and mushrooms wherever the possibility of new, loosely monitored routes for the transshipment of illicit substances might exist. The smallest territories are often the most vulnerable to this scourge since their security and wider institutional structures cannot withstand the power and resources wielded by wealthy drug lords. It is within this general context of region-wide social alienation coupled with increasing violence, growing unemployment, and a burgeoning drug trade, that the example of Jamaica is useful. In Jamaica, all of these problems are particularly well defined.

In February, government minister Portia Simpson Miller was narrowly elected president of Jamaica's ruling—and nominally social democratic—PNP, making her the nation's new prime minister. Before a massive crowd of cheering supporters outside the PNP headquarters, and amid a sea of the yellow T-shirts of her campaign, Simpson Miller read from the prophet Isaiah, called for party unity, and then issued a message of hope: "I come to you with a promise of hope as we continue the transformation of the PNP and a promise of hope that all of us will unite and work for a better and brighter Jamaica."[6]

She is the first woman and the seventh person to lead Jamaica since its independence in 1962, replacing P.J. Patterson, who is also from the PNP and Jamaica's longest-serving prime minister. In the days following Simpson Miller's victory, commentary in the newspapers and on the talk shows that dominate the Jamaican airwaves did not miss the significance of a woman coming to power, noting she was also someone who was genuinely from Jamaica's grassroots and who—at least in the popular perception—had never severed her linkages with those roots. Most significant, though, were the powerful expectations that the victory seemed to have generated among her supporters and even deep within the rank-and-file of the opposition Jamaica Labor Party (JLP).

Elmore Briscoe, from the working-class community of Vineyard Town, felt that a woman needed the chance to rule the country: "I feel good for a woman. Mek a woman get a chance. I feel crime is going to reduce because she's a woman, she knows how to deal with things, and she's down to earth."[7] Even would-be critics like Winnifred Stoddart, a party delegate and supporter of opposition candidate Peter Phillips, recognized the significance of the victory. Stoddart said the new prime minister stood out from the other higher-ups of the PNP: "They've allowed things to go too low with the workers of the party; they are helping people who can do without it; she's from the grassroots, she understands when somebody says they are hungry."[8]

Jamaica, while far from the "failed state" as described by some of its more pessimistic analysts, has oscillated between periods of marginal growth (as in recent years) to flat periods of no growth at all.[9] It is evident that Jamaica fits into the pattern of many "middle income," non-oil-producing developing countries that respond to the impulses of the global economy, though with a broadly negative outlook for their prospects in the middle to long term. The Jamaican economy's stagnation can be understood as part of the broader process of hegemonic dissolution, in which the old ruling bloc that defined Jamaica's social and political path in the pre- and immediate post-independence periods is moribund.

Insurgent social forces from below are questioning the terms of the old hegemony across the gamut of symbolic and substantive spheres of the social terrain. For more than a decade, this contestation has manifested itself in the culture wars surrounding the appropriateness of the Jamaican "nation language," a new assertive sense of blackness, and in the quintessential space for popular expression: the dancehall and its music.[10] Jamaican popular music in the post–Bob Marley era has moved from a period mostly defined by the glorification of symbolic wealth and macho sexual conquest (*slackness*) to a more recent period of "consciousness" in which themes of unity, resistance, and rebellion have once more come to the fore.[11]

Artists like Bounty Killer, Sizzla, Anthony B, Capleton, and many more, chant a message of renewed interest in the Rastafarian religion, but with a decidedly militant twist. Perhaps fittingly, one of the newer and most popular voices is Marley's son, Damian "Junior Gong" Marley. In his new album *Welcome to Jamrock*, he raises themes of uprising and revolution that are now part of the stock-in-trade of the contemporary deejays: "Now we foreparents sacrifice enough / Dem blood sweat and tears run like syrup / Any day a revolution might erupt / And the skies over Kingston lighting up / For the new generation rising up."[12]

Marley's lyrics, while located within the sphere of cultural contestation, are however only part of a wider social upheaval, which is increasingly taking more overtly confrontational forms. Three recent incidents, chosen for their locations across widely separated parts of the island, suggest the tensions in the social sphere and the depth of the emotions that have been unleashed.

Under the headline "Rage in Mandeville: Town Loses Its Cool Over Beating of Supermarket Employee," *The Jamaica Observer* describes an incident last January in which popular anger burst into spontaneous demonstrations after the alleged beating of two SuperPlus supermarket employees.[13] The supermarket's director, Jeremy Chen, two of his managers, and two other accomplices reportedly apprehended the employees for stealing three cases of Guinness from the store. Newspaper reports said they whisked the two workers to a nearby house, tied them up, and beat them, even attacking one of the employees with a dog. When Chen and his cohorts were detained and taken to the courthouse, an indignant crowd of protesters arrived to denounce the violent act. Angry crowds even appeared at locations of SuperPlus, Jamaica's largest supermarket chain, forcing many of the stores to temporarily close. Police were called to make sure the situation did not spin out of control. "We are convinced that if we had not acted as we did, they would have burnt down Mandeville," one investigator told the *Observer*.

Similar to Mandeville, the rural district of Farm Town in the parish of St. Ann is not normally associated with popular upheaval, but when a businessman was suspected of involvement in the shooting death of a local resident on February 1 and appeared to be escaping the net of justice, Farm Town erupted.[14] Newspapers called the third day of protests a "rampage," reporting that residents burned down the man's house, two of his cars, his bar, and his liquor store. "The fuming residents," as the *Observer* called them, were demanding that the investigation into the killing be reopened.

The volatile city of Spanish Town, some 15 miles west of Kingston, has gained notoriety as the battleground between two rival gangs: the Clansman, reputedly sympathetic to the PNP, and One Order, to the JLP. When police killed Clansman leader Donovan "Bulbie" Bennett in late 2005, widespread protests and the burning of property led authorities to place the city under curfew. The same thing happened in February 2006, when unknown assailants gunned down One Order leader Andrew "Bun Man" Hope. After his death, in which some residents claimed police involvement, armed men presumed to be One Order members overran sections of the city. "The gangsters also set fire to the town's old courthouse, which was used for sittings of the night court, as well as several cars parked in front of the building," reported the *Observer*. "Irate at the death of their 'leader,' residents shouted support for the torching of the courthouse. They also prevented firemen from putting out the blaze."[15]

These three brief examples—of which there are countless more—share some common features. First, there is the common popular perception, evidently fed by numerous concrete provocations, that there are two categories of law: one for those with power and influence and one for those without. The examples also illustrate a willingness to take popular action for what is conceived to be in the interest of justice. The notion of justice deployed in these instances dictates that if the agents of the law are unable or unwilling to execute it, then it is within the right of the populace to execute the law on their own behalf. Finally, the form of this popular execution of justice includes not only the apprehension of the alleged perpetrators, but also the elimination of their property and, if necessary, the property of other symbolic representatives of the formal and unjust system of law.

The rapidity of the popular mobilizations, the similarity and the severity of the actions taken, particularly in the instances of Farm Town and Spanish Town, all suggest the paper-thin acceptance of legitimacy and the depth of the disconnection. Using the earlier terminology, this might best be described as an advanced phase of hegemonic dissolution. The Jamaican state, and the social bloc that operates within its circles, remains in power, but mounting evidence suggests that its hold is increasingly tenuous.

It is in this moment of advanced hegemonic dissolution that Simpson Miller's ascendancy to a position of leadership has occurred. She has won a party election, buoyed by broad popular support, with a simple message bringing hope to the poor and calling for unity among the people of Jamaica. The problems she faces, however, are formidable. Within her own party, she has few cabinet or senior technocratic supporters with the experience and ability to run the complex machinery of government. She will therefore have to rely on many persons who have been lukewarm or openly hostile toward her ascendancy to power. And within the PNP, the majority of leaders have long been won to the notion that even if it is possible to disagree with the war in Iraq and to protest the expulsion of Aristide from Haiti, there is little room to maneuver around the macroeconomic "certitudes" of the Washington Consensus. She will therefore need the sort of technical talent coupled with political skill that can forge a policy sensitive to job creation and poverty alleviation, conscious of the constraints of global capital and yet willing to initiate hard negotiations with it.

Her support is undoubtedly strongest among the Jamaican poor, but whereas Jamaican working people have shown the ability to mount impressive, spontaneous community mobilizations around local concerns, as in the three instances cited, there is little evidence of deep, layered community-based organization that builds from the local to address national and global issues. The political bases then, for a Bolivia-type movement—like Evo Morales's Movement Toward Socialism (MAS), building on a history of popular militancy and organization around indigenous, trade union and national issues—does not as yet exist. Nevertheless, given conditions in Jamaica and the Anglophone Caribbean, where politics more often than not flows through the conventional channels of the dominant nationalist parties, Simpson Miller's election remains powerfully symbolic.

PNP delegates, riding on a national wave of hostility to "business as usual," have elected a president whom the poor and the dispossessed perceive to be their own. If she chooses to deny her mandate and operate within the tight confines of business as usual, then her widespread popularity will ebb and Jamaica will continue along its rocky path of high interest rates, widening income gaps and low growth. If she chooses, however, to resist such a path, then she may help to initiate a different kind of politics.

Such a trajectory, while not the most likely outcome in the remarkably difficult constraints of the present moment, is nonetheless made possible by the presence of a powerful and palpable desire for a change of direction among the majority of the Jamaican people. If this course is taken, it would have profound consequences not only for Jamaica but also for the wider Caribbean—moving the region toward a deeper democracy, greater accountability, and a new approach to how the local might negotiate with the global in the 21st century.

NOTES

1. Brian Meeks, "The Political Moment in Jamaica: The Dimensions of Hegemonic Dissolution," in Manning Marable, ed., *Dispatches From the Ebony Tower* (Columbia University Press, 2000), 32–52.
2. United Nations Development Program, *Human Development Report 2005* (Oxford University Press), 219.
3. However, the pragmatic response to the sudden termination of Soviet aid saved Cuba from destruction and laid the basis for economic recovery. See Susan Eckstein, "From Communist Solidarity to Communist Solitary," in Aviva Chomsky et al., eds., *The Cuba Reader: History, Culture, Politics* (Duke University Press, 2003), 607–22.
4. For critical discussion of this turning moment in Jamaica and the Caribbean's recent history, see Kari Levitt and Michael Manley, "The Michael Manley/Kari Levitt Exchange," *Small Axe* no.1 (1997): 81–115.
5. Prachi Mishra, "Emigration and Brain Drain: Evidence from the Caribbean," IMF Working Paper WP/06/25 (January 2006), downloaded from www.imf.org.
6. *The Sunday Observer* (February 26, 2006).
7. Ross Sheil, "Church Members React to Victory," *The Gleaner* (February 27, 2006).
8. Howard Campbell, " 'I Dream It . . . ' — Women Respond to Portia Simpson Miller's Historic Victory," *The Gleaner* (February 27, 2006).
9. See, for instance, William Clarke, "The Disappointment of the Promise," *The Sunday Gleaner* (May 22, 2005).
10. Deborah Thomas, "The Emergence of Modern Blackness in Jamaica," *NACLA Report on the Americas* 39, no. 3 (November/December 2005), adapted from *Modern Blackness: Nationalism, Globalization and the Politics of Culture in Jamaica* (Duke University Press, 2004).
11. See, for instance, Carolyn Cooper, *Sound Clash: Jamaican Dancehall Culture at Large* (Palgrave Macmillan, 2004) and Norman Stolzoff, *Wake the Town and Tell the People: Dancehall Culture in Jamaica* (Duke University Press, 2000).
12. Damian "Junior Gong" Marley, "Confrontation," *Welcome to Jamrock*, Tuff Gong/Universal Records 80005416-02 (2005).
13. Garfield Myers, "Rage in Mandeville: Town Loses Its Cool Over Beating of Supermarket Employee," *The Jamaica Observer* (January 20, 2006).
14. Carl Gilchrist, "Violent Protest in Farm Town: Residents Burn Cars, House and Businesses of Man Released by Cops," *The Jamaica Observer* (February 14, 2006).
15. Vaughn Davis, "Spanish Town Erupts Again: Anger Over Gangster Slaying," *The Jamaica Observer* (February 9, 2006).

NEITHER LEFT NOR RIGHT:
SANDINISMO IN THE ANTI-FEMINIST ERA

BY KAREN KAMPWIRTH
NACLA Report, January/February 2008

In October 2006, Nicaragua became one of a handful of countries, including Chile and El Salvador, where abortion is illegal without exception. This included the abolition of what Nicaraguans call "therapeutic abortion," that is, legal abortion under very limited circumstances, especially to save the life of the pregnant woman. A little more than year later, at least 80 women have died because of the new law.[1] Most died as a result of a miscarriage, like 22-year-old Francis Zamora, who died in a hospital in January 2007, leaving behind three children. "They let my daughter die," Zamora's mother told a newspaper, recounting how the doctors had said the laws had changed and that they were required to wait until Francis expelled the fetus before they could perform a lifesaving D and C procedure.

The vote in the Nicaraguan National Assembly that resulted in the new law took place 10 days before the presidential election. The unanimous votes of representatives from the traditional party of the revolution, the Frente Sandinista de Liberación Nacional (Sandinista Front for National Liberation, or FSLN), were critical. Without them, the exception to save the life of the woman, a reform dating to the late-19th-century Liberal revolution of José Santos Zelaya, would not have been overturned. Although the Sandinista representatives had always upheld therapeutic abortion in previous years, they voted against it in 2006 out of fear that the party would otherwise lose the upcoming election.

The subsequent victory of Daniel Ortega, the FSLN's longtime leader and candidate, after 16 years out of power, seemed to confirm this. But there is little reason to believe that FSLN votes in favor of the abortion ban affected the electoral outcome. Most of the Sandinistas I interviewed disagreed with the abolition of therapeutic abortion, but they voted for the FSLN anyway. Similarly, none of the anti-abortion activists I interviewed gave me reason to believe they had voted for the FSLN. In fact, many suggested that the FSLN's vote against therapeutic abortion was only a response to the election, so they voted for one of the two right-wing parties (the Partido Liberal Constitucionalista or PLC, and the Alianza Liberal Nicaragüense or ALN), which better represented their values.

Nationwide, none of the FSLN's strategies—expensive advertising, the rhetoric of love and reconciliation, the electoral alliances with Contras and Somocistas, the alliance with the Catholic Church and various evangelical leaders, the vote against therapeutic abortion—seem to have made any difference. As analysts from the journal *Envío* noted, the FSLN "won without growing," that is, it won with the votes of its traditionally loyal voters, and few others, and it would have lost had the right not been divided between the traditional Liberal Party and the ALN.[2] But whether or not they win votes, electoral strategies have consequences. They set the stage for the government that is to follow, and they may serve to reset the balance of power among different groups in society. The gendered components of Ortega's 2006 electoral strategy certainly had the effect of weakening feminists, who had formed part of the FSLN's base, and strengthening anti-feminists. That strategy also had the consequence of making life more precarious for pregnant women who depend on public health services.

With Ortega's election, Nicaragua joined a regional trend to the left, what has sometimes been called Latin America's "pink tide." In some countries in the region, the pink tide has brought with it a limited expansion of reproductive freedom.[3] But not in Nicaragua. On the contrary, the 2006 election illustrated a second regional trend: the rise of politically sophisticated anti-feminist movements in response to the second wave of feminism. In the Nicaraguan case, these two trends are related.

In 2006, the FSLN seemed to reimagine the legacy of the revolution. And that new vision of what it meant to be a revolutionary was traditional rather than liberation-theology Catholic, anti-feminist rather than feminist. One could question in what sense this legacy of the revolution was truly revolutionary. On the billboards that sprung up everywhere in Nicaraguan cities during the months leading up to the November election, little of the FSLN's traditional red and black was to be seen. Instead, FSLN propaganda used an array of brilliant colors, especially hot pink, and Ortega the Marxist-Leninist in military uniform was replaced by Ortega the practicing Catholic in white shirt and jeans. The rhetoric of peace and reconciliation supplanted that of anti-imperialism and class struggle. In fact, many historic enemies of the FSLN joined the Sandinistas' electoral coalition, most prominently vice presidential candidate, and former Contra commander, Jaime Morales Carazo.

One of many signs that Ortega had changed was his marriage to Rosario Murillo, his partner of 27 years, in a Catholic ceremony presided over by former archbishop Miguel Obando y Bravo, a little more than a year before the 2006 election. Not only did Ortega marry Murillo, the mother of six of his eight children, but he often allowed her to speak for him. Ortega was conspicuously silent when his wife, who also headed his electoral campaign, advocated the abolition of therapeutic abortion, firmly allying herself with the Catholic Church.

In an interview on *Radio Ya*, Murillo was asked about the position of the Gran Unidad Nicaragua Triunfa (Great Nicaragua Unified Triumphs, the electoral coalition to which the FSLN belonged) on therapeutic abortion. "Precisely because we have faith, because we have religion, because we are believers, because we love God above all things . . . for those reasons we also defend, and we agree completely with the church and the churches, that abortion is something that affects women fundamentally, because we never get over the pain and trauma that an abortion leaves us!" She added, "The [Sandinista] Front, the Great Nicaragua Unified Triumphs, says no to abortion, yes to life!"[4] With these words, Murillo cemented the pact with the Catholic Church, and in particular with Obando y Bravo (whom she praised elsewhere in the interview), representing a real shift in the position of the Sandinista party, which had not legalized abortion when it was in power but had never before opposed therapeutic abortion.

But despite long-standing tensions between the leadership of the FSLN and autonomous feminists, it is highly unlikely that the FSLN would have voted to abolish the exception for the mother's life if not for the fact that the election was days away. In other words, the FSLN's newfound opposition to therapeutic abortion does not indicate an ideological shift to the right. What it does show is that, after a decade and a half out of power, and close to a decade of political pacts with the right—with Arnoldo Alemán's Liberal Constitutionalist party and with Obando y Bravo's faction within the Catholic Church—the FSLN was quite willing to oppose its former base in the women's movement, to say nothing of the vast majority of Nicaragua's medical establishment, if that is what it took to return to power. Rather than a shift to the right, it was a shift to cynicism. It was part and parcel of the FSLN's long-term evolution from a revolutionary party to one that is often a personal vehicle for Ortega and his family.

While the vote to abolish therapeutic abortion tells us much about the evolution of the FSLN, it perhaps tells us even more about the evolution of Nicaraguan civil society, both feminist and anti-feminist, in the years following the Sandinista revolution. By 2006, the feminist movement, one of Nicaragua's largest and most effective social movements, was divided. There was no disagreement over the need to defend therapeutic abortion, but the movement was damaged by personality clashes and disagreements regarding language and symbolism. One position, promoted by activists in the feminist organization Puntos de Encuentro, among others, was that therapeutic abortion should be defended using "positive messages." They participated in various vigils dressed in white and carrying candles.

"From the perspective of Puntos," Evelyn Flores, the organization's director of institutional relations, told me in November 2006, "it was very worrisome that other women [from the Movimiento Autonomo de Mujeres, or MAM] were calling for a carnival-style march [i.e., dressing up in costumes]. . . . Later the MAM began to have a public presence with a message that was quite full of negativity: 'murderers,' 'killers of women,' 'you don't know your own laws,' 'don't vote for a rapist.' "

Ana María Pizarro, director of the women's clinic Sí Mujer and member of the MAM, was on the other side of this disagreement over tactics, but she also saw the divide as being over whether radical or moderate strategies were the most effective. In her opinion, the cause had been hurt by the moderation of many members of the women's movement, who over the years took the position that "therapeutic abortion is the maximum demand, and don't even talk about legalizing abortion." The problem from her perspective was not that the tactics were too forceful, but that they were not forceful enough and that organized women would never successfully lobby if they continued to forgive, and vote for, the Sandinista party no matter what it did.

In contrast with the feminist movement, the anti-feminist movement had never been so united and sophisticated as it was in 2006. The activists I identify as "anti-feminist" rarely use that term to describe their own work. Instead, they call themselves pro-family or pro-life. But I contend that the term *anti-feminist* is appropriate for at least three reasons: First, feminist activists also favor families (albeit egalitarian ones), and their work against maternal mortality and domestic violence is clearly pro-life. Second, activists in this movement are not simply social conservatives any more than feminist activists are simply social liberals. In both cases, the movements are centrally concerned with the politics of intimacy and daily life. Finally, the term anti-feminist identifies it as a backlash movement.

Anti-feminist organizations do not compose a "movement" in the same sense that feminist organizations do. Hundreds of Nicaraguan organizations identify with the feminist movement, but a relatively small number of them actively oppose organized feminists. The most extensive list I have seen comprises nine organizations that identified themselves as pro-life and pro-family. So the feminist movement is far more significant than the anti-feminist movement if measured in terms of organizations; however, counting organizations is not the only way to gauge the strength of a movement. In fact, up until Ortega's taking power in early 2007, the anti-feminist movement was more powerful than the feminist movement if power was measured in terms of the movement's access to the Nicaraguan state and to the hierarchy of the Catholic Church.

Probably the most important source of support for the Nicaraguan anti-feminist movement is the Catholic Church as an international organization, and conservative interpretations of Catholic faith more generally. The Nicaraguan Catholic Church is divided between a conservative branch that adheres strictly to Vatican teachings regarding questions of sexuality and reproduction, and a liberation-theology branch that is more concerned with social justice than with individual sexual behavior. Many Nicaraguan feminists trace their histories as activists to the liberation theology movement and continue to identify in some way with a Catholicism informed by liberation theology. In contrast, all of the anti-feminists whom I have interviewed or whose works I have read identify strongly with the hierarchy of the Catholic Church or with conservative evangelical organizations.

Some of the most prominent leaders of the movement are active in international conservative Catholic organizations. For example, former education minister Humberto Belli and Max Padilla, former minister of the family, belong to Opus Dei, and Elida de Solórzano, an adviser to Padilla and founder of Asociación Nicaragüense de la Mujer (Nicaraguan Women's Association, or Animu), told me she is a founding member of Ciudad de Dios, or City of God, a Catholic lay organization.[5] Moreover, Nicaraguan opponents of feminism have been supported by a variety of international organizations. The U.S.-based evangelical organization Focus on the Family has provided materials to the Ministry of Education and to the Asociación Nicaragüense Provida (Nicaraguan Pro-Life Association, or Anprovida), a leading anti-abortion group.[6] Vida Humana Internacional (based in Miami) and the Catholic Church also have provided money and materials to support Anprovida's work, as members of that organization told me, and the Catholic Church in the United States has provided the model for Animu's Proyecto Raquel, aimed at counseling women who have had abortions. Padilla has participated in the activities of the Rockford, Illinois–based World Congress of Families.[7] Finally, the U.S.-based Heritage Foundation has provided support for the work of Padilla and Solórzano.[8]

Government delegations from Nicaragua (headed by Belli and Solórzano) have been some of the most prominent opponents of feminism at the United Nations, especially in the events surrounding the Cairo population conference and the Beijing women's conference.[9] Nicaraguan governmental delegations have been at the forefront of global anti-feminist organizing in alliance with governmental delegations from Argentina and several Muslim countries, right-wing Christian NGOs based mainly in the United States, and the Vatican.[10]

This movement, which is an indirect legacy of the revolution—reacting against the autonomous feminist movement that traces its roots to the revolution—first became identifiable in the 1990s. It was a group of organizations with strong ties to the state, especially to the ministries that deal most directly with personal politics: health, education, and the family. In the years following the Sandinista revolution, one of the anti-feminists' major goals was to abolish Article 165 of the penal code, the article that gave doctors the right to perform therapeutic abortion.

In November 2006, Rafael Cabrera, a gynecologist and president of Anprovida, told me that abolishing Article 165 was a good thing because it was a 19th-century anachronism. In that time before the invention of antibiotics, before tuberculosis had been brought under control, before cardiac problems could be treated, Nicaragua was characterized by what he called "a hostile environment." In the 19th century, pregnancy could threaten a woman's life, and so therapeutic abortion was permitted to allow doctors to try to save patients faced with life-threatening pregnancies. But over the course of the 20th century, that medical environment became less hostile, until the point when, according to Cabrera, all pregnancies could be safely carried to term. I brought up a case of a Nicaraguan woman I knew personally who died at the age of 27 after her first pregnancy caused irreparable heart damage. He dismissed that example, telling me that since she died months after the baby was delivered by cesarean, her death could not be attributed to the pregnancy. Cabrera's position—that therapeutic abortion was never medically necessary, so Article 165 was just a loophole to permit abortion for social reasons—was the most common position among the anti-therapeutic-abortion activists I interviewed, although it was not the only position.

Cabrera and like-minded Nicaraguans had opposed therapeutic abortion for many years prior to 2006. That they succeeded in abolishing that 19th-century medical reform in 2006 cannot be understood outside the electoral context, which abortion opponents had not taken advantage of previously. Perhaps more critically, while there were both Catholic and evangelical abortion opponents, they had rarely worked together. But that started changing in the late 1990s.

Elizabeth de Rojas, a minister with Alianza Evangélica (Evangelical Alliance), explained that her work first came to the attention of traditional Catholic leaders in December 1998, when she helped organize what she called a "crusade" and "campaign" called Festinavidad. More than 300,000 gifts were distributed to Nicaraguan children at this event, gifts that had been provided by supporters of the U.S.-based evangelical minister Franklin Graham. Festinavidad culminated in a massive two-day cultural event in the Dennis Martínez National Stadium. The event attracted press coverage and the attention of Padilla, then minister of the family, Rojas said. Believing that the evangelicals behind this event shared values with traditional Catholic opponents of feminism, Padilla invited Rojas to a meeting at his government office. It was there that she met Solórzano of Animu; Evangelina de Guirola, also of Animu and the founder of Sí a la Vida (Yes to Life); and Cabrera of Anprovida.[11]

This alliance between Catholic and evangelical abortion opponents culminated in a mass march against therapeutic abortion in early October 2006, and the vote in the National Assembly, three weeks later, to abolish the life-of-the-mother exception to the civil code. During the march, a team from the feminist organization Puntos de Encuentro interviewed some of the approximately 200,000 participants. Many agreed with a young woman who explained that, in case of threat to a pregnant women's life, "That would have to be left to God: the mother or the child. If it is put in God's hands, He will decide if the two of them will live or not." But many anti-therapeutic-abortion marchers seemed uncomfortable with the reality of banning the procedure and its logical consequence: letting some pregnant women die.

One teenage girl proposed the pro-choice position (though she did not call it that). "If it is a situation like that," she said, "it would depend on the person. In my case I would prefer to have my child with the risk. Like a personal decision." And a 54-year-old women explained that she was at the march "as the Catholic that I am, to support the ideas of our priests." But if the pregnant woman would die along with her unborn baby? "Yes," she said, "[the abortion] would be just."

For many anti-feminist activists or their supporters, abolishing therapeutic abortion is not the final goal. Instead, it could be seen as part of a broader project of restoring or imposing a particular model of gender relations. Asked about the poor care pregnant women generally receive in the public health care system (which makes the abolition of therapeutic abortion more dangerous than it would be in a country with good pre-natal care), Noel Pereira Majano, congressman from the Liberal Party and president of the National Assembly's Justice Commission, responded:

"One has to keep one's cool in making statements about the effects of abortion. We have to study the causes; there has to be a coordination of governments and state agencies to avoid prostitution and free love. There must be an imploring against the situation of the liberated woman, who thinks she can control all the parts of her body."[12]

Perhaps it is not surprising that a congressman from the right-wing Liberal Party should take this sort of position, although the Liberal Party itself has changed significantly from the days of the Somoza dictatorship, when it was considerably more secular and liberal regarding women than its main rival, the Conservative Party. What is surprising is that this agenda has been furthered with the active support of the FSLN. This alliance between anti-feminism and the nationalist party of the revolution complicates our view of politics. Though we tend to speak of movements as left- or right-wing, liberal or conservative, they may in fact be all of these things at once—simultaneously resisting imperialism, rejecting dictatorship, and promoting gender inequality.

Some have even suggested that it may be time to talk of a "Sandinismo of the right."[13] But that may go too far. Certainly seen from the grassroots, Sandinismo still is a left-wing project. Seen from the perspective of Ortega and Murillo, Sandinismo may be a left-wing project drained of principle or, to put it more kindly, a flexible left-wing project. This is something that arguably has happened to the left across the region.[14] But whether flexible or cynical, the return to the left in Nicaragua does not look very left-wing, at least not from a feminist perspective.

NOTES

1. José Adán Silva, "Un año de muertes y agresiones: más de 80 muertes, justicia retardada y ataques contra movimiento feminista, ONU declara preocupación por proyecciones de aumento en mortalidad materna," *El Nuevo Diario* (October 26, 2007).
2. "Daniel Ortega presidente: del poder 'desde abajo' al gobierno," *Envio* 25, no. 296-297 (November/December, 2006): 7.
3. Stan Lehman, "Brazil Offers Morning-After Pill to Poor," *The Washington Post* (June 26, 2007); James C. McKinley Jr., "Mexico City Legalizes Abortion Early in Term," *The New York Times* (April 25, 2007).
4. "Extracto de la entrevista ofrecida por Rosario Murillo, jefa de campaña del Frente Sandinista de Liberación Nacional, a la emisora Nueva Radio Ya," downloaded from www.izquierda.info.
5. Luis Felipe Palacios, "Cardenal acusa a Belli de pedir que lo retiren: Belli dice que Obando está mal informado, que sólo visitó a sus amigos en El Vaticano," *La Prensa* (December 5, 2002); Opus Dei, "Después de la canonización: el primer sello de San Josemaría" (2002), downloaded from www.opusdei.org.
6. Tom Neven, "Your Tax Dollars at Work in Latin America," downloaded from www.family.org.
7. Max Padilla, "La autonomía de la familia," speech given to the World Congress of Families II, November 15, 1999, Geneva, Switzerland, downloaded from www.thefamily.com.
8. Edgar González Ruiz, "Imperialismo 'profamilia,' la Fundación Heritage," *Red Voltaire* (March 29, 2004), downloaded from www.redvoltaire.net.
9. Humberto Belli, "The Anti-Family Cairo Proposals," *Social Justice Review* (July/August 1994): 113–6; Anick Druelle, "Right-Wing Anti-Feminist Groups at the United Nations" (2000), downloaded from http://netfemmes.cdeacf.ca; Ana María Pizarro, "We Urgently Need a Secular State for the Sake of Women's Health," *Envío* 22, no. 266 (2003): 29–38.
10. Druelle, "Right-Wing Anti-Feminist Groups at the United Nations"; Elina Vuola, "God and the Government: Women, Religion, and Reproduction in Nicaragua," paper presented at the 2001 meeting of the Latin American Studies Association, Washington, D.C. (September 6–8, 2001).
11. On these organizations, see Karen Kampwirth, "Resisting the Feminist Threat: Antifeminist Politics in Post-Sandinista Nicaragua," *NWSA Journal* 18, no. 2 (summer 2006): 73–100.
12. Quoted in Lourdes Arróliga, "FSLN, ALN, PLC alineados con Iglesia," *Confidencial* 10, no. 507 (October 15–21, 2006).
13. Edelberto Torres-Rivas, "Nicaragua: el retorno del sandinismo transfigurado," *Nueva Sociedad* no. 207 (January/February 2007): 4–10.
14. Francisco Panizza, "Unarmed Utopia Revisited: The Resurgence of Left-of-Centre Politics in Latin America," *Political Studies* 53, no. 4 (December 2005): 716–34.

LATIN AMERICA'S LEFT OFF TRACK

BY MATÍAS VERNENGO
Dollars & Sense, May/June 2005

For several years, electoral results in Latin America have been shifting leftward. The victory of Tabaré Vázquez in Uruguay is the most recent example; the list also includes Néstor Kirchner in Argentina, Luiz Inácio Lula da Silva in Brazil, Ricardo Lagos in Chile, Lucio Gutiérrez in Ecuador, and Hugo Chávez in Venezuela. The new left governments are a mix in their political provenance. Lagos is from the well-established Socialist Party, while Lula and Vázquez represent newer parties gaining power for the first time. Kirchner, from the Partido Justicialista (Peronists), Chávez, and Gutiérrez are more typical of the old Latin American populism in which personalities are more important than political parties.

Beyond these center-left electoral victories, it is clear that the majority of civil society in Latin America rejects the neoliberal policies imposed during the 1990s. Popular demonstrations against privatization and trade liberalization are widespread. Last October saw a dramatic revolt in Bolivia, for example, where a coalition of labor unions and indigenous peoples, spurred by the government's plan to privatize the nation's gas reserves, brought about the resignation of President Gonzalo Sánchez de Lozada and strengthened the position of the indigenous leader Evo Morales.

The resurgence of the left is a momentous step in Latin America. The election of Lagos, Chile's first Socialist president since the 1973 military coup against Salvador Allende, is a landmark, as are the victories in Brazil and Uruguay of new-style left governments embedded in deep-seated social movements. The political changes under way in Latin America today are comparable to the victories of Felipe González after the long night of Franco's dictatorship in Spain, and the more recent revival of the Labor Party under Tony Blair following Margaret Thatcher's conservative reign. These victories are significant, especially because they reflect the region's long process of redemocratization, a political shift which has gone hand in hand with the revival of civic life: the rise of empowered indigenous movements, renewed struggles for land reform, worker occupations of factories to keep them operating in the face of economic collapse, the rise of *asambleas* (neighborhood assemblies) meeting to discuss the way forward for anti-neoliberal protests.

Observers of the region have usually credited this left turn to dissatisfaction with the neoliberal, "Washington Consensus" policies imposed during the

1990s. The Washington Consensus basically required deregulating markets, liberalizing trade and finance, and privatizing public firms. The emphasis was on price stabilization, fiscal austerity, and market-friendly policies, a mix that ultimately favored international financial markets and the local elites who could benefit from a more open financial environment. Arguably, if the left is to stake out a new direction and change the region for the better, economic policies will have to be at the center of the social transformation. Notwithstanding the political importance of Latin America's recent left turn, however, there is little reason for progressives to be optimistic about the economic policy direction of Latin America's new leaders.

ACCEPTABLE LEFTISTS

Many observers have tried to sort the new left-leaning leaders into "good" and "bad" camps. Rutgers' Tomás Eloy Martínez, an Argentine writer, sees two antagonistic economic models at play. In his view, a "negative left," embodied by Chávez's Bolivarian Revolution, uses the windfall gains from higher oil revenues to promote an unsustainable redistribution policy without laying the foundations for future growth. The "positive left" is represented by Lula and his policy of macroeconomic austerity as the necessary prerequisite for sustainable growth, allowing, in a hoped-for second phase, redistribution of the fruits of prosperity to the less privileged.

Jorge Castañeda, ex–foreign affairs minister of Mexico and former adviser to Cuauhtémoc Cárdenas, also argues that Latin America has voted two lefts into power. In his view, Lagos and Vázquez should be included with Lula in the responsible and pragmatic left that has learned that market discipline and macroeconomic stability are important for development. Castañeda groups Kirchner and Mexico City mayor and possible presidential contender Andrés Manuel López Obrador with Chávez as representatives of a nationalist and populist left of the past, one that has been less receptive to modernizing influences. (Despite parallels with Chávez, Ecuador's Gutiérrez was timid in distancing himself from Washington and fulfilling his campaign pledge to overturn neoliberal policies, which may explain, in part, his recent fall from power.)

Unlike Eloy Martínez, Castañeda sees macroeconomic orthodoxy dominating the region as a whole, Chávez and Kirchner included. Unfortunately, his view is closer to the truth. Apart from some anti-imperialist rhetoric, the economic policies of the new governments in Latin America cannot be classified as leftist. Like the U.K.'s Blair, the new center-left leaders in Latin America have embraced so-called "Third Way" economic policies that are largely indistinguishable from neoliberalism. In a sense, everyone has caved in to Thatcher's infamous notion that there is "no alternative." María da Conceição Tavares, a prominent Brazilian economist and member of Lula's Workers' Party, recently said that there is no such thing as left-wing macroeconomics.

GOOD LUCK, NOT GOOD POLICIES

If Keynesian fiscal policies—progressive taxation, increased spending on social programs, and deficit spending to maintain full employment—are the hallmarks of a progressive government, then the new left governments in Latin America cannot be seen as particularly progressive.

Despite variations in political discourse, the countries' macroeconomic policies are broadly similar, and represent little change from those of the previous regimes. The continuity of macroeconomic policies is most evident in the arena of fiscal policy. All the center-left governments in the region have accepted the logic behind an emphasis on fiscal discipline: that high fiscal deficits cause inflation, and, by generating fears of default, cause capital flight and lead to balance-of-payments problems. All accept the dictum that they cannot pursue more progressive fiscal policies because international financial markets would punish their countries with a run on their currencies.

All of these center-left governments are prioritizing fiscal austerity to control government debt accumulation and are committed to maintaining primary surpluses even in periods of recession. (Primary surpluses correspond to the difference between spending and revenues, but excluding interest payments on outstanding debt. In other words, a government with revenues of $100 that pays $35 in interest payments and $70 on other expenditures would have a nominal deficit of $5 but a primary surplus of $30.) This is a significant change compared to the Keynesian approaches that dominated policy-making in the region prior to the 1990s and is more extreme than the anti-Keynesian bias in the developed world. The consequences are stark: Maintaining primary fiscal surpluses has squeezed public investment and spending on social programs, dampened economic growth, and favored financial interests and the well-to-do.

Although exchange-rate policies vary somewhat, most Latin American governments across the political spectrum today emphasize the role of exchange rates in controlling inflation. Their role in promoting external competitiveness has become secondary. By controlling exchange rates, governments are able to keep down the prices of imported goods, which crucially affect inflation. But this also means that the prices of domestic products are less competitive, and so hobbles the development of domestic industries.

At times exchange rate controls are seen as a temporary device to avoid balance-of-payments crises, but not as instrumental in promoting development. For example, Argentina adopted capital controls after the December 2000 crisis, but these are intended to be temporary. None of the left governments has made capital controls (such as foreign exchange controls or Tobin taxes) central to its economic agenda. Capital controls reduce the outflows and inflows of foreign currencies. With capital controls in place, the rate of interest does not need to be hiked to avoid capital outflows and can be adjusted for domestic purposes. Hence, capital controls put national governments in control of monetary policy.

If the macroeconomic policies of the region's left regimes are successful, perhaps it doesn't matter whether or not they are progressive. In fact, recent economic performance in Latin America has been exceptional. According to the Economic Commission for Latin America and the Caribbean (CEPAL), the economies of the region exceeded expectations in 2004, with an average regional GDP growth rate of 5.5%, surpassing the world average rate of 4%. Venezuela grew by an incredible 18%, Argentina by around 8%, and Chile and Brazil by slightly above 5%.

However, these strong growth rates have more to do with external drivers than with any innovative policies of the region's new leaders. Ultimately, the remarkable expansion of China, which has increased its trade with Latin America considerably, the United States' mild recovery, and an improvement in the terms of trade—the relative price of Latin America's exports—explain the positive Latin American performance. That external factors are propelling the region's economies casts serious doubt on the sustainability of their growth. The economic policies pursued by the left will not be of much help if economic growth in China and the United States slows down in the near future, as many analysts expect. Good luck more than good policies is behind the new prosperity.

MACROECONOMIC CONSERVATISM AND DISTRIBUTION

Economic growth alone is not enough to improve the lot of the region's poor anyway. Brazil's story illustrates the distributive consequences of the current fiscal policies in the region, and highlights the continuity with the policies of past administrations. Last year Lula signed his second agreement with the International Monetary Fund (IMF). The agreement, which requires Brazil to adopt the usual litany of neoliberal policies, particularly cutting government spending, was all but necessary, and Lula decided to sign it only to gain credibility with international financial markets.

In Brazil's case, the primary surpluses (4.25% of GDP in 2003) go hand in hand with large nominal deficits (5% of GDP in 2003). The difference between a primary surplus and a nominal deficit represents interest payments made to the owners of government bonds. That is, almost 10% of Brazil's GDP was transferred last year to bond holders, mostly corporations and wealthy individuals. Interest payments represent almost half of Brazilian government expenditures, and are considerably higher than the amounts spent on Zero Hunger, land reform, or First Job, to name a few of the well-publicized social programs of Lula's Workers' Party. The result is that the income distribution in Brazil, one of the world's most unequal countries, is no better now than when Lula took office in 2003, and probably slightly worse. The share of wages in total income in Brazil fell from 36.1% in 2002 to 35.6% in 2003.

Argentina and Venezuela face similar constraints, but because of more closed capital accounts and lower rates of interest, their plight is less extreme. In Argentina, Kirchner is negotiating fiercely with the IMF and the private creditors who allowed the country to obtain a favorable rescheduling of foreign debt. Yet last year his government maintained a primary surplus even greater than the 3% of GDP its prior agreement with the IMF called for. The IMF has let it be known that future approvals of the debt-restructuring program, and hence additional money, will be forthcoming only if Kirchner maintains fiscal austerity.

More important, Argentina has tentatively agreed to gradually scrap all the capital controls implemented since its currency crisis in 2001. Argentina's interest rates today are considerably lower than Brazil's, and close to the U.S. real rate of interest. (Brazil does not impose controls on capital flows.) If Argentina complies, the country can expect higher interest rates in the near future.

Kirchner has been accused of promoting irresponsible economic policies and favoring unsustainable redistribution toward the poor, but it's hard to see why. Argentina's current fiscal stance will require continued primary surpluses to pay for debt servicing. It's true that the government established a program of transfers to the unemployed (Plan Jefes de Hogar), but the benefits are insufficient, and other public investments are simply not being made. Maintaining primary surpluses means that the resources available for social transfers, including the Plan Jefes de Hogar, are severely constrained. Overall, then, with the exception of the fixed exchange-rate system, Kirchner's government is adhering to basically the same set of macroeconomic policies that prevailed through the 1990s.

The Venezuelan story is similar. Chávez's 1998 government program (*La propuesta de Hugo Chávez para transformar Venezuela*) designated inflation as the country's central macroeconomic problem. Since then, an overvalued exchange rate has been his administration's main instrument for reducing the price of imported goods and keeping inflation in check. Lula also uses a managed and appreciated exchange rate to control inflation, as did his predecessor Fernando Henrique Cardoso; Argentina, under the 1991 Convertibility Plan, which pegged the country's currency to the dollar; and Ecuador, with dollarization. In each case, overvaluation of the currency damaged external competitiveness, reducing the rates of output growth. Eventually, speculation forced depreciation.

More importantly, Chávez generated great expectations about using oil revenues to pay for social programs. His government did indeed implement a massive program of social spending, including an expansion of health assistance and distribution of foodstuffs; social spending as a share of total government spending did go up. Deficits soared, but less as a result of the increase of government spending than as the consequence of lower non-oil revenues due to recession. The social conflicts associated with the political resistance against Chávez exacerbated the fall in non-oil government revenues and forced the government to increase the amount of debt finance. Public debt has soared; interest payments on outstanding debt corresponded to around 40% of total spending last year.

Like Argentina and Brazil, Venezuela has kept substantial primary surpluses—reaching 3% of GDP in 2004—even as its nominal deficits have grown. According to Leonardo Vera, a professor at the Central University of Venezuela, a vicious circle has developed in which reduced revenues lead to more indebtedness, and indebtedness, in turn, leads to higher debt service costs. As this vicious circle turns, wealth is redistributed, but not in the way Chávez hoped—rather, from the poor to the wealthy owners of public bonds.

Across Latin America, governments both center-right and center-left have pursued fiscal policies aimed at containing deficits and trying to reduce the burden of debt. As a result, they have shunned countercyclical spending programs and neglected the effects of fiscal policy on income distribution. The region as a whole obtained a primary surplus of 1% of GDP in 2004, while the nominal deficit was close to 2% of GDP. This means that Latin America, a region of highly unequal income distribution, transferred on average 3% of GDP to the owners of government bonds last year.

With Latin American governments maintaining primary surpluses even in times of crisis and channeling a sizable share of spending into interest payments—in other works, redistributing it to the wealthy—it is not surprising that unemployment remains high across the region. The average rate of unemployment in 2003, according to CEPAL, was above 10%, with Argentina (15%) and Venezuela (18%) heading the charts. As high as these official measures of unemployment are, they underestimate the problems of underemployment and low-productivity jobs typical in the region. These numbers are particularly problematic because leveling the income distribution and reducing unemployment are essential to addressing the region's high poverty rate. Poverty fell in 2004, but not enough to make up for the increase between 2001 and 2003; around 43% of Latin Americans still live below the poverty line. And nothing in the macroeconomic policies of the new left governments suggests that their outcomes are likely to diverge from those in the rest of the region in the coming years.

FISCAL POLICY AND INTERNATIONAL FINANCIAL REFORM

Fiscal policy was central to the development of the systems of welfare in the developed world, and for industrialization in the Global South, including in Latin America. What is often forgotten about the role of fiscal policy is that it was most effective during the Bretton Woods period, the so-called Golden Age of capitalism from the end of World War II until the 1970s. The Great Depression and the rise of fascism and communism had led the leaders of the rich countries to adopt a fiscal pact that allowed higher levels of social spending in order to save capitalism from itself. Under the Bretton Woods regime, capital controls forced interest rates to low levels. This allowed governments to increase spending, while keeping the burden of debt service within reasonable levels.

Today, a more comprehensive reform of the international financial system along the lines of Keynes' proposals at Bretton Woods, as advocated by some heterodox economists, is necessary not just to stabilize financial markets and reduce balance-of- payments crises, but to promote more just fiscal policies. Controls on capital flows would allow lower rates of interest, reduce spending on debt service, and allow for more public investment and higher levels of social transfers. These policies should be complemented with trade polices that promote full employment, and a coherent set of industrial policies to promote international competitiveness. The experience of the new left-leaning governments in Latin America suggests that as long as the existing rules of the international financial system remain in force, Global South governments will be unable to adopt progressive economic policies whatever their political stripes.

Furthermore, international financial reform is unlikely to come as a result of the victory of the left in developing countries. (Admittedly, progressive observers hoped there would be less subservience to international financial markets in Latin America with left-of-center governments in power. China and India, for example, adopt strict capital controls.) Historically, reforms of the international financial system result from crises at the center, not at the periphery, of the global economic system. But it is still important to see things for what they are. The center-left governments in Latin America have maintained or implemented macroeconomic policies that redistribute income toward financial markets and elites. Only Latin American magical realism explains how these policies could be seen as progressive alternatives to neoliberalism.

SOURCES

Philip Arestis and Malcolm Sawyer, eds., *The Economics of the Third Way: Experiences From Around the World* (Edward Elgar, 2001); Jorge Castañeda, "Las dos izquierdas latinoamericanas," *La Nación*, January 4, 2005; CEPAL, *Estudio económico de América Latina y Caribe, 2003–2004*; Martínez, Tomás Eloy, "Bolívar quería otra cosa," *La Nación*, December 31, 2004; José Antonio Ocampo, "Half a Lost Decade," *ECLAC Notes* no. 24 (September 2002); Leonardo Vera, "Interpretando la agenda económica de Chávez," downloaded from www.analitica.com; Matías Vernengo, "Fear, Hope and Wishful Thinking in Brazil," *Dissent* 50, no. 1 (Winter 2004): 28–30.

BY MEANS LEGAL AND OTHERWISE: THE BOLIVIAN RIGHT REGROUPS

BY BRET GUSTAFSON
NACLA Report, January/February 2008

Two years into Evo Morales's tenure as president of Bolivia, he and his party, the MAS, face difficult challenges. In pursuing its "democratic and cultural revolution," as the MAS (Movimiento al Socialismo, or Movement Toward Socialism) calls its program, the party is grappling with its own missteps and with tensions between the indigenist, leftist, and nationalist wings of the movement. Meanwhile, the right-wing opposition seeks to frustrate the MAS agenda to the point of failure, since it cannot be defeated outright. Though weakened by its collapse in 2003, the right is regrouping through a two-pronged strategy of promoting a regionalist vision of departmental "autonomy" and rebuilding a national party apparatus.

Branko Marinkovic and Jorge "Tuto" Quiroga are two exemplars of this new strategy. Marinkovic hails from Santa Cruz, Bolivia's wealthy eastern city and the capital of the department of the same name. His parents arrived there from Croatia in the 1950s, just in time for an agrarian boom fueled by Bolivian state funds and U.S. aid dollars. Silvo Marinkovic, Branko's late father, founded IOL S.A., now the largest domestically owned exporter of soy and sunflower oil. With soy-related industries second only to hydrocarbons in export importance, Marinkovic is a major player among the business elite. He led the private businessmen's chamber of Santa Cruz by the age of 35; now 40, he leads the Santa Cruz Civic Committee, the self-(s)elected council of regional elites that has spearheaded the demand for autonomy and business opposition to the MAS.[1]

Like other moneyed immigrants, the Marinkovics built wealth the Cruceño way. They hold large tracts of productive and nonproductive land (though many titles, acquired during military regimes, are of questionable legality). They run a business that grew under state credits, protection, and subsidies (though IOL S.A. is under investigation for tax fraud). And they control a sizable share of Bolivia's Banco Económico, one of several strategies elites have employed to weather the vicissitudes of a commodity-dependent export economy. Marinkovic also followed a traditional path into Cruceño high society. He graduated from the U.S.-style Santa Cruz Cooperative School alongside "traditional" Cruceño elites (the Molina, Franco, Gutiérrez, Barbery, and Suárez families, for example). He married a Bolivian beauty queen (of German descent) and went to college in Texas, following others on circuits linking two oil-rich and business-friendly regions.

Though a lightning rod for critics who see in his Croatian heritage a link to the region's racially charged calls for autonomy, Marinkovic has tactfully distanced himself from the separatist rhetoric of more extreme regionalists (some conspiracy theorists associate Bolivia's Croatian community with the World War II–era pro-Nazi Ustashe regime, many of whose members fled to South America). Yet the paradoxes of wealth and a transnationalized identity make Marinkovic a perfect icon of the regionalist turn: Though regionalism revolves around claims of deeply rooted historical particularity, it also thrives on accommodations with transnational sources of wealth and power.

Quiroga, 47, more of a technocrat than Marinkovic, is at the forefront of attempts to rebuild a conservative party apparatus. A native of Cochabamba, he grew up in Santa Cruz, where his father worked in the oil business. There he graduated from the Colegio La Salle, a traditional high-society Catholic institution. He also went off to Texas A&M and St. Andrew's of Austin, and eventually found a U.S.-born wife. Drawing on political networks in both Cochabamba and Santa Cruz, Quiroga joined the Democratic Nationalist Action (Acción Demócratica Nacionalista, or ADN) party and became a protégé of its leader, former military dictator Hugo Bánzer. At 32 he served as finance minister during the early years of neoliberal structural adjustment, when the ADN was taking a corruption-filled turn at the state trough alongside its former nemesis, the Movement of the Revolutionary Left. When Bánzer was elected president in 1999, Quiroga returned as his vice president and took over after the old general resigned due to cancer in 2001.[2]

Barred from reelection when his term ended in 2002, Quiroga left the country to make the rounds of Washington think tanks and development agencies. Meanwhile, Bolivia continued its slide into social discontent as the violence and corruption of the neoliberal era took its toll on traditional parties. (The ADN polled a little more than 3% in 2002, and shortly thereafter the party virtually disappeared.) Gonzalo Sánchez de Lozada's National Revolutionary Movement (Movimiento Nacionalista Revolucionario, or MNR) won that election but soon collapsed during the bloody Gas War of 2003. The right was in tatters. The MAS and its allied movements surged forward to demand new elections and a new constitution. At this point Quiroga returned relatively unscathed to Bolivia at the head of a new party called Podemos (Social Democratic Power). He was Morales's main opponent in the 2005 elections, but the MAS won in a landslide. Podemos managed to secure the strongest minority bloc in congress and did well, especially in Santa Cruz, in later elections for the national constitutional assembly. Quiroga now leads the formal party opposition to the MAS, and among the right-leaning parties, Podemos has the broadest national base of support.

The stakes in the right's resurgence are high. Bolivian natural gas, all of it located in the country's eastern lowlands, generates millions of dollars of annual revenue disputed in a tug-of-war between national, regional, and local governments. Eastern agrarian and forestry lands constitute the extractive frontier of an export-oriented economy, and with mineral prices having risen in recent years, private cooperatives allied with transnational capital have clashed with the government over its plans to rebuild a state-run mining company. Massive deposits of iron ore in Bolivia's far-eastern Mutún field (in Santa Cruz department) will soon be exploited by India's Jindal Steel. The new markets in Asia promise yet another flood of income into a state already destabilized by gas. Resources and territorial power, pure and simple, have mobilized expectations and interests into an explosive frenzy.

Yet a deeper geopolitical struggle also exists. Although much has been made of the east-west divide between the people of the highland Andes (known as Kollas) and those of eastern Bolivia (known as Cambas)—with pundits and observers anxiously predicting a slide toward an ethnoracial civil war—this is a misreading.[3] It ignores the strong right-wing presence in the Andes and the equally significant MAS presence across eastern Bolivia. The east-west optic also collapses identity, ideology, and territory by conflating Andeanness, indigeneity, and the MAS regime. This feeds the right's racially charged rhetoric of "autonomy" yet it fails to capture the tensions between the MAS agenda and that of the right-wing opposition. Whereas the MAS speaks of regrounding sovereignty (sentar soberanía) across national territory (reflected in its defense of a strong developmentalist state and its network of support linking small towns, marginal urban neighborhoods in all major cities, and rural provinces), the right (entrenched in major urban centers, with weaker tentacles reaching into provincial outposts) envisions a weak, neoliberal state of interconnected capital-friendly regions detached from the regulatory and redistributive pressure of national populations and politics.

A mapping of this right-wing vision would link Santa Cruz (with its easterly ties to soy-rich, energy-hungry Brazil and on to the Atlantic coast), Cochabamba, a crucial political linchpin, and pro-business La Paz (with its orientations west toward cities in Chile and Peru), along with Tarija and Trinidad, appendages of Cruceño dominance. In this language of productive chains, clusters, and corridors, parts of Bolivia become transit zones for capital, while others are broadly excluded. If carried to its extreme, the vision would create exclusionary divisions between regional identities and detach democracy, citizenship, and sovereignty from the more profound project of nation building. Bolivia is not, then, on the verge of an east-west civil war. Rather, it faces a choice between recrafting the national project or converting the country into a series of regionally administered resource and labor pools that constitute production and extraction nodes on global market circuits.

Here the complementarity between the right's pro-autonomy and party-building strategies represented by Marinkovic and Quiroga come together. The one seeks to intensify regionalist discourse against the nationalist agenda; the other, to construct a national-level party apparatus to defend and administer a hollowed-out neoliberal state. "Autonomy" represents not merely the pursuit of efficiency, local democracy, and accountability, but a demand for regionalized sovereignty. As testified in the Santa Cruz draft "autonomy statute," a de facto regional constitution, autonomists want control over the means of legitimate violence; the signing of contracts with multinationals; the administration of schools, health care, and justice; the distribution of public forests, subsoil resources, and land; and even "internal migration."[4] This is something more than moderate federalism or decentralization.

To this end, the regionalist and party right have found success in a range of tactics, legal and otherwise. Their most powerful tools are newspapers and TV channels, owned largely by representatives of the pro-autonomy business class. Regionalist papers in Santa Cruz (*El Deber*, *El Nuevo Día*) and its allied city Tarija (*El País*) are closely aligned with the autonomist agenda. In La Paz, the major paper *La Razón* plays a more moderate role, like that of Quiroga, in defending the integrity of Bolivian territory while also railing against the MAS agenda. (It and the Santa Cruz *El Nuevo Día* are controlled by the Spanish media conglomerate Prisa Group.) In Santa Cruz, investors' groups also control major TV outlets. Autonomy spots flood the airwaves with emotionally charged calls for "liberty" and "democracy."

In recent months eastern Bolivian and Andean media outlets have synchronized "reporting" on three recurring threats posed by the MAS: Communist totalitarianism, inflation, and race war. In a country already wracked by nervous tensions and unsettled expectations, the media have played heavily on racialized fear and uncertainty against the imagined chaos brought on by the indigenous-led MAS government. The results of the national referendum on autonomy are a good measure of media success (and the fact that the message of autonomy resonates with many Bolivians). In Santa Cruz (department) the "yes" passed with more than 70% of the vote; in La Paz, it received only 26%.

The right has also turned to public culture and spectacle. Bolivian politics has long thrived on the power of dances, parades, and festivals, especially in the Andes. Yet Cruceños are now also increasingly concerned with "culture." Elites have hitched autonomy talk to carnival, to folkloric celebrations of regional identity, and even to intimate markers of speech, dress, and consumption. One cannot now eat *majado*, an eastern Bolivian rice, meat, and plantain dish, without thinking of oneself as an autonomist. (And one must pronounce it *majao*, like a good Cruceño.) One must embrace and desire the (light-skinned, tall, definitively not indigenous) "beauty" of Cruceña women who appear in public events, just as one should embrace and desire Santa Cruz and autonomy. Called "sovereigns" (*soberanas*), these beauty "queens" (like the region) are to be defended by true men like Marinkovic.

New forms of political spectacle have also been successfully used. Huge crowds are convoked to proclaim their support for "autonomy" in events known as *cabildos*, mass street assemblies said to represent popular democracy. The events are sheer pageantry, with helicopter flyovers, rock bands, civic notables, and much flag-waving. Crowds chant "*Au-tono-mía! Au-tono-mía!*" and the region's colors—green (for natural abundance) and white (for noble, that is, racial, purity)—are ubiquitous. Though undoubtedly reflecting real anti-MAS sentiment, these urban spectacles reduce politics to colors and slogans that echo the carefully choreographed orange, rose, and velvet-style "revolutions" of Eastern Europe.

The right has also taken up Bolivia's rich tradition of social movement protest and language. In the days of corporatism, right and left were largely fungible stances that revolved around nationalism and state patronage. Many leaders of the new right (not a few ex-leftist statists among them) are intimately familiar with the power of populist symbols—Quiroga's Podemos party emblem is a red star, no less. The racist and separatist Camba Nation branch of Santa Cruz's autonomy movement takes up indigenous rights discourse, demanding "self-determination" and "land, dignity, and freedom." It also mimics the language of anti-imperialist class struggle, chanting "*El pueblo / unido / jamás será vencido!*" The rancher-governor of Santa Cruz, former left-leaning Rubén Costas, speaks of defending autonomy through a "democracy of peace." Marinkovic himself declares their struggle a battle against "authoritarianism" and "totalitarianism."

The right has also used hunger strikes and marches, classic tools of social movement and union struggle in Bolivia. During the first sustained challenge to the constitutional assembly, the right and the MAS faced off over a procedural issue. The MAS hoped to approve articles by simple majority, while the right wanted to maintain an ambiguously written rule requiring a two-thirds majority. Andean and eastern elites went on hunger strike to defend the "2/3." In a melodramatic show, Cruceño business leaders were joined by the likes of would-be novelist (and La Paz native) Juan Claudio Lechín, son of the legendary Juan Lechín, who led Bolivia's powerful miners' unions from the 1950s through the 1980s. Though the show of wealthy people playing the part of hungry, oppressed, sacrificial victims was widely mocked by the "real" social movements, the right eventually succeeded in defending the 2/3.

During other conflicts over MAS proposals, the right has also staged marches in and around urban centers. Unlike the historic marches of popular and indigenous movements that move to and generally besiege centers of power, these marches are staged as spectacles to define public space as anti-MAS space and capture the sentiment of the urban middle and lower classes. To protest Morales's land law, for instance, wealthy landowners staged a six-mile jaunt from the suburbs into Santa Cruz. Eastern Bolivia's indigenous leaders rolled their eyes. They, of course, had exploded onto the national scene in 1990 with a march of more than 372 miles from the Amazon to La Paz. Other marches have erupted to protest MAS education proposals that seek to strengthen the place of indigenous knowledges and languages in public schools, remove Catholicism from the official curriculum, and regulate the business of private schooling. Organized by the regionalists and the Catholic Church hierarchy, parents and private school groups marched through the streets of Santa Cruz with signs suggesting Communism and Satanism were threatening their children. Other marches echo the tactics of the anti-Allende right in 1970s Chile, like the one staged by the "housewives" of the elite-led Feminine Civic Committee (a counterpart to the masculine group led by Marinkovic), which denounced inflation in defense of the "family basket." In a country where the practice of popular protest is a deeply cherished tradition, these appropriations reflect both the collapse of the right wing's institutional hegemony as well as the self-positioning of elites as oppressed minorities struggling against a brutal state.

Given that the right lost access to legitimate state violence, it now also relies on extralegal violence. Fistfights started by Podemos in Congress, disruptive violence at the constitutional assembly, and harassment of MAS activists is increasingly common. The MAS has also used the tactic of provocation, though its violence is generally defensive. More significant is the escalation of organized street violence, especially in Santa Cruz, where assaults on people and public institutions are the preferred tactic. The most notorious example is the Cruceñist Youth Union (Unión Juvenil Cruceñista, or UJC), the young men's counterpart to Marinkovic's civic committee. The UJC merges violent cultural substrates linked to sports hooliganism, martial arts, weightlifting, and youth fighting into a directed instrument to enforce civic strikes, attack peasant and pro-MAS marches, and assault disputed public institutions like tax agencies, school administrations, labor unions, and water management entities.

The UJC's tactics are spreading to other urban centers. The bloody confrontation between urban youth and MAS supporters in Cochabamba in January 2007, for which the MAS bears some responsibility, is an example. Though said to be marching for democracy, young urban men armed with sticks, bats, golf clubs, and homemade shields set out to provoke coca growers (also armed with sticks and machetes). In Tarija, a young men's civic group also attacked a pro-MAS urban homeless peoples' movement. When the right introduced the nonissue of moving the national capital to Sucre from La Paz, young men attacked the constitutional assembly and threatened MAS assembly members, all in an ostensible effort to defend Sucre's demand. In the most recent case, the civic committee and the UJC mobilized to "defend" the Santa Cruz airport, that is, to effectively seize power over the airport administration to resist central government appointees. The military had to be deployed to maintain federal control.

In the rural areas, especially north of Santa Cruz, another kind of violence is emerging. Rural elites backed by the civic committee and business leaders have organized "land defense councils" and "self-defense committees," the basic outlines of rural paramilitarism. These moves are backed by agrarian and cattlemen's chambers reminiscent of Guatemala's notorious Committee of Agricultural, Commercial, Industrial and Financial Associations during the 1980s. One of them is led by a fiery rancher who has already declared that Bolivia's next war, after the water and gas wars, will be the land war. On several occasions between 1999 (the onset of neoliberal collapse) and 2005 (the electoral victory of the MAS), armed thugs and landowners assaulted peasants who "invaded" contested lands. Attacks on NGO lawyers and peasant and indigenous rights' activists escalated. Provincial elites also mobilized attacks on indigenous and peasant movement offices and installations of the state land reform agency, physically threatening and kidnapping land surveyors. These are the extralegal means on which the party and regionalist right relies.

There is a moderate opposition as well. "Soft" Cruceño regionalists like former governor Carlos Molina pursue decentralization yet distance themselves from the fascistic tendencies of the Civic Committee and the UJC. Many have been accused of "betraying" the region. In La Paz and the Andes, the moderate right includes the professionals who occupied the NGOs, think tanks, and consultancy offices of Bolivia's 1990s development boom. They now face deep questioning of their market orthodoxy, the loss of their party vehicles (the MNR, among others), and their discredited links to neoliberal-era corruption. Yet with continued support from entities like USAID and other donors, these figures pursue a new developmentalism that touts regional tourism, small-scale entrepreneurialism, micro-enterprise, and decentralization. They are defined by an intellectual commitment to the market (and a pragmatic fear of national-popular democracy). Their position overlaps with the Quiroga-Marinkovic right in the language of "regional development"—neoliberalism's answer to the contradiction between democracy and free markets. An influential think tank called Fundación Libertad y Democracia, with ties to the Cato and Heritage foundations (and with Marinkovic on its board), now preaches freedom by way of autonomy. In La Paz, Nuevo Norte is a similar holding tank for technocrats out of power. Those who once sought to liberalize Bolivia have downsized their visions to now speak of developing "the department of La Paz."

Meanwhile, the intellectual right attacks the social justice agenda of the MAS by calling it irresponsible populism. Yet it turns to cultural racism to dismiss the indigenous character of the MAS agenda and its creative exploration of new languages and epistemes to rethink economy, polity, and society. Writers like H.C.F. Mansilla, a Mario Vargas Llosa–type liberal, represents this erudite anti-indigenous stance. Mansilla argues that Andean (i.e., indigenous Aymara, Quechua, and mestizo-cholo) "mentalities" are culturally conservative. Andeans resist "modernization," the thinking goes, because of the baggage inherited from the Spanish colonial bureaucracy and its fateful collision with Inca totalitarianism. Forward-thinking easterners are more open to change and progress.[5] *Mentality* is, of course, a codeword for race, and implicitly dismisses the MAS agenda as anti-modern primitivism.

This intellectualized racism dovetails with anti-statist regionalism. Cruceños openly scorned Morales's overtures to Andean ritual at his inauguration and mock MAS indigenous ministers who invoke Andean spiritualism. By reviving a vision of Bolivia as divided into modern and premodern (indigenous) peoples and places, parts of the country can be imagined as modernizing "autonomous" spaces fit to manage their own resources and "mentalities." Other parts, as pro-autonomy Cruceños have acknowledged, may not want autonomy and will still cling to the state, but will choose autonomy in the future after they have "evolved." This more palatable cultural racism underlies a long-standing alliance between the nonindigenous conservative elite of the western Andes and the agro-industrialists of the east.[6]

Against the challenge of the right, the MAS faces its own authoritarian temptations. The party's leaders acknowledge that their party struggles between two logics: that of the older Bolivian left, which pursued state capture through blockades and petitions, and that of a new, emergent left infused with a decolonizing indigenous agenda that seeks to reconstitute the state itself and redefine political subjectivities in alliance with a social justice platform.[7] Natural gas provides resources to defend this agenda, yet it also generates conditions ripe for corrupt authoritarianism. Whether democracy can be preserved without losing sight of the progressive agenda, decaying into state patronage politics or morphing into the right's vision of a hollowed-out electoralism, is still an open question.

NOTES

1. Miguel Lora, "Los capitanes del comando camba," *El juguete rabioso* (La Paz, February 5, 2005).
2. See www.podemosbolivia.com/tuto.htm.
3. See, for example, Dan Keane, "Civil War Talk Stokes Bolivian Fears," *The Washington Post* (September 30, 2007).
4. Estatuto de Autonomía del Departamento de Santa Cruz (2006), p.11, downloaded from www.asamcruz.org.
5. See, for example, H.C.F. Mansilla, *El carácter conservador de la nación boliviana* (Santa Cruz, Bolivia: Editorial El País, 2004).
6. On cultural racism, see Charles Hale, *Más Que un Indio (More Than an Indian): Racial Ambivalence and the Paradox of Neoliberal Multiculturalism in Guatemala* (School of American Research Press, 2006).
7. See Álvaro García Linera, *Horizontes y límites del estado y el poder* (La Paz, Bolivia: Comuna, 2005).

CHAPTER 2
ARMED FORCES, VIOLENCE, AND HUMAN RIGHTS

LAWS AND INJUSTICE:
FIGHTING FOR HUMAN RIGHTS IN MEXICO

BY CHRIS TILLY AND MARIE KENNEDY
Dollars & Sense, March/April 2007

In a February statement, Amnesty International described Mexico as a country with "laws but no justice." The organization was talking about the criminal justice system, but the statement describes Mexico more broadly, in a couple of ways. First, the application of laws in Mexico is often arbitrary and driven by covert or overt economic and political interests. Second, Mexican society (like most others, including U.S. society) institutionalizes injustice toward a number of groups of second-class citizens—such as indigenous people, the poor, and women.

But the story is more complex. Mexico today also is registering some unexpected breakthroughs in civil rights, including gay/lesbian rights. And popular organizations, sometimes with allies in the mainstream parties and sometimes without, are continuing to push forward the struggle for social justice.

WHOSE LAW?

Totalitarianism, according to one description, is a situation in which laws are constructed so that absolutely everyone must violate them in the course of daily life, rendering everyone vulnerable to selective application of the law. Mexico does not meet this definition of totalitarianism, but the country certainly has some things in common with it. Tax evasion is virtually universal. There are often multiple land ownership claims based on conflicting government policies or actions—agrarian reform, indigenous reservations, patronage gifts by some governor or other, eminent domain, and so on. And politicians often interpret broadly written laws to their own advantage, as well as supplementing legal actions with extralegal and illegal ones.

Perhaps the most celebrated recent example of arbitrary application of the law took place in 2004, in the political jockeying preceding the 2006 presidential campaign. The popular center-left mayor of Mexico City, Andrés Manuel López Obrador (popularly known as AMLO), was leading in early polls. The government of President Vicente Fox, of the right-wing National Action Party (PAN), contrived charges against López Obrador for taking a small slice of private land by eminent domain for a hospital access road. An open criminal proceeding would have barred him from being a candidate. He responded by organizing a protest movement, and the federal prosecutor finally dropped the charges. Fox stirred up a furor a couple of weeks ago by commenting that López Obrador had beaten him that time, but "I got even when my candidate"—Felipe Calderón, the PAN's presidential candidate—"won at the polls." López Obrador and his supporters maintain the election was stolen with Fox's collusion.

López Obrador's plight is just one of many such cases. Journalist Lydia Cacho, who accused the governor of Puebla of shielding powerful political and business figures who were procuring sex with minors, spent a year in prison awaiting trial on libel charges before a judge finally ordered her released last month. In the case highlighted by Amnesty International, indigenous activists in Oaxaca languish in prison on trumped-up charges for taking part in the movement against that state's governor. Environmental activists in Morelos and elsewhere have suffered a similar fate. Because Mexico's laws do not include a presumption of innocence, people accused for political reasons have limited tools to fight their incarceration.

Unjust imprisonment is bad enough, but those with political power sometimes go well beyond that in clamping down on dissidents. Mexico, historically a land of *caudillos* (regional political-military leaders) and *caciques* (local bosses controlling patronage and enforcement systems), has not completely escaped its legacy. In San Salvador Atenco (Mexico State) and Oaxaca, where governors savagely repressed demonstrations last year, human rights observers have documented cases of detention without charges, beating, torture, rape of women and men, disappearance, and assassination. Some such actions are targeted, others appear designed to indiscriminately sow terror— one account describes apolitical ice cream vendor Ismael Cruz, who was unlucky enough to get caught in the wrong place at the wrong time, was beaten and tortured, and remains under detention. In Chiapas, similar tactics have been used against the Zapatistas and communities suspected of being sympathizers. The National Human Rights Commission recently reported that in the last six years, 31 journalists have been assassinated and five disappeared in Mexico—more than a third of these in the last year—making it the second-most dangerous country for journalists after Iraq (some of the killings are presumed to be the work of organized crime).

Typically the worst abuses are carried out by non-uniformed troops or police, paramilitaries, or thugs, giving government officials "plausible deniability." Those ordering and carrying out such acts of violence generally enjoy impunity. In fact, it's only in the last few years that the Mexican system of justice has begun to investigate the "dirty war" the Mexican government pursued against militants in the late 1960s and 1970s.

MULTIPLE JEOPARDY

The most vulnerable groups suffer most. Indigenous people, many of whom are among Mexico's poorest—start out with three strikes against them: race, class, and language. This combination disadvantages them in property rights—land thefts from indigenous communities are legion—and in the courtroom as well. Rodolfo Stavenhagen, the UN's special rapporteur on indigenous people's rights, issued a February report that condemned the state of Yucatán's treatment of the indigenous, who make up the majority of the state's population. Stavenhagen highlighted the case of Ricardo Ucán, currently serving 22 years in prison. Ucán, who speaks no Spanish, killed a man who was pointing a gun at him and his family. Because his court-appointed lawyer spoke only Spanish and the proceedings were never translated, the fact of self-defense was never raised.

Women, who only gained the vote in national elections in Mexico in 1953, also suffer more violations of their rights. An anthropologist colleague commented: "In Mexico, men can accept women being politicians, professionals, even their bosses—but they are machos in the home." Domestic violence is a serious problem—suffered by 44% of women living with a partner, according to a survey by Mexico's National Institute on Women. The hundreds of killings in Juárez remain unsolved, leading many to suspect official complicity. And criminologist Rocío Santillan Ramírez characterizes the criminal justice system as "patriarchal and misogynist," pointing out that women murderers receive longer sentences on average than men, even though they have often killed a partner after years of abuse and violence.

In both substance and symbolism, Calderón's government is giving off signs of worse things to come. Calderón has done a phenomenally large number of photo-ops with the military, including one occasion when he posed in fatigues (maybe he's getting PR lessons from George W. Bush?). He gave troops a 46% raise while refusing to raise the minimum wage. The president's most visible policy initiative has been a series of military raids—so far without significant success—against the organized criminals running the drug trade. The violent acts of these gangsters are indeed a serious public concern, but given the range of economic and social problems facing Mexico, making this priority number one sends a clear message (as well as winning points with the United States). Calderón is not alone in playing the law-and-order card. Marcelo Ebrard, current mayor of Mexico City and a stalwart of López Obrador's Party of the Democratic Revolution, has been carrying out mass evictions of public housing projects where drug-dealing is allegedly taking place. The state of Guerrero just authorized its state legislators to carry arms and is paying for bodyguards.

Calderón's rhetoric targets not just criminals, but dissidents. "In this country, we will no longer confuse illegality with respect for rights," he intoned ominously in late January. It's true that in Atenco and Oaxaca protesters broke the law by violating police orders to disperse. But one could argue that when protest and criticism are made illegal, protesters and critics will necessarily become criminals. In any case, Calderón's Presidential Guard (Estado Mayor) went well beyond punishing illegal acts when he visited the National Governor's Conference here in Oaxaca. The Estado Mayor roughed up seven reporters—all from mainstream publications—without warning, throwing one to the ground and kicking him in the head, breaking his nose and sending him to the hospital. "We've never known the Estado Mayor to act like this," one friend commented. Calderón's officials have also blocked López Obrador's TV talk show from going on the air.

Meanwhile, the assistant attorney general for human rights, Juan de Dios Castro, as much as threw his hands in the air when he declared in mid-February that "we have a problem of violation of human rights that unfortunately the federal government . . . so far does not have in its hands the possibility of totally eliminating." He blamed state governments, complaining that in some states, "a climate of impunity is facilitated because democracy doesn't exist," but claimed that Mexico's federal system limits the central government's ability to intervene. (If the U.S. federal government had adopted this view in the 1960s, we'd probably still have Jim Crow in the South today!) Human rights advocates slammed Castro the next day for abdicating federal responsibility.

Though the actions of Calderón and his cabinet anger and worry government critics, they have gained favor in other quarters. Columnist Julio Hernández López reports that mega-capitalist Alberto Bailleres (major stockholder in financial, mining, commercial, and agribusiness interests), commented publicly in mid-February that the rule of law requires a strong government that compels all to obey, "even in the face of factional interests."

He reportedly added that "the civilizing way of law" should not be detained by "the hesitations of any actor or any political tendency." Interesting words coming from a major stockholder of Peñoles, in whose coal mine 65 miners perished in an explosion a year ago after years of safety violations. One year later, no action has been taken against the company.

SURPRISING BREAKTHROUGHS

But the news on human rights from Mexico is not all bad. Mexico's governments are naming domestic violence (*violencia intrafamiliar*) and conducting educational campaigns to raise consciousness about it. The federal government passed a law criminalizing domestic violence last year, and is conducting a hard-hitting radio campaign to publicize it ("Señor Martínez, you are sentenced to two years in prison for hitting your wife!").

Perhaps even more surprising in a land where machismo is so deeply rooted, laws recognizing gay and lesbian rights are taking new strides. The first same-sex civil union in Latin America, between two lesbians, was celebrated at the end of January in the gritty border state of Coahuila, best known for coal mines (including the Pasta de Conchos mine were last year's disaster took place) and maquiladoras. (Coahuila's law was championed, not by the left-leaning Party of the Democratic Revolution, but by the centrist Institutional Revolutionary Party, which ruled Mexico from 1929 to 2000.) The Distrito Federal (the federal district containing Mexico City) passed a similar law that takes effect in March, and already hundreds of same-sex couples have symbolically registered their intentions. Of course, Mexicans have long had an ambivalent relationship toward homosexuality. On the one hand, there are few insults harsher than *puto* (faggot). On the other hand, perhaps the most popular marchers in the recent carnival parade in Santa Ana, where we are living, were the dozens of *lindas marinas* (drag queens)—a fixture in many Mexican carnivals. Some were clownish objects of ridicule, but others were glamorous figures (including quite a few androgynous sylphs of ambiguous gender) who attracted appreciative whistles and propositions from male onlookers.

Mexican laws and views on reproductive rights, the rights of the HIV-positive, and even ex-offenders' rights are also changing. The morning-after pill was approved in Mexico in 2004, two years before the U.S. FDA finally gave it the nod. Abortion is illegal but tolerated. The Mexican Supreme Court just ruled that the Army may not discharge soldiers for being HIV-positive, and the secretary of health has initiated legal action for "crimes against public health" against the National Movement for the Refocusing of Science, which promotes a theory that the AIDS virus doesn't exist. The state of Coahuila even passed a law prohibiting discrimination against ex-convicts in government employment (with the exception of the police).

And in the shadow of brutal repression in Oaxaca and Atenco, in spite of the echoes of Calderón's tough-guy speeches, Mexicans continue to organize for basic human rights. A "citizens' jury" of well-known cultural and political figures traveled to Oaxaca to hear testimony from victims of the government crackdown there. A crowded field of human rights organizations pursues its crucial work of documentation and denunciation. Brave journalists face down death threats and worse to tell the stories of Ismael Cruz, Ricardo Ucán, and many others. And ordinary Mexicans, including growing numbers of indigenous people and women, challenge arbitrary power by lobbying, litigating, meeting, demonstrating, and creating autonomous, community-based institutions—building alternative structures of power founded on recognizing the rights of all.

FREE MARKETS AND DEATH SQUADS

BY RICKY BALDWIN
Dollars & Sense, September/October 2004

On February 29, a right-wing coup took control of the Haitian capital, Port-au-Prince, and sent President Jean-Bertrand Aristide into exile. Within two days, the same right-wing troops began attacking Haitian factory workers and sharecroppers at the behest of factory managers and large landowners, according to the grassroots labor federation Batay Ouvriye (Workers' Struggle).

The first assault came in the Codevi Free Trade Zone (FTZ) in the border community of Ouanaminthe. Thirty-four workers at the Dominican-owned sweatshop Grupo M, a subcontractor for Levi Strauss, had been fired for involvement with the union SOKOWA, an affiliate of Batay Ouvriye. The Codevi workers were demonstrating outside the plant on March 2 to demand that the 34 workers be rehired when management made a call, and in rolled troops fresh from overthrowing the elected government.

Armed men beat and handcuffed many of the demonstrators, then forced them—except for the original 34—back to work, sans union. Being fired is no small matter when there are only about 100,000 permanent full-time jobs in a nation of almost 8 million inhabitants, according to Charles Arthur, director of the U.K.-based Haiti Support Group.

Once the richest colony in the world, Haiti is now universally recognized as the poorest nation in the Western Hemisphere. The World Bank puts the poverty rate there at over 75%. The CIA's *World Fact Book* (2004) reports that "80% live in abject poverty" and three-fourths of the 3.6 million Haitian workforce have no formal jobs. Moreover, most of the formal jobs that do exist are seasonal or part-time, according to local observers.

Neoliberals, in the U.S. government and in Haiti, wholeheartedly supported the coup (or the "liberation," as some Haitian business leaders have dubbed it). Their support quickly proved to have little to do with freedom, marketwise or otherwise, and everything to do with enforcing the domination of local and international elites.

FREE TRADE AT GUNPOINT

Armed attacks like the one at Grupo M were soon repeated elsewhere, says Yannick Etienne, lead organizer with Batay Ouvriye. Large landowners in the Northwest communities of Ma Wouj and Bombardopolis called in troops to battle sharecroppers campaigning for a larger share of their produce. "Rebels," as the forces who overthrew Aristide are commonly called, have also attacked members of the active peasant group Tet Kole, as well as wage-earning farmworkers demanding the legal minimum wage.

The "rebel" troops had crossed into Haiti in the vicinity of the Codevi FTZ from the Dominican Republic, where several of their leaders had been in exile, facing charges of mass murder stemming from the first U.S.-backed coup against Aristide in 1991. Among them, Guy Philippe and Gilbert Dragon had been trained by the CIA in Ecuador, and Louis-Jodel Chamblain and Jean-Pierre Baptiste had been leaders in the CIA-organized Front for Haitian Advancement and Progress (FRAPH).

In the three bloody years following the 1991 coup, FRAPH functioned as an umbrella group for right-wing death squads that terrorized Haiti's democratic movement and drove its nascent labor unions underground. FRAPH itself was originally composed of army veterans from the brutal U.S.-supported Duvalier dictatorships that ruled Haiti from 1957 to 1986. Then as now, Etienne says, the motivation of U.S. and Haitian armed action has been the same: "cheap labor."

After this year's coup, Haitian business leaders immediately began meeting with coup leaders, calling them "liberators" even as U.S. Secretary of State Colin Powell admitted they were murderous "thugs." This collaboration between "thugs" and Haitian businessmen is hardly surprising, Arthur notes, because the Haitian elites owe their power to thuggery of another era: the 1915–34 U.S. occupation. Then, U.S. Marines slaughtered 20,000 resisters, disbanded the Haitian parliament, and rewrote the country's constitution—effectively turning Haiti into a U.S. cheap-labor plantation.

U.S. Senator Mike Dewine (R-Ohio) continued this tradition when he proposed the Haiti Economic Recovery and Opportunity (HERO) Act, S. 489, this spring. The bill, supported by the Haitian business sector and opposed by Haitian labor unions, would essentially extend the existing free-trade zones to include the whole of Haiti. (A free-trade zone is a designated area where a government, typically in the Global South, lifts normal trade barriers such as tariffs, gives tax breaks, suspends environmental, labor, and other regulations, and takes a range of steps to encourage investment by foreign corporations.) The bill, currently in the Senate Finance Committee, encourages foreign direct investment, for example, by awarding garments assembled in Haiti duty-free status for import into the United States.

"The HERO Act will ensure the multinationals' power to profit from the terrible misery of the Haitian people," Etienne says. "It will allow them to obtain cloth[ing] at preferential prices . . . without the slightest concern for workers' rights. They are concerned, rather, with stifling these rights."

NO SAVIORS

Yet, contrary to some expectations, Batay Ouvriye and other worker groups are not agitating to bring Aristide back this time. When the Clinton administration reluctantly returned him to power in 1994, under intense international pressure, there were strings attached. Aristide was forced to accept neoliberal austerity measures that reversed most of his government's populist reforms. Massive privatization, a suppressed minimum wage, and the establishment of new free trade zones such as the Codevi FTZ were among these requirements.

When Aristide was re-elected in 2000, labor unions began to make a comeback, and in 2003 the government nearly doubled the legal minimum wage. The Haitian minimum in 1994 was 36 gourdes a day, or about $2.40. But by the time it was raised to 70 gourdes in 2003, over the strident objections of the USAID, the higher amount was equivalent to only around $1.70, about one-third of the cost of living in Haiti. Many workers had to fight for enforcement of even this abysmally low minimum wage, receiving little help from the Aristide government.

More disturbingly, the Aristide government also began cracking down on emerging workers' organizations. In 2003 riot police beat and shot at garment assembly workers demonstrating at a Port-au-Prince factory belonging to Wilbes & Co., a supplier of Wal-Mart, K-Mart, Target, Sears, and other discount outlets. When orange pickers unionized the year before at the major liqueur supplier Guacimal, they faced beatings, imprisonment, and death by dismemberment at the hands of Haitian police.

As a consequence, says Etienne, many Haitian workers now see Aristide as a collaborator and are looking elsewhere for salvation, even as their situation quickly worsens. "The forces lining up for power now represent the bosses' interests even more directly," she says. "But we, at Batay Ouvriye, are very clear that neither one has nor had workers' organization on its agenda. Of course, it is we, workers, who have to roll back our shirt sleeves to fight for our rights independently."

SHIRT SLEEVES AROUND THE WORLD

Batay Ouvriye has been fighting for workers' rights since the mid-1990s in the Port-au-Prince garment district, where workers assemble goods for export under Dickensian conditions. At HAACOSA, for example, a subcontractor for uniform giant Cintas, workers earn well below the minimum wage, have no access to clean water, and work behind locked gates in suffocating heat and filth. Attempts to unionize have been met with beatings or firings, but the workers persist.

A great deal of Batay Ouvriye's work consists of education, including basic literacy classes (adult literacy is about 53%, and much lower among workers) and legal rights training. The group ties into a network of local and international unions and solidarity groups that lend support by pressuring employers and government officials with letters, faxes, e-mails, and phone calls. But the system requires constant vigilance, as at Grupo M.

Grupo M's contract employer, Levi Strauss, has a code of conduct that requires respect for union rights among its subcontractors. Thanks to the anti-sweatshop movement of the 1990s, such codes are common in big corporations, including several in Haiti. Most are difficult to enforce. But the Grupo M plant in the Codevi FTZ had received a startup loan of $20 million from the World Bank, and with the help of international supporters Batay Ouvriye campaigned successfully to make the loan conditional on respect for workers' rights.

So when the troops attacked workers at Grupo M, Batay Ouvriye quickly mobilized an international call for the World Bank and Levi Strauss to intervene. They did, and Grupo M promised to rehire the 34 fired workers. Managers later balked at rehiring them all, although eventually all 34 did return to work.

At the same time, the plant forced workers to accept mysterious "vaccinations," which the workers feared were sterilizations. Their fears may have been justified: The Haitian Doctors' Union reports evidence that the injections contained contraceptives, including several miscarriages and numerous menstrual problems among workers who received the shots. And one worker says a doctor at the local hospital told her that Grupo M was running a "family planning program." When the workers went on strike in protest in June, plant managers brought in armed troops, this time from the Dominican Republic, to strip and question female workers at gunpoint. Workers say the soldiers also beat up a pregnant woman and threw her in a mud puddle.

Two days into the strike, management agreed to negotiate and the strikers agreed to return to work. However, when the workers arrived at the plant the next day, they discovered that management had locked them out. Now Grupo M is threatening to close the plant in the Codevi FTZ. But Haitian workers will not give up, says Yannick Etienne, at Grupo M or elsewhere. "The struggle," she says, "is just beginning."

To help, visit www.batayouvriye.org or www.haitisupport.gn.apc.org.

SOURCES

Lydia Polgreen and Tim Weiner, "Haiti's President Forced Out; Marines Sent to Keep Order," *The New York Times* (February 29, 2004); Paul Farmer, *The Uses of Haiti* (Common Courage Press, 1994); the International Centre for Trade Union Rights, *International Union Rights* 10, no. 2 (June 2003); *Haitian Times* (October 15, 2003); Clara James, "Haitian Free Trade Zone," *D&S* (November/December 2002).

POLITICS AS ORGANIZED CRIME IN COLOMBIA?

BY FORREST HYLTON
NACLA Report, May/June 2006

As the rest of Latin America continues its seismic political shift to the left, Colombia moves starkly in the opposite direction. In the March 12 congressional elections, 22 of the country's 32 departments swung to the right, and now that President Álvaro Uribe has re-engineered the 1991 Constitution, he is widely expected to win a second term in the May 28 elections.

Uribe's reelection bid and the paramilitary entry into official politics have split the Liberal Party, and the parliamentary duopoly—shared by the Liberals and the Conservative Party—that endured for more than 150 years appears to have ended. The Conservative Party, which put forth candidates with paramilitary ties and is merely one of a handful of parties in the pro-Uribe camp, has been losing ground to the Liberal Party since the 1940s. But in the recent elections, the Conservatives made their first significant gains against the Liberals since 1930.

The congressional election had several other significant features: the abstention rate of 60% was typically high; the Liberal Party suffered a historic setback with the defection of many of its *caciques* (political bosses) to pro-Uribe parties, which ended up winning 70% of the seats in the House and Senate; and the remarkable showing—by Colombian standards—of a united electoral left led by professor and jurist Carlos Gaviria. The results highlight the growing degree of political polarization under Uribe and the overwhelming dominance of the pro-Uribe right. Perhaps most revealing of the country's current political conjuncture and its future directions was the extent to which the elections confirmed the paramilitaries' increasing reach into Colombia's official political landscape.

Paramilitarism began in Colombia as a counterinsurgency strategy against the expansion of a durable left insurgency that exercised sovereignty, levied taxes, and challenged private property rights in huge swaths of Colombia's territory. In the 1980s and 1990s, with the support of landowners, sectors of the Colombian police, military, and intelligence, and the two main political parties, the right-wing counterinsurgency went from operating locally and regionally to operating nationally. Paramilitaries quickly moved beyond the designs of their creators to become the country's largest, most powerful landlords and cocaine exporters, with regional power bases that translated into electoral gains.

In the hothouse of the narcotics trade, paramilitary activities also became a business enterprise premised on the violent concentration of land as well as the promotion of large-scale agribusiness, mining, transport, and infrastructure projects. As human rights groups have documented, paramilitaries are responsible for an estimated 80% of all human rights violations in Colombia, helping to create, after Sudan, the second-largest internally displaced population in the world; 2 million Colombians have been dispossessed in the first five years of this century. This massive displacement facilitated the expropriation of land, which provided the paramilitaries and their allies one way to launder fortunes acquired mainly through drug trafficking.

IMMUNITY AND IMPUNITY

One of Uribe's first acts upon coming to power in 2002 was to declare a "peace process" with the paramilitaries. But it is not a peace process in the accepted sense of the term, since paramilitaries have always claimed to be fighting in support of the Colombian government in its war against left insurgencies—a factor that partially explains why the demobilization process continued even though paramilitaries doubled their attacks from 2004 to 2005. Half of paramilitary commanders are wanted for extradition to the United States on cocaine trafficking charges, but the Colombian government would be hard-pressed to fight the paramilitaries and left insurgencies at the same time. So in March the U.S. government requested the extradition of commanders from the Revolutionary Armed Forces of Colombia (FARC) on trafficking charges, sending a clear signal of impunity to paramilitaries. But in delegating repression to right-wing paramilitary forces, the Colombian state has weakened an already fragile legitimacy in the eyes of citizens. President Uribe appears to recognize this, and has sought to integrate the paramilitaries into public life via demobilization under the terms of the "Justice and Peace Law."

Rafael Pardo, who lost the presidential nomination as the Liberal Party candidate, used the phrase "a political model based on organized crime" to describe the implications of the "Justice and Peace Law" passed by the Colombian Congress in June 2005. The law gives a team of 20 prosecutors a maximum of 60 days to investigate all paramilitary crimes, and it provides the legal framework regulating the "demobilization" of 30 paramilitary blocs composed of 28,000 fighters. Colombian senator Jimmy Chamorro aptly described it as "a law of immunity and impunity." And a surprisingly frank *New York Times* editorial argued that it should have been called the "Impunity for Mass Murderers, Terrorists and Major Cocaine Traffickers' Law."

The law makes no provisions for official reparations to victims and provides only minimal investigation of paramilitary crimes. If the demobilized commanders serve jail time in Colombia—as one of the most powerful is now doing at the prison of his choice—they would only do a maximum of five and a half years, after which they could claim double jeopardy in the face of U.S. government extradition requests. Numerous human rights organizations have documented that commanders of the regional paramilitary blocs have not "demobilized" their private armies, except for photo-ops during official ceremonies. Paramilitary armies, landed empires, investments, bank accounts, transport corridors, political connections, and the dominance of cocaine exports are likely to remain intact.

Through the pomp and ceremony of demobilization, paramilitaries have disappeared through official fiat, but their power is suspected to be greater now than it was before the demobilization ceremonies began. In February, the U.S. government pressured Uribe's cousin, Senator Mario Uribe, to remove two openly paramilitary candidates from the list of congressional candidates of one of the most powerful parties backing the president's reelection bid—the Democratic Colombia party. In a strikingly uncharacteristic response, the president demanded that Washington stay out of Colombia's internal affairs. The candidates barred from Mario Uribe's party quietly passed into the ranks of another pro-government party, Citizen Convergence, led by Luis Alberto Gil. Pressed by a journalist about his connections to paramilitaries, Gil replied, "Me? A paramilitary? But paramilitarism is over in Colombia. . . . And it's not me saying this, it's our president, Álvaro Uribe Vélez." Gil was one of the top 10 congressional vote-getters, and his party picked up 14 seats. Amid widespread criticism in the run-up to the elections, nine paramilitary candidates were purged from the congressional lists of the two strongest pro-Uribe parties: the National Unity Party—commonly known as "La U" and led by former Liberal caciques—and the Radical Change party. But four of those candidates still won seats by getting on the ballots of other, lower-profile pro-Uribe parties, especially in the northern coast. Yet paramilitaries dumped two of their staunchest congressional supporters, both women, after the U.S. Embassy demanded their expulsion from the lists of La U.

It is in Colombia's northern Caribbean region straddling the Sierra Nevada de Santa Marta—namely, the departments of Magdalena, César, and La Guajira—that the growing paramilitary reach over politics and the economy has been strongest. Hernán Giraldo and Rodrigo Tovar (a.k.a. "Jorge 40"), who demobilized in February and March 2006, respectively, control the department of Magdalena. In 2003, their candidate for governor won the race after running unopposed (the other candidates had resigned, citing paramilitary threats). They also secured victory for three senators and three representatives to the national legislature. And in late 2002, when one opposition candidate braved threats from the AUC and insisted on running for mayor in the municipality of Concordia, he was assassinated. Fourteen of 30 mayors in the department ran unopposed in the 2003 local elections.

In La Guajira, which straddles the Venezuelan border, the mayor and 10 city council members were arrested in the capital, Riohacha, in September 2004 for funneling health care block grants to Jorge 40. In Santa Marta, the capital of

Magdalena, everyone from street vendors to store owners pay taxes levied by paramilitary groups. As elsewhere, in Magdalena and La Guajira, Giraldo and Jorge 40 control intelligence, gambling, prostitution, private security, protection rackets, contraband, money laundering, and much of the cocaine business.

Jorge 40's strategy of enlisting candidates with backgrounds in traditional politics, rather than recruiting newcomers with direct and overt paramilitary association, proved successful in the congressional elections. All but one of the four candidates expelled from other pro-Uribe parties ended up winning in Jorge 40's fiefdom, along with traditional caciques. For the time being, the paramilitaries have shown a clear preference for politicians not publicly associated with them, choosing influence over direct representation, but they reelected congressmen and senators on the coast. In the wake of demobilization, paramilitaries have become a mafia state within the state, but their future ultimately rests on Uribe's willingness to refuse U.S. government requests for their extradition. Warriors like Jorge 40 have said that only reelection can guarantee their "peace," which requires, in the words of one of the last of the paramilitary Castaño dynasty, nothing less than "judicial bullet-proofing."

THE FALCON REMEMBERED

BY KAREN ROBERT
NACLA Report, November/December 2005

At noon on March 4, 2005, a green Ford Falcon pulled up next to a woman in Centenario, a municipality of Neuquén, in southern Argentina. Three men and a woman forced her into the car and then spent the next several hours threatening, torturing, and mutilating her. The victim, whose name has been kept secret, was the wife of an employee at the Cerámica Zanon tile factory, one of the flagship worker-controlled enterprises that have sprung up in Argentina since the 2001 crisis. While the Zanon workers have successfully resuscitated the plant, they have also faced growing intimidation, as exemplified by this attack. The victim's abductors released her with the message: "This is for Zanon. Tell them that the union will run with blood. . . . You're all going to have to move into the factory because we're going to kill all of you."

Such tactics of violence and intimidation carry a pedigree as long as Argentina's history of authoritarianism. Yet the automobile used in this attack has a much more specific association with the terror of the 1970s Dirty War, when the Ford Falcon was the car of choice used by police, military, and paramilitaries alike. Ford's exclusive contracts with the Argentine security forces throughout the dictatorship eventually made the Falcon the single most recognizable icon of repression, one that clearly still resonates today. "Whenever a Falcon drove by or slowed down, we all knew that there would be kidnappings, disappearances, torture, or murder," reflects renowned Argentine psychologist and playwright Eduardo "Tato" Pavlovsky in a recent article. "It was the symbolic expression of terror. A death-mobile."

AN END TO IMPUNITY?

The attack on the Zanon workers also chillingly recalls the violence used nearly 30 years ago against the very workers who were building Falcons for Ford. A lawsuit currently being prepared against Ford Motor Company alleges that the company's relationship with the military junta went beyond that of a privileged supplier.

Pedro Troiani and 14 other former Ford employees are seeking to bring criminal charges against the company for its role in their disappearance, torture, and detention during the first two years of the dictatorship. They allege that Ford management conspired with military officials to rid themselves of the factory's union delegates and to intimidate the rest of the workforce into submission. The plaintiffs accuse the company of providing the military with a list of "subversives" and then supplying information from personnel files to facilitate the men's abduction from their homes or from the factory premises, where they also allege that an illegal detention center operated from the first day of the coup.

The Ford case and a parallel lawsuit against Mercedes Benz owner DaimlerChrysler mark the first attempts in Argentina to charge private corporations for complicity in human rights violations. The latter case concerning the disappearance of Mercedes Benz workers implicates DaimlerChrysler in Germany, the United States, and within Argentina. The case names the company's Argentine subsidiary, the military, and José Rodríguez, president of SMATA, the autoworkers' union. These cases also break new ground in multinational corporate accountability by naming the parent companies located outside Argentina as also bearing ultimate responsibility for these crimes.

For now, the Ford investigation remains in the hands of lawyer Tomás Ojea Quintana and prosecutor Federico Delgado, who must determine whether sufficient evidence exists to pursue criminal charges against individual Ford managers and executives from the 1970s. Ojea Quintana must then build the larger case against Ford Argentina and Ford Motor Company step-by-step, moving from the culpability of individuals to the complicity of the corporation itself. To do so, he must prove that the factory in General Pacheco was not taken over by the military but remained under Ford's managerial control during the dictatorship. He also has to establish that the disappearances of Ford employees resulted from a management directive and not from the excessive zeal of a few overseers. If the Ford case successfully passes these obstacles, Ojea Quintana's Los Angeles–based colleague Paul Hoffmann will use the U.S. Alien Tort Claims Act to challenge the Ford Motor Company in U.S. courts.

Soon after the return to democracy at the end of 1983, Argentina set an example within Latin America by pursuing criminal charges against military officers in a series of trials that saw all the junta leaders convicted and briefly imprisoned. Pioneering human rights lawyers successfully proved that the violations of the Dirty War had been meticulously planned and directed by the junta, and were not the result of accumulated "excesses" committed by lower officers. However, the so-called impunity laws passed by presidents Raúl Alfonsín and Carlos Menem stalled and eventually reversed these landmark achievements. Menem's blanket pardon of 1990 seemed to end all possibilities of justice. Yet the political and economic crisis of 2001 revitalized efforts to reform the judicial system, culminating in the Supreme Court's repeal of the impunity laws in June 2005. According to Ojea Quintana, this new juncture has made it possible to take the legal struggle for human rights into areas of corporate accountability that were previously all but unimaginable.

The connivance between business and military leaders at the time of the coup is a recognized fact in Argentina, though one that has not been proven in a judicial forum. Both parties feared the left-wing Montoneros guerrillas and the People's Revolutionary Army (ERP), but their greater worries were reserved for Argentina's organized and combative labor movement. For the military, organized labor represented the most enduring and disturbing legacy of Peronism. Though plagued by corruption and fractured by political polarization in the 1960s, the unions had survived efforts at cooptation and repression since Juan Perón's overthrow in 1955 and represented a major political obstacle to the far-reaching goals of the junta's bloody "Process of National Reconstruction."

Organized labor's strength also had concrete implications for Argentine industry, especially in large-scale establishments where shop-floor delegates challenged management's control over the pace and organization of the labor process. Tensions ran especially high in the automotive sector once the bureaucratic leadership of SMATA, lost control over some factories to a generation of more combative, *clasista* shop-floor delegates. The most dramatic example of that challenge was the Cordobazo of 1969, a massive general strike in the city of Córdoba that began as a labor dispute at a plant of Italian automaker Fiat.

BUSINESS-MILITARY REPRESSION

In a new study of the dictatorship, historians Marcos Novaro and Vicente Palermo describe a virtually seamless collaboration between business and the armed forces in 1976. In one instance they point to a pamphlet prepared jointly by the Army and the Argentine Employers Institute for Development (IDEA), a leading executive forum, which recommended that managers denounce "subversive" or even suspicious employees to the security forces. The response was apparently so enthusiastic that by the end of the dictatorship virtually all the shop-floor delegates had been disappeared from the country's biggest firms, among them several auto manufacturers, such as Mercedes Benz, Chrysler, and Fiat.

The fact that 15 Ford workers survived their disappearances and have lived to challenge Ford in court may, ironically, be a testament to the effective paternalism that the company exercised in its huge plant in General Pacheco, a suburb of Buenos Aires. It has taken years for the plaintiffs against Ford to even conceive of their former employer as criminally responsible for their disappearances. Pedro Troiani, today the most outspoken among the survivors, was an avid Ford racing fan even before he started building Falcons at the new Pacheco plant in 1963, at the age of 21.

"It was a real novelty to work in an auto factory, because it was one of the first ones in the country," Troiani remembers. "You really felt privileged to get a job there. There was lots of talk about the 'Ford family,' and they'd have a big

Christmas party every year and raffle off a new Falcon." Troiani remained a company man even after he was elected as a union delegate in 1970. He dedicated himself to workplace safety and salary-related issues while also remaining so moderate within the union that the Marxist ERP guerrilla movement marked him for death in the early 1970s as a stooge of both Ford and SMATA.

Ford invited the army into the factory in 1975, months before the coup. Ford spokesperson Rolando Ceretti told *The New York Times* that this military presence was a response to guerrilla threats and attacks against executives. From the perspective of the shop floor, the factory was like an armed camp; soldiers roamed between the machinery and checked workers' identification daily against lists of union activists.

Rumors about detentions of union delegates from the premises of the Ford plant began circulating during the dictatorship and were confirmed in 1984 in *Nunca Más*, the official report of Argentina's National Commission on the Disappeared (CONADEP). The most damning evidence regarding Ford management's complicity with the military appeared in the testimonies of several former union delegates who were all present at a meeting with Ford's labor relations manager, known only as Galarraga. Although two of the witnesses dated this meeting on or after the date of the coup (March 24, 1976), Juan Carlos Amoroso, who was also at the meeting, recalled that it occurred on March 23—the eve of the coup. After announcing that management would no longer recognize the men as the workers' delegates, Amoroso remembers that Galarraga taunted them with words that, at the time, meant nothing to him: "Amoroso, give my regards to Camps!" When Amoroso asked whom Camps was, Galarraga replied laughing, "You'll find out soon enough." Ramón Camps, then an obscure Army Colonel, would soon become one of Argentina's most notorious architects of terror in his role as chief of the Buenos Aires provincial police and would be sentenced in 1986 to 25 years in prison for his role in 600 murders.

Galarraga's was not an empty threat, and the disappearances began immediately. Two union delegates among the cafeteria workers, Luis María Giusti and Jorge Costanzo, were abducted from the cafeteria on March 24 by two armed men wearing civilian clothes; they tied their hands with wire, hooded them, and forced them into a green Ford Falcon. The two workers were held for four hours in the sports center inside the plant, where they were beaten and kicked. They were then transported in another Ford Falcon and later a pickup truck to the Tigre police station in the province of Buenos Aires. Along the way they were subjected to a mock execution.

The next day, March 25, Francisco Guillermo Perrotta, a Ford accounting employee who was working as a paid union delegate outside the plant, got a call from Ford management ordering him to present himself at the factory the following day. When he arrived, two men met him in the secure parking lot, called him by name and forced him into a green Ford Falcon. They carried his photograph, which they claimed was obtained from Ford's human resources office.

Pedro Troiani says his supervisor had advance notice of his abduction on April 13, 1976. Far from warning him when he arrived at work that morning, the supervisor ordered Troiani not to move from his place on the line: "You can't move because they're watching you." When a truckload of soldiers descended on the plant, the factory foreman, Miguel Migliacchio, identified Troiani to them. The plant manager came out of his office to watch as they pulled Troiani off the line and paraded him around the factory, hands behind his head.

Troiani, Carlos Alberto Propato, and five others rounded up that day were taken to the same makeshift detention center within the plant's athletic facilities, where they were kept for seven hours. They were then transferred to the Tigre police station, where they encountered co-workers from Ford and union delegates from other firms who had also been kidnapped. "When we arrived Perrotta was already there, delirious because they'd beaten him and worked him over so badly with a cattle prod," recalls Propato. Eleven men were crowded into a 10-square-foot cell for roughly six weeks and subjected to continuing rounds of torture while officials refused to confirm that they were being held there. The men allege that they saw copies of their Ford credentials in the hands of police at the Tigre police station. The workers' lawyer also has the testimony of witnesses who saw the military commander of the detachment stationed in the plant with a list of the men's names on Ford letterhead.

After roughly six weeks as "disappeared," authorities officially recognized the men as detained under National Executive Power (PEN) and were sent to regular prisons. While theoretically less likely to be killed now, they continued to suffer torture and abuse until their eventual release roughly a year later. Carlos Alberto Propato still does not know why he was later moved from Devoto prison to Sierra Chica, a maximum-security prison reserved for the country's most dangerous criminals. During the five-hour flight he and other prisoners were beaten and told they were going to be thrown into the ocean. Propato remained in solitary confinement for several months at Sierra Chica, where he was constantly beaten and subjected to at least three simulated executions. In May 1977 he was inexplicably released.

Back in General Pacheco, meanwhile, panic ran through the factory as other union delegates abandoned their activism or resigned altogether. "Lots of people left without claiming one cent, because they were scared," observes Propato. Several families of disappeared workers received telegrams from Ford warning that employees absent from work would be fired, even in cases like Troiani's in which management had witnessed the arrest. When Troiani's wife protested by telegram that the Ford managers knew exactly why her husband was absent from work, the message was returned to her.

NEVER AGAIN

The survivors from Ford gradually recovered their freedom throughout the months of 1977, but they lived in terror for the remainder of the military years, unable to return to their old jobs and blacklisted from other factories. Having briefly counted themselves among the most privileged and organized industrial workers of Argentina, they now found themselves living as ghosts. Perhaps they survived to spread word of their ordeal because they were deemed less dangerous or more "redeemable" than the Mercedes or Fiat workers who had fatally challenged not only their employers but also their own union leadership. SMATA president José Rodríguez, whose control of the union has continued unbroken since 1973, is himself implicated in the Mercedes Benz disappearances. In fact, Propato and Troiani recall a meeting from before the coup when Rodríguez warned them that they should calm union activism at the Ford plant because the military would soon be taking power.

Ironically, as corporate entities both SMATA and Ford have enjoyed an institutional continuity that stands in dramatic contrast to the upheavals that have broken down and remade the Argentine state several times since 1976. They have remained as durable as the old Ford Falcons themselves that still roam the streets and are occasionally brought out for intimidation operations. That same continuity may yet be used against Ford in court, however, just as it has been used against firms that profited from slave labor in Nazi Germany (including Ford and its subsidiary Ford Werke).

Memory is also a form of endurance, and memories of Ford's association with the dictatorship remain vivid in Argentina. Artists continue to evoke the Falcon in sculpture, film, and photography as the physical embodiment of terror, and at least one Falcon owner in Buenos Aires feels compelled to drive with a sticker in the back window that reads, "My Falcon was not to blame. Nunca más" (Never again). The plaintiffs seek to bring their own memories to light through their case against Ford. In the words of survivor Carlos Alberto Propato, "We are part of the Falcon, too."

CHAPTER 3
LATIN AMERICA, NEOLIBERAL POLICY, AND THE GLOBAL ECONOMY

IS CHILE A NEOLIBERAL SUCCESS?

BY JAMES M. CYPHER
Dollars & Sense, September/October 2004

Chile is commonly portrayed as the great exception to Latin America's long and difficult struggle to overcome economic backwardness and instability. In 1982, conservative economist Milton Friedman of the University of Chicago pronounced the market-driven policies of Augusto Pinochet's military dictatorship "an economic miracle." Friedman was hardly an impartial observer. He and other Chicago economists had trained many of the dictatorship's ultra-free-market economic advisers, a group of Chilean economists who became known as the "Chicago boys." Other prominent U.S. economists, however, also tout Chile's "economic miracle." In 2000, Harvard economist Robert Barro asserted in *BusinessWeek* that Chile's "outstanding performance derived from the free-market reforms instituted by . . . Pinochet." Even Nobel laureate Joseph Stiglitz, a strong critic of the Chicago School, described Chile in his 2002 book *Globalization and Its Discontents* as an exception to the failure of unregulated free markets and free trade policies in developing nations.

Neoliberalism, a term first employed in Latin America, describes the experiment in unregulated capitalism that the Pinochet dictatorship embraced in the years following the 1973 coup that toppled the elected government of Socialist president Salvador Allende. Chile has seen three elected governments since Pinochet's fall in 1990. None, however, including the present Socialist-led government, has broken sharply with the neoliberal economic model instituted by the dictatorship. For years, these post-Pinochet Concertación governments (a coalition of the Christian Democratic and Socialist parties) were content to administer the economic boom that had begun in the latter years of the dictatorship.

But the boom turned to stagnation in 1997: Average per capita income rose only 0.7% per year between 1998 and 2002, while unemployment stayed above 9% through 2003. Export growth, widely viewed as the engine of the Chilean "miracle," stagnated, with total exports barely rising from $17 billion in 1997 to $17.4 billion in 2002.

While both the Concertación economists and those of the far right sought to blame Chile's woes on outside factors—the Asian crisis of 1997, the Argentine implosion of 2000, the U.S. slump of 2001, and so on—a few dissident economists had predicted all along that the boom would inevitably reach an impasse. One, economist Graciela Moguillansky of the United Nations' Economic Commission for Latin America and the Caribbean, argued that the large Chilean finance/

resource-processing conglomerates which dominate the economy had exhausted the easy resource-processing opportunities handed to them by the government through programs created decades ago. The "Chilean miracle" had reached its own self-imposed limits. Along similar lines, Orlando Caputo, director of the Santiago-based Centro de Estudios sobre Transnacionalización, Economía y Sociedad, argued that the underlying cause of the crisis was Chile's breakneck overproduction of copper. The price of copper fell so sharply between 1995 and 2002 that dollars received for copper exports actually declined over this period even while total output increased by 85%.

Rather than grapple with the need to realign economic policy and adopt a new model of development, however, the leaders of the Concertatión have decided to intensify the free-trade, export-oriented model—for example, by signing as many free-trade agreements as possible. In 2003 Chile was able to sign agreements with the two largest trading areas of the world, the European Union (EU) and the United States. These agreements would allow Chile's exports to surge, Concertación politicians and economists argued, pulling the rest of the economy along. The Chilean ruling elite is once again basking in self-satisfaction. But can they expect another lengthy period of export-fueled growth?

A review of recent Chilean economic history suggests that it's not likely. Despite the claims of free marketeers, Chile's economic performance has been mixed, and its successes owe more to state intervention than to the invisible hand of the free market. In fact, it would be hard to find any major sector of the economy that did not owe much of its existence to state intervention—intervention which continued in a variety of forms under the nominally neoliberal Pinochet dictatorship.

THE REAL TARGET: LABOR'S POWER

While the Chicago school is known for its devotion to free-market policies and its hostility to government regulation, the chief target of the Chicago Boys (and other right-wing economists), along with the military dictatorship and the business class, was not state intervention in economic life, but rather the organized power of the Chilean working class.

Through protracted struggles over many decades, Chilean unions had grown, spreading from the mining sector into manufacturing and eventually into agriculture. The 1973 coup destroyed the power of the working class in the political and economic systems. Its union and party leaders were tortured, assassinated, imprisoned, or exiled. Political parties were banned and unions made virtually illegal. The dictatorship introduced a "flexible" labor system that left workers with the formal right of individual contract, but stripped them of any right to organize and bargain collectively. Power shifted to the employers in the mines, factories, fields, and ports. The dictatorship spared no form of state intervention to crush workers' power.

The core political and economic strength of the unions when Pinochet came to power was in the industrial sector. Given the dictatorship's anti-labor aims, its economic development policy thus had to be an anti-industry policy. This meant abandoning the longtime basis of Chilean development policy, import substitution industrialization (ISI). When the Great Depression of the 1930s hit Chile harder than any other nation in the world, advocates of ISI argued that Chile had to stop exporting natural resources (e.g., nitrates, copper, and other minerals), at falling prices, and importing machinery and consumer products, at rising prices. ISI advocates claimed that nations such as Chile would be better off and more stable if they developed domestic industries and an internal market. To sustain industrialization, infant industries needed to develop behind a tariff wall so firms could learn, adapt, and grow. A developed internal market requires mass-based consumption (rather than just elite consumption of imported luxuries), trained workers, and the diffusion of production knowledge. Unions thrived in this environment: High wages provided the mass consumption base, while unions helped maintain morale and skill levels, which facilitated higher productivity.

The economists associated with the military dictatorship realized that an economic development strategy based on industrialization could not exclude a real voice for labor. One that drew upon Chile's vast treasure of untapped natural resources, however—the unceasing ocean, the endless forests of the south, the exceedingly fertile farmlands—could do just that. (Peter Winn's *Victims of the Chilean Miracle* brilliantly documents the pivotal anti-labor focus, particularly in the agricultural, forestry, and fishing sectors.) Thus, the creation of a "nontraditional" export sector became the keystone of the dictatorship's economic strategy.

The plan worked—for a time. Exports soared from 14.5% of GDP in 1974 to 31.4% in 1999. Copper fell to 40.5% of exports by 1995, while nontraditional exports such as salmon and resource-based "manufactured" products such as wood pulp, paper, cardboard, disposable diapers, and processed woods boomed. By 2002 all of the new resource-based exports combined—fresh produce and processed foods, forestry products, wine, and fishing—totaled $6.7 billion, less than total mining exports of $7.3 billion, but ahead of copper at $6.3 billion.

The export boom undeniably fueled the country's economic growth. After enduring a deep recession from 1982 to 1985 (unemployment reached 20% in 1982), Chile's economy more than bounced back. Between 1987 and 1998, per capita income grew by 88%.

MARKET OR STATE?

But it was not the invisible hand of the market that caused the new boom in resource-based exports. Most of the credit belongs to the state: Most of the strategies—such as new product development, risk capital, technical training and advising, marketing, quality control—and many of the personnel involved in the new Chilean "miracle" were products of the old, and much derided, state interventionism of the ISI era.

How could the core changes generating the "miracle" come from the detested state sector? One part of the answer is that many military officers in the upper ranks of the dictatorship were "developmentalists"—believing that the economic growth of Chile was partly a by-product of an agile and creative state. (When the nationalized copper giant CODELCO fell into the military's control, it *remained* a state-owned corporation. The military reluctantly permitted the privatization of the electric grid and the telephone system, but not copper, the state-owned oil corporation, or several other key state entities.) Another answer is that nations cannot quickly change their economic structure. The Chilean economy was put on a particular development path in 1939 with the creation of the CORFO, the state agency mandated to carry out the ISI strategy and build the national production base. CORFO's many new public and mixed public/private firms accounted for the great bulk of Chile's industrial growth from 1940 to 1974: A 1993 study pointed out that of the 20 top private exporting companies, at least 13 had been *created* by CORFO.

For a while under the dictatorship, it seemed that CORFO's mission was nothing more than to sell off all the state-owned firms, then disappear. But the agency still exists, and after the 1982–85 recession it became more active in the funding and development of new resource-sector firms.

In one key instance, CORFO was responsible for the funding and creation of the forestry sector—a strategy that it had advocated and supported for decades prior to the coup. The Chicago school economists have portrayed the boom in forestry products, now the largest export sector after mining, as a result of good policy and private initiative. The real story is that, while private capital lacked the initiative and foresight to develop the forestry sector, CORFO introduced forest-management techniques, provided credits and subsidies, financed projects for technological development and labor training, and fostered the development of the allied paper, cardboard, and wood industries. CORFO also created an affiliate, the Forestry Institute, which launched a marketing and information campaign designed to promote forestry exports, while carrying on massive reforestation programs and introducing new tree varieties.

The same basic story holds for the fishing industry, as well as for most of the developments in fresh produce and processed food. Rather than the invisible hand moving through market forces, the visible (but largely ignored) hand of Fundación Chile—a public-private agency designed to develop firms in new areas where private capital would not invest, then sell them to the private sector—was responsible for most of this diversification. Fundación Chile began in 1976, with the assistance of a prominent economist, Raúl Sáez, who had headed CORFO for many years. Like many of the military officers in the highest ranks of the dictatorship, Sáez was contemptuous of the pretensions and ignorance of the Chicago school neoliberals. With CORFO under attack from this quarter, Sáez moved laterally and gathered a group of experts who achieved major changes in the productive apparatus of the Chilean economy. (Incubating institutions similar to Fundación Chile have played a key role in the recent history of economic development in Korea, Taiwan, and much of East Asia—but these nations have consciously avoided neoliberal free trade policies. Instead of *accepting* the dictates of the market, they have sought to *govern* the market.)

Likewise, the dictatorship created ProChile in 1974 to assist the private sector in locating and selling to foreign markets. Today, many of the activities of ProChile are coordinated with support programs fostered by CORFO. Through its Export Promotion Fund, ProChile has co-financed export projects, providing up to 50% of the necessary capital—often using funds obtained from or through CORFO.

In yet another instance of state intervention, the government facilitated a boom in the private mining sector from the 1980s by allowing the mines to operate essentially tax-free. The tax rate was an all but invisible 0.8% of sales in 2002. From 1992 to 2002, eight of the top 10 private mining companies paid no taxes, in spite of the fact that Chile has the most profitable copper mining companies in the world. (Meanwhile, the poor pay a value-added tax of 19% on their consumption, including food and medicine.)

What all this adds up to should not be too surprising. In spite of a brutal military dictatorship that sought the total restructuring of the economy and the elimination of the state's guiding role in it, the state sector was a crucial ingredient in Chile's efforts to build an export-led economy in the Pinochet years and beyond. Thus, although neoliberals occasionally imposed their free-market ideas in the financial sector, the restructuring of the economy was led by a *stealth* government development policy. (Even in the financial sphere, the Chicago boys were forced by real circumstances to retreat, imposing protective tariffs in the 1980s and accepting capital controls on imported short-term "hot" money.) While Chile is nearly always portrayed as a *neoliberal* success story, the reality is that Chile's transformation was *not* neoliberal at its core—that is, within the system of production.

END OF AN ERA?

Why has the Chilean "miracle" stagnated? CORFO, the Fundación Chile, and ProChile—the core triangle of state institutions responsible for the stealth development policy—are no longer receiving the funding to create new export sectors. In theory, the large forestry companies and others involved in resource processing *could* expand and upgrade their exports, but Moguillansky's work has demonstrated that these corporations are unwilling to take risks and plow their profits into new economic activities. They have no intention of making the long-term investments in machinery and equipment, personnel, and technology, and marketing that would be necessary to develop, for example, a strong, dynamic furniture-making sector. The same criticism was raised by the vice-president of Chile's Institute of Mining Engineers and by the Association of Metallurgy Industries, who argued that Chile needed an industrial policy (i.e., state intervention directing investment to strategic new sectors) to develop copper processing and the manufacture of copper-intensive products. Currently, only 1% of the copper mined in Chile is processed or turned into manufactured products in the country.

As Moguillansky stresses, Chile's financial/industrial groups are not interested in technological modernization. In a study of 15 similar nations, the United Nations ranked Chile next to last in its index of technological capabilities, and 13th in terms of expenditures on research and development by private firms. Yet, in spite of all this, and because of the role of state intervention in the past, Chile *does* have a somewhat competitive manufacturing sector: Metalworking exports in the manufacturing sector in 2002 were larger than processed food exports and nearly equal to fresh produce exports. Other manufactured exports include plastics, containers, and textiles. With large investments and a new government policy fostering technological research and development and massive labor training, Chile could develop high value-added manufacturing. High wages flowing from a strongly unionized manufacturing sector could, in turn, enlarge the internal market for industrial products.

Both forestry and mining have great potential in terms of expansion into clusters of high value-added industries. Both would demand the massive participation of a trained, skilled industrial workforce. Support for these sectors is logical from the standpoint of development economics; however, it would create more favorable conditions for unionization and, because independent unions in Chile have always been political as well as economic organizations, this would help bring the working class back into the political arena. Such a development would threaten to revive fundamental struggles not only over the distribution of income, but also over the institutional organization of the economy—the worst fear of Chile's economic, political, military, and religious elites.

THE FREE TRADE OPTION?

For now, the elite is hoping that the new free-trade agreements will cure the country's economic stagnation. Exports to Europe are up, along with copper prices, and Chile now awaits a further opening to the U.S. market. The new trade agreements are expected to increase foreign direct investment, but no one has attempted to quantify it. Chile has been so wide open to foreign investment, and foreign investors have enjoyed the assurance of a pro-investor climate for so long, that it is difficult to imagine much of a surge of new investment from either Europe or the United States.

Thus, if the new free-trade agreements are to be the next short-term fix for Chile's unraveling economic model, the impact will have to come through more export opportunities. Chile has an edge in trade with the European Union and the United States because its fresh produce is largely grown and harvested during the summer in the southern hemisphere, which coincides with the winter months in Europe and the United States. This edge is tenuous, though, since other southern nations can also grow and transport these crops.

Chile may be a few years ahead of its competitors, but it has nothing unique to offer. Since 1996, reforestation has stagnated and Chile's two largest forest-product companies have shifted investment to Argentina and Brazil. Another successful niche has been aquaculture, particularly farmed salmon. Salmon production and prices are up for the moment and Chile has a huge coastline well adapted to fishing. But other countries can become competitors in this sector as well. In short, although Chile has developed some important niche markets like high-end produce, fish, wine, and wood products, there is no reason to believe that these nontraditional exports will long be immune to global competition. The result, as always: overproduction and falling prices, a problem that has cursed Latin America for centuries.

There is, of course, another side to free-trade agreements. The United States did not sign the 2003 agreement with Chile out of goodwill. While Chile's pundits foresee huge export growth, they are virtually silent about surging U.S. imports. Which parts of the production system will be knocked out by competition from U.S. firms? The Chilean government has conducted some relevant studies, which predict that the agreement's overall results will be positive for Chile, but small. Between 2004 and 2010, when the stimulus of the trade agreement is expected to end, Chile's GDP growth might rise between one-half and one percentage point per year. Since 1997, Chile's growth has slowed to 2.3% per year. Thus, in the most optimistic scenario, the U.S. trade agreement could lift the growth rate for a six year period to 3.3%. The EU free-trade agreement may have a similar impact, since the EU market is of similar size. If so, Chile could project, at best, a 4.3% growth rate. Chilean government economists claim U.S. imports will essentially *complement* Chile's expansion, providing machinery and equipment that will permit more exports. But competition from U.S. wheat, potato, corn, sugar beet, and dairy producers will probably destroy much of the farm sector.

Still, all this is just toying with economic models. Back in the real world, if Chile manages to keep an edge in its nonmineral exports, it will only be by keeping wages down. If growth does pick up modestly for a few years, the benefits of that growth will not flow to the mass of Chileans.

Unfortunately for them, the two new free-trade agreements will probably prolong the life of the export-led model a bit longer. Rather than facing the inherent limitations and injustices of this development model, the Concertación government has sidestepped the real question: After export-led policies fail, what next?

In the absence of a critical dialogue, it is hard to imagine Chile turning away from its free-market, free-trade orientation. Even a devastating economic crisis might not spur change if no critical vision can be put forward. Unfortunately, the legacy of the dictatorship still lingers over Chilean public opinion and political discourse: The economics departments (with one or two small exceptions) all speak with a single, free-trade voice, the independent research centers are silent, and the government and the press laud the idea of more and greater export possibilities. In this climate, as a Chilean colleague said: "*You* can be critical, but if *we* say these things we will be committing economic suicide—our careers will be destroyed." Less than 15 years removed from the end of the military dictatorship, in Chile dissent is still largely an unpracticed art.

BOOM FOR WHOM?

The Chilean economy unquestionably enjoyed a boom in the late 1980s and 1990s. Some Chileans enjoyed the boom more than others, however. Even as Chile's average per capita income nearly doubled between 1987 and 1998, workers' average wages increased by only 53%, and because of wage losses over the 22 years between 1970 and 1992, real wages in 1998 were only 29.5% higher than in 1970. Chile now has the third most unequal income distribution in Latin America (behind Brazil and Guatemala). According to official government data, the top 20% received 57.5% of the national income in 2000; the top 10% received 42.5%. Tax evasion is widespread, with an estimated 23% of total income going unreported, virtually all of it flowing to the top 20%. So in reality, income distribution is even more unequal than official figures acknowledge. The skewed distribution of income, more unequal than it was in the 1960s, is a deliberate result of government policy. One element of the policy is to keep income taxes low—the average income tax rate on the top 10% is a mere 2.5%. Another is to keep wages low in the export sectors to keep them internationally competitive. But this also means that wages must be low throughout the economy.

Redistribution policies instituted by the Concertación have brought the official poverty rate from 45% in 1987 to 21% in 2000. Certainly this is a laudable accomplishment, but it fails to address the inequality and the near-poverty status of workers that result from the neoliberal strategy. Those in power may simply have no interest in addressing these problems on a systemic level. For the top 20% (and this includes the political class—right, left, and center), Chile is a great country full of expensive imported SUVs, cheap servants, spiffy private schools, marvelous skiing, and exquisite weekend beach houses. No matter that monthly tuition in one of the private schools exceeds the entire monthly wage of the average worker, or that one day of skiing would cost that worker three to four days' income. Unlike in most of Latin America, the poor are kept out of sight of the comfortable, thanks to homogeneous neighborhoods on the U.S. model.

SOURCES

Rafael Agacino, "Reestructuración productiva, flexiblidad y empleo" (unpublished manuscript, 2003); Carlos Álvarez, "La CORFO y la transformación de la industria manufacturera," in *Estudios y informes de la CEPAL* no. 84 (Santiago, Chile, 1993); Orlando Caputo and Juan Radrigán, "Economía chilena: agotamiento relativo del modelo" (October 2003), downloaded from www.cetes.cl; Graciela Moguillansky, *La inversión en Chile: ¿el fin de un ciclo en expansión?* (Mexico: Fondo de Cultura, 1999); Peter Winn, ed., *Victims of the Chilean Miracle: Workers and Neoliberalism in the Pinochet Era, 1973–2002* (Duke University Press, 2004).

FROM NAFTA TO THE SPP

BY KATHERINE SCIACCHITANO
Dollars & Sense, January/February 2008

Which is closer to your vision of North America?

Vision A: Three interdependent countries with vibrant social movements, respect for labor rights, and environmentally sustainable economies anchored in provision of social needs and respect for cultural autonomy? Or Vision B: An unequal alliance dominated by the United States, complete with pumped up oil and gas production, increasing militarization, corporate transnational planning groups, and guest-worker programs to ensure cheap, vulnerable labor?

If your answer is Vision A, there's good news and bad news. The good news is that this past August at a summit of the leaders of the United States, Canada, and Mexico in Montebello, Quebec, labor, environmental, and globalization activists braved riot police and tear gas to demand democratic input into North American decision making.

The bad news is that the summit was about the Security and Prosperity Partnership (SPP) of North America—the real-world name of Vision B.

While left activists and researchers in Canada and Mexico have been spreading the word about the SPP for several years, so far in the United States the SPP, which was officially launched in March 2005, has mainly caught the attention of the right wing, which sees it as a stealth plan to impose a European Union–style government on the continent.

The SPP is *not* a North American version of the European Union. But it *is* a stealth plan—one aimed at bypassing the kind of international solidarity that halted the Free Trade Agreement of the Americas and the Multilateral Agreement on Investment. The European Union emerged after years of public debate and a treaty ratified by member states. By contrast, the SPP is not a treaty and will never be submitted to the U.S., Mexican, or Canadian legislatures. Instead it attempts to reshape the North American political economy by direct use of executive authority. And while the European Union maintains an explicit role for government in addressing inequality within and between countries, the SPP's foundation is an unequal alliance where the United States retains the political and economic trump cards.

Designed to shore up the United States' weakening position as a global hegemon, the SPP's primary goals are to link economic integration of the three countries to U.S. security needs; deepen U.S. access to oil, gas, electricity, and water resources throughout the continent; and to provide a privileged—and institutionalized—role for transnational corporations in continental deregulation. The stakes for labor, the environment, and civil liberties in all three countries couldn't be higher. Yet because of the SPP's reliance on executive authority to push the agenda, many of the SPP's initiatives remain virtually invisible, even to many activists.

SPP BASICS

The North American Free Trade Agreement (NAFTA), which went into effect in 1994, was designed to enhance the access of transnational capital from the United States to cheap Mexican labor and Canadian natural resources. The SPP deepens these relations and harnesses the so-called war on terror to an expanded U.S.-Mexican-Canadian trade agenda and a lopsided energy grab to secure U.S. access to dwindling continental oil and gas reserves.

As its name implies, the SPP has two basic parts: the Security Agenda and the Prosperity Agenda. Both are rooted in the United States' deteriorating global position, particularly its increased competition for access to global oil and gas reserves and worsening trade balance with China.

With the explicit aim of securing North America from "internal" as well as external threats, the Security Agenda coordinates intelligence activities among the three countries and streamlines the movement of "low risk" goods and people (especially so-called NAFTA professionals) across borders. It also involves extensive military coordination, much of it focused on protecting energy and transportation infrastructure. (Consolidating a North American military structure no doubt also serves as an offensive hedge against Venezuela's attempt to shape an independent South American energy policy.)

The Prosperity Agenda continues the Security Agenda's focus on energy. World demand is growing as traditional sources from the Middle East, Russia, and South America are becoming less secure; and the resulting price increases and realignment of power threaten a redistribution of wealth and power in favor of the oil and gas producers, many of them in the Global South. The Prosperity Agenda aims first and foremost at consolidating U.S. control over North American energy supplies, first by expanding production in Canada and Mexico, and second by increasing U.S. access to that production by deregulating energy markets.

In addition to expanding energy production, Prosperity Agenda activities include a trinational framework for "minimizing" regulatory "barriers"; special committees on the auto and steel industries; removal of constraints on movement of capital and financial services; and expanded and streamlined cross-border transportation networks—networks that will facilitate not only trade within the continent, but more outsourcing to Asia.

The official SPP website posts official documents, but ongoing discussions are shrouded within tightly controlled annual summits, ministerial level meetings, and working groups that exclude civil society participation. Corporations, however, have a privileged view of the road ahead and provide guidance and direction through a specially created North American Competitiveness Council. U.S. members of the NACC include Wal-Mart, Merck, GE, UPS, FedEx, and Kansas City Southern. The U.S. Chamber of Commerce and the Council of the Americas—whose website brags that its blue-chip members represent the majority of private U.S. investment in Latin America—serve as the U.S. secretariat.

NACC advice is taken seriously. In February 2007, the NACC issued detailed recommendations for energy integration, streamlining regulatory processes, and the speedy resumption of trade after emergencies. Six months later at their August 2007 summit, the countries announced an energy cooperation agreement, an avian flu preparedness plan with emergency border-management procedures, and a regulatory cooperation framework. The regulatory framework—complete with goals and action plan—specifically incorporates NACC recommendations to increase reliance on voluntary standards and to analyze regulations for their cost to trade. Although the framework doesn't say exactly how principles would be applied to different industries, the NACC's 2007 report gives several telling examples, including regulations harmonizing "hours of service" for truck drivers that would expand permissible weekly driving hours, which safety advocates are already challenging in court. Canadian plans to "harmonize" pesticide use to U.S. levels—an action that will raise exposure levels for most regulated pesticides—also provide a glimpse at the kinds of regulatory changes we can expect from the SPP.

"COMMUNITY" FROM THE TOP

In the United States, the best-known proponent of the SPP is Robert Pastor, director of the Center for North American Studies at American University. NAFTA broke new ground by linking Mexico (a developing economy) with the United States and Canada (two major industrialized nations) in a pact to increase trade and investment. Predictably, NAFTA increased rather than decreased inequality. But for Pastor, NAFTA's real problem was its failure to build continent-wide institutions to push integration even further. He sees the SPP as a means of building those institutions and envisions it as a new model for global governance—by and for elites—that could be used to link other developed and developing countries.

Building a North American Community, a 2005 independent task force report of the Council on Foreign Relations on which Pastor served, reveals the breadth of SPP's ambitions. The report called for a security perimeter around the three countries by 2010, so that goods and people would be checked once on entry and then move freely—while being tracked—within the continent, greatly diminishing the costs of trade. There would be a common tariff for goods from outside North America. Currently, NAFTA rules of origin require checking goods to ensure they contain sufficient North American content to qualify for duty-free treatment under NAFTA. A common external tariff would save money by eliminating the need to check for North American content. It would also facilitate expanded supply chains and outsourcing.

"Full labor mobility" would be preceded by greatly expanded guest-worker programs tying immigration status to employment. "Development" funds for Mexico would translate into transportation and energy infrastructure to help foreign investment push past the *maquila* zone on the border into central and southern Mexico where poverty is greatest and wages lowest.

Intelligence sharing and joint military exercises would increase "interoperability" and protect strategic energy and transportation infrastructure. Mexican reticence to accept U.S. troops on its soil—the result of eight U.S. invasions since its independence—would be overcome in small steps such as joint disaster coordination and plans for fighting organized crime.

Academic and political exchange programs and North American studies centers would help build a North American identity. Policy areas not touched by NAFTA or never implemented would be revisited. As one SPP participant put it, during NAFTA negotiations, the Canadians wouldn't talk about exporting water, the Mexicans wouldn't talk about privatizing oil, and the United States wouldn't talk about immigration. Barriers to maximizing energy production and cross-border trade in oil, gas, and electricity would be eliminated and pressure put on Mexico's state-owned energy company, Pemex, to dramatically open itself to private investment. Air, rail, and trucking companies would be given unlimited access to all three countries.

Meanwhile, a common regulatory scheme would make "harmonized" (read: lower) North American standards the default approach to new regulations, and countries would have to justify more stringent requirements. A seamless North American market would create economies of scale for the largest corporations. Delays and costs of checking goods for compliance at the borders would be minimized. A rule of "tested once" would eliminate "duplicative" reviews of product safety and—according to the council—substantially raise profits for biotechnology and pharmaceutical firms.

THE PERILS OF BEING CLOSE

U.S. corporations and elites that dominate continental production chains clearly stand to gain the most from the SPP. But in fact, the SPP's earliest roots lie in proposals by Canadian businesses and think tanks for what Canadians call "deep integration."

Essentially a strategy for bypassing U.S. protectionism, deep integration seeks to leverage Canada's geographic proximity for greater access to U.S. markets. The idea received a serious boost in the days after 9/11. The United States buys 80% of Canada's exports, and so when the United States closed its borders following the attacks, Canadian businesses lost millions of dollars every hour. Canadian elites promptly concluded—correctly—that the price of continued access to U.S. markets was deeper cooperation on security matters.

Canada, like Mexico, quickly signed a "smart-border" agreement and began conforming its security practices to the needs of the Bush administration's war on terror. In 2002 Canadian officials provided information that helped the U.S. deport a Canadian citizen, Maher Arar, to Syria, where he was tortured. The Canadian government has since apologized, and Arar, a software engineer whose wife stood as a candidate for the New Democratic Party in 2004, has signed on to a public demand that SPP provisions be submitted to Canadians for a vote.

But the SPP's dangers for Canadians go beyond threats to civil liberties. Like NAFTA and the Canadian U.S. Free Trade Agreement (CUFTA) before it, the SPP is a Trojan horse aimed at trapping Canadian workers into a downward spiral of global competition and neoliberal policies.

Both NAFTA and CUFTA were sold to Canadians on the grounds that increasing trade would boost employment and productivity; that would in turn solidify the economic base for Canadian social spending, including the deeply popular single-payer health insurance program. Instead, elites used the logic of competition to tighten first monetary and then fiscal policy—much as Reagan did in the United States in the 1980s. As in the United States, recession followed. Canadian exports, particularly of raw materials, increased, but overall competitiveness came largely from pushing up unemployment and driving down wages. Meanwhile, budget politics were used to squeeze rather than support social spending. The resulting deterioration in services became the pretext for experiments in private health care provision that could jeopardize the entire single-payer system. In many cases, it is Canadian divisions of U.S. transnationals that are profiting.

Not surprisingly, Canadian activists began arguing for abrogating NAFTA and reversing cutbacks in health care funding and other public services. With its security trump card and stratagem of rule by executive order, the SPP helps sidestep popular opposition to belt-tightening and the more expansive deep integration agenda.

DEEP INTEGRATION AND NATURAL RESOURCES

Energy provides the strategic example of how the SPP and deep integration would merge the interests of Canadian and U.S. elites at the expense of ordinary Canadians.

The United States is the world's largest energy consumer, and by 2025 it will be importing one third of its supply. Canada is the largest supplier of crude oil and natural gas to the United States, and has been deregulating its energy sector since the 1980s to increase access to U.S. markets. Now that rising oil prices have increased the financial feasibility of oil production from the vast Alberta oil sands, total Canadian oil reserves are second only to Saudi Arabia's. Canadian oil concerns are more eager than ever to increase sales to the United States.

In a fully integrated, privatized North American energy market, U.S. users would buy the lion's share of energy resources; at the same time, demand would increase for Canadian production, and so would prices. Not surprisingly, fully integrating North American energy markets figures prominently in the hopes of both U.S. and Canadian elites.

But the same mechanism would make energy more expensive for Canadian consumers, who will be in direct competition with U.S. buyers. In addition, easily tapped Canadian conventional reserves are dwindling rapidly. Raising oil production accelerates their depletion and risks Canadian energy and environmental security. The huge quantities of gas and water needed for production from the oil sands increase environmental risks even more, and also make economic feasibility dependent on continued high oil prices.

Finally, Canada is home to a quarter of the earth's freshwater. Although it is not mentioned in official SPP documents, Canadian activists believe that SPP includes discussions of bulk water exports to the United States, threatening Canadian water security just as the world enters a period of anticipated severe water shortages.

FROM NAFTA TO THE SPP

If Canada's path to the SPP can be described as a voluntary regression from developed welfare state to exporter of natural resources, Mexico's reveals the combination of coercion and repression running through the SPP and NAFTA.

Mexico bought into NAFTA and neoliberalism as a result of the 1980s debt crisis. U.S. banks made huge low-interest loans to developing countries and then ratcheted up interest rates. When Mexico defaulted, the United States and the International Monetary Fund renegotiated Mexico's loans and saddled Mexico with free-market reforms that opened the country to foreign investment. Wages and living standards plummeted. Mexico abandoned what remained of its development plans and turned to neoliberalism, free trade, and the promise of increased foreign direct investment to pay its bills.

Foreign investment never materialized on the level expected. Meanwhile, Mexico enthusiastically reduced agricultural tariffs under NAFTA even as the

United States flooded it with subsidized corn. Two million small farmers were driven from their land, increasing unemployment and driving down wages. Today half of all Mexicans live in poverty, with 15 million in extreme poverty. Half of new labor-market entrants can't find employment in Mexico, and remittances from migrants to the United States outstrip foreign direct investment. The situation will become even more dire when all remaining agricultural tariffs under NAFTA expire later in 2008.

Any economic plan actually centered on the needs of the Mexican people would include renegotiating NAFTA's agricultural provisions. Instead, agriculture is off the table, and immigration has taken center stage. Rebuffed by the anti-immigrant backlash in the United States, Mexico is turning to Canada for an expanded guest-worker program, and the two countries have set up an SPP working group to discuss labor mobility.

Meanwhile, SPP negotiators are discussing funds to address "uneven development." In practice this means connecting central and southeastern Mexico—regions that have some of Mexico's highest poverty rates and lowest wages, but also some of its richest gas reserves—to U.S. markets. The region is also the target of former president Vicente Fox's 2001 Plan Puebla Panama, an $8 billion infrastructure program aimed at integrating southern Mexico with the CAFTA countries. The overall vision: stepped-up development of energy and gas reserves, an even lower-wage workforce for maquila production than on the U.S. border, and transportation and energy networks needed to produce and carry finished goods to U.S. consumers.

Of course, appropriating land for highways and other projects requires massive dispossession of farmers and indigenous peoples. Since many of the peasants NAFTA has displaced have already crossed the border to the United States, stepped-up immigration control and labor repression are both in the offing. So far, the two countries appear poised to limit migration from the CAFTA countries into southern Mexico, regulate the flow of Mexican immigrants to the United States in the north, and seal a captive, repressed workforce in between. Mexico's participation in the SPP's security perimeter will greatly stiffen security along its southern border, where several hundred thousand migrants annually try to cross into Mexico from Central America to get to the United States. And the United States has already tightened security along Mexico's northern border, where 500,000 cross annually.

Bush's $1.4 billion request to the U.S. Congress for a "Plan Mexico," which he hopes eventually to extend to Central America, is linked to this plan. Billed as a "new paradigm" for security cooperation and fighting drug crime, in reality it's another step toward a U.S.-led continental military and security structure. It won't position U.S. soldiers on Mexican ground, but it will deepen coordination and provide intelligence, training, and equipment to Mexican military and police. The resources are certain to be used against Mexico's growing social movements. Mexico's anti-terrorism law has already made it easier to criminalize protest. In 2002, the People's Front for Defense of the Land managed to halt construction of an airport that was part of Plan Pueblo Panama, and the Front also participated in the Zapatista campaign to boycott the last presidential election. In April 2006 the group came to the aid of flower growers and vendors in a confrontation with police in nearby San Salvador Atenco. Thirty five hundred police beat 200 of the town's 300 inhabitants; arrested 150; sexually assaulted 30 women; and killed two youths. For his part in the resistance, the movement's leader was sentenced to 67 years in prison—the first prosecution under Mexico's post-9/11 anti-terrorism law.

MEXICO'S ENERGY MATTERS TOO

As with Canada, Mexican energy is where the largest stakes are being played. Mexico is currently the third largest supplier of oil to the United States, yet estimates are that Mexican oil and natural gas reserves could be exhausted in as few as 10 years. The SPP's plan to step up Mexican oil production by completely privatizing gas production and increasing private investment in its oil sector will strip Mexico of crucial resources for development at a time when world oil prices make them most valuable.

The main barrier to the SPP's privatization strategy is the Mexican constitution, which guarantees the benefits of the energy sector to the Mexican people and places management of oil and gas in the hands of state-owned Pemex. Pemex is a symbol of national sovereignty, and Mexico refused to commit to privatizing Pemex during NAFTA negotiations. But legislation in the 1990s chipped away at Pemex's jurisdiction while expanding the scope for private sector contracts. More importantly, Pemex was severely undermined during the 1980s debt crisis, when oil and gas revenues were chained to foreign debt repayment.

As a result, Pemex has been chronically starved for funds for exploration and development. The shortage is routinely used as an argument for privatization. The SPP has plans to release a report this year highlighting Pemex's purported inefficiencies and need for private capital. Sixty percent of Pemex's revenues go to supplying nearly 40% of Mexico's national budget; no private firm could survive under similar constraints.

Ironically, the 1970s loans that led to the 1980s debt crisis were made so Mexico could develop newly discovered oil during a period of record prices. Those record prices were the result of the 1973 OPEC oil boycott. OPEC deposited the profits from those price hikes in U.S. banks, and those funds in turn became the capital U.S. banks used to lend to Mexico. Chaining Pemex's revenues to debt repayment in the 1980s meant Mexico was forced to increase output and add to what by then was a glut of world energy supplies—thereby contributing to lower world prices and weakening its own revenues. In effect, Mexico went into debt slavery to help undermine OPEC and cheapen the cost of energy for U.S. corporations. SPP's agenda brings the cycle full circle, with the United States willing to accelerate exhaustion of Mexico's remaining reserves to bolster its own increasingly precarious international energy position.

UPPING THE ANTE

The SPP ups the ante for activists. Until now, labor and progressives—at least in the United States—have tended to focus on specific targets such as trade agreements or demands for debt relief. And when we analyzed NAFTA, we analyzed it in class terms, not in geopolitical terms. But the SPP's goals are broader and deeper even than NAFTA's goals. They aim at nothing short of remaking the political and economic governance structure of North America.

The wishes of Canadian and Mexican elites notwithstanding, the SPP's primary purpose is to buoy U.S. capitalism's flagging international position, from its trade deficit to its energy deficit. U.S. security, energy, and transportation needs are the touchstones, and the draft agreement aligns the policies of Canada and Mexico—and appropriates natural resources—to meet those needs. Economic integration is conditioned on military integration, which in turn aims at consolidating the U.S. position in the hemisphere.

While the United States maintains most of the economic leverage in the triad, most hot-button issues are in Mexico and Canada. For U.S. activists in particular, bringing these issues alive will first require a much deeper understanding of our neighbors, and an ability to link their issues to domestic U.S. concerns.

Chief among the dangers for ordinary people in all three countries are the environmental consequences. Increasing rates of fossil-fuel extraction in North America may feed the U.S. energy habit, but the solution is short term. The contributions to global warming for North America and the world, however, will not be.

The SPP's bundling of security with economic concerns also fuels Bush's war on terror, the accelerating militarization of U.S. foreign policy, and continued U.S. leadership of neoliberal globalization. Canada's commitments of troops in Afghanistan, increased military spending, and willingness to find common ground with the United States on Latin America and the Caribbean are one product of the noxious mix. Another is Mexico's willingness to serve as a counterweight to Venezuelan attempts to harness its oil wealth to alternative regional and global development strategies.

In terms of daily governance, the SPP privatizes the regulatory functions of government on an international scale not seen before in industrialized democracies. NAFTA and other WTO agreements limit the legislative and regulatory powers of member states by imposing global standards such as "market access" and "national treatment" on how countries treat foreign investors. These standards create "one way roads" to privatization once countries begin liberalizing a sector. Applied to Canadian experiments in private health care, they could end up forcing Canada first to open its doors to for-profit foreign providers and insurance companies, and then to pay them the same subsidies given to Canadian public and nonprofit operators. In the United States (where health insurance is already private), they could be used to prevent the United States from putting its own single-payer system in place.

By contrast, the SPP bypasses national authority to create formal, trinational structures for corporate regulatory input *prior* to involvement by legislatures or citizens. Many SPP goals are thus hidden at their inception; even after they emerge, most will be buried in the daily workings of executive agencies who have been directed to give maximum attention to corporate needs and trade. In the United States, a short list of agencies already involved in the SPP includes the Department of Justice, the Department of State, the Federal Trade Commission, the Federal Communications Commission, the Departments of Agriculture and Energy, and the Department of Homeland Security.

Finally, the SPP is a frontal assault on labor and civil liberties. Plan Mexico should be seen as a threat to human rights throughout the continent. The North American labor movement desperately needs a democratic Mexico where independent organizing and labor rights can be exercised without threat of violence. Instead, the SPP will intensify exploitation of Mexican labor and deepen the low-wage neoliberal model in both the United States and Canada, as well.

WHAT IT WILL TAKE

Currently, Bush is politically weakened by the Iraq war, Mexico's president Felipe Calderón by his election scandal, and Canadian prime minister Stephen Harper by his lack of a parliamentary majority, raising the question of whether the SPP will survive the leaders' terms in office.

But even if it were stopped in its current form, much of the SPP would continue. A Framework for Regulatory Cooperation has been signed, complete with goals for action and annual work plans. The North American Energy Working Group—now integrated into the SPP—was actually established in 2001. Plan Mexico, once funded, will take on its own life, and the push to privatize Pemex will continue.

Opposition to Plan Pueblo Panama gives some indication of the depth and breadth of the activism that will be needed to be effective with the SPP's agenda. Calderón recently revived Plan Puebla Panama, with an added military component—no doubt inspired by the SPP. Yet it was stalled for many years by protests against displacement of farmers and destruction of the environment, and a vibrant cross-border network of activists has grown up around it. The breadth of the Plan Puebla Panama led activists to conclude that opposing environmentally destructive infrastructure projects wasn't sufficient: what is necessary is a deeper understanding of the economic and political vision behind Plan Pueblo Panama, and development of an alternative analysis.

An effective response to the SPP agenda will require the same kind of expanded cross-border contacts and focused study of the North American and global political economies. This is the very work the left needs to do to begin creating economic and political alternatives that reflect its values.

The challenge is particularly difficult for activists in the United States. Unlike the left in countries where domestic agendas have been affected by U.S. actions for many years, most in the United States think of domestic issues as controlled by domestic politics. But as rising oil prices combine with a falling dollar, and U.S. economic autonomy begins to be more constrained, more people in the United States may understand the need for different allies.

U.S. activists need a democratic Mexico with strong labor rights and a Canadian welfare state that survives the ravages of neoliberal globalization. We need to build an environmental agenda based on conservation and renewable resources and an economic agenda based on diversity and human rights. We need a progressive voice that can drown out right-wing cries that the problem of globalization is the loss of U.S. dominance and power. Most of all, we need an international, powerful, and organized response from the left, and popular forces to challenge the more deeply coordinated and increasingly militarized forces of international capital. Reasoned opposition is no longer enough.

SOURCES AND RESOURCES

Alejandro Álvarez Béjar, "Pemex: de la reestructuración a la privatización," *Revista venezolana de economía y ciencias sociales* no. 4 (October–December 1998); Alejandro Álvarez Béjar, "Predatory Oil Exploitation in the South East Region of Mexico and Alternatives to Neoliberal Structural Change," Latin American Studies

Association conference paper (2007); Laura Carlsen, " 'Deep Integration'—the Anti-Democratic Expansion of NAFTA" (May 2007)and "Plan Mexico and the Billion-Dollar Drug Deal" (October 4, 2007), America's Program, Center for International Policy, americas.irc-online.org; Council on Foreign Relations, *Building a North American Community*, Independent Task Force Report no. 53 (2005), downloaded from www.cfr.org; Robert A. Pastor, *Toward a North American Community* (Institute for International Economics, 2001); Ricardo Grinspun and Yasmine Shamsie, eds., *Whose Canada? Continental Integration, Fortress North America, and the Corporate Agenda* (Canadian Centre for Policy Alternatives, 2007); Integrate This!/SPP Watch, Council of Canadians website, canadians.org/integratethis; Canadian Centre for Policy Alternatives, www.ccpa.org; Canadian Council of Chief Executives, www.ceocouncil.ca; U.S. Department of Energy website, www.doe.gov (for data on North American energy reserves); *La Jornada* (progressive Mexican daily), www.lajornada.unam.mx; Official U.S. government website for the SPP (includes press releases and NACC reports), www.spp.gov; Maude Barlow, "Ten Reasons to Stop the SPP," available on www.youtube.com; video of union leader stopping provocateurs at the Montebello protests, available on www.youtube.com.

CAFTA'S DEBT TRAP

BY ALDO CALIARI
Dollars & Sense, July/August 2005

Critics of the Central American Free Trade Agreement (CAFTA) have focused on concerns that the treaty will devastate Central American farmers by forcing them to compete with heavily subsidized U.S. agribusiness. Others point out that the deal will perpetuate low-road development based on poverty wages and lax environmental enforcement, while undermining governments' authority to ensure basic services. These are all valid concerns, but CAFTA poses yet another danger that deserves equal attention.

Rules buried in the technical language of the investment chapter of the agreement would make it more difficult for the six Central American nations to escape their heavy debt burdens or recover from debt crises should they, for example, find themselves unable to meet their obligations to holders of government bonds and other creditors. The investment provisions of CAFTA— like the 1994 North American Free Trade Agreement between the United States, Canada, and Mexico—are based on the argument that strong investment protections encourage foreign private investment. CAFTA subscribes to this same precept, and, like NAFTA, it would require governments to comply with a long list of investor protections and even grant foreign private investors the right to sue governments for damages if those obligations are violated.

Both treaties require governments to treat foreign investors at least as favorably as domestic investors, a principle known as "national treatment." Governments must also ensure "most favored nation" treatment for other treaty members, meaning they cannot give special preferences to, or discriminate against, the investors of any one country that is a party to the agreement. As a result, member governments can no longer favor domestic interests or investors even to support social goals or other national interests.

But whereas NAFTA's investor protections explicitly exclude "sovereign debt" (the bonds, loans, and other securities issued from or guaranteed by national governments) from investor protection rules, CAFTA specifically includes these forms of public liabilities.

As the U.S. House deliberates on CAFTA, it's important for the public to recognize that in subjecting government bonds and other forms of sovereign debt to stringent investment protections, the deal would place huge constraints on indebted countries' ability to prevent or survive debt crises—and to protect the basic needs of their citizens.

NATIONAL TREATMENT AND MOST FAVORED NATION STATUS

The "national treatment" and "most favored nation" principles were originally born in agreements dealing with trade in goods, only later extending to investment. Their application to sovereign debt introduces a number of serious problems.

1. CAFTA dismantles essential tools governments need to recover from crisis.

Requiring that foreign creditors be offered favorable treatment equal to domestic creditors is dangerous for the developing-country members of CAFTA, since they all, with the exception of Honduras, owe a significant share of public debt to domestic creditors. In some countries, including Costa Rica, domestic debt is actually higher than external debt.

When undergoing a debt restructuring, a government makes an "offer" to all creditors, typically reducing the value of outstanding bonds and loans substantially. Once the offer is agreed to, the country can regain its footing and restart the flow of investment.

There are a variety of reasons why a country might want to offer domestic creditors preferential conditions in restructuring its sovereign debt. In a financial crisis, domestic creditors often take a double hit. They're forced to accept a reduction in the value of their loans, and they face high interest rates and other costs. Yet domestic capital markets are critical in a recovery. By addressing the needs of domestic investors first, a country will be better able to return to domestic capital markets quickly during what is likely to be a sustained interruption in access to foreign capital. This can feed a resumption of growth, which, in turn, can facilitate repayment of other obligations and reverse the precipitous fall in a country's standard of living that typically accompanies a debt crisis. Even the International Monetary Fund (IMF), a staunch defender of the rights of foreign private investors, acknowledges that "the restructuring of certain types of domestic debt may have major implications for economic performance, as a result of its impact on the financial system and the operation of domestic capital markets."

Prioritizing domestic debt may also be necessary to protect a country's banking system. Argentine economist José Luis Machinea has pointed out that sovereign debt restructuring has a double impact on domestic holders of debt: On the one hand, the value of their bonds is reduced. On the other, they suffer the general impact of the crisis on the real economy and on their access to finance. The IMF has stated that in crises, affording special treatment to domestic debt might help protect "a core of the banking system by ensuring the availability of assets required for banks to manage capital, liquidity, and exposure to market risks."

More generally, countries may need to provide special treatment to domestic debtors as part of their national development strategy—that is, for the same legitimate reasons that can lead them to accord special treatment to domestic industries.

2. CAFTA prevents states from paying salaries and pensions.

Under CAFTA, member governments would no longer be able to prioritize domestic debts consisting of, among other things, wages, salaries, and pensions. This could have dire ramifications for state workers. According to the national-treatment principle, governments are bound to treat these obligations the same way they treat foreign debts held by transnational banks and foreign investors. If the state has only enough resources to cover a portion of its debts, it will be prohibited from choosing to direct those funds first to wages and salaries. In this way, too, CAFTA would deal a setback to national governments' ability to prioritize their obligations to the basic human rights of their citizens and put their own economic development above the claims of foreign creditors.

Unlike a private corporation in bankruptcy, an indebted nation has human rights obligations and social responsibilities toward its people. That's why civil society groups have called for developing new debt-crisis protocols that take into account the broader mission of the state and its role in society. Models already exist—for example, Chapter 9 of the U.S. bankruptcy code which applies to municipalities. Even the IMF's proposed rules for restructuring sovereign debt excluded "wages, salaries and pensions" from their application.

3. It reduces the leverage of domestic debtors.

A government's debt restructuring offer can take on added clout if it has first cut a deal with supportive domestic creditors. Giving these domestic creditors preferential terms is a way for the state to win back their support. If the principles of national treatment are applied to sovereign debt, however, any incentive offered to domestic creditors would have to be offered to the foreign creditors as well, effectively foreclosing this avenue of recovery.

Argentina's offer of preferential conditions to domestic creditors was a crucial element in enhancing the government's leverage in negotiating with its foreign private creditors after it suffered the largest sovereign default in history in December 2001. In September 2003, the government released its initial proposed debt restructuring conditions, which included a 75% cut in the value of its bonds. Some groups of bondholders quickly rejected this offer, claiming that it was woefully insufficient and, in light of the country's latest growth figures, below what the country could repay. The creditors also strongly lobbied the G7 group of industrialized countries, which, both directly and through the IMF, put more pressure on Argentina to sweeten its offer. With pressure mounting from the G7 and the IMF, Argentina turned to its domestic pension funds. By granting domestic pension funds preferential conditions, Argentina was able to reach an agreement with them. The funds held more than 17% of the country's total debt and their coming on board was a critical first step in Argentina's eventually garnering the support of a full 76% of its creditors.

The government's ability to treat domestic bondholders differently from foreign ones was crucial to reaching an agreement with the majority of creditors. This option would have been out of the question if the government had been bound by CAFTA's national treatment principle.

4. Investor-State Lawsuits

Under CAFTA, governments that violate these investor protections can face expensive lawsuits. As under NAFTA and numerous bilateral investment treaties, CAFTA grants private foreign investors the right to bypass domestic courts and sue governments in international tribunals.

Such "investor-state lawsuits" are highly controversial for a number of reasons. First, many arbitration tribunals operate with an absolute lack of transparency, having no obligation to disclose relevant documents or allow any form of public participation. The system for choosing arbitrators has also drawn criticism, as the arbitrators can be chosen from the ranks of practicing investment lawyers, with no obligation to appoint people who will be independent, that is, who have no stake in the treaty interpretation. These unelected tribunals may well rule on difficult questions with far-reaching social and economic implications that rightfully belong under the domestic jurisdiction of states.

CAFTA's application of investor protections to sovereign debt would suppress the few options available to countries trying to prevent or exit from debt crises. History shows that the inability to exit a crisis situation causes economic losses far outweighing any commercial gains achieved through a free trade agreement.

Central American activists are already calling on their governments to reject CAFTA. In the United States, activists must also urge Congress to reject CAFTA because in addition to all the concerns that have been voiced already, it will tightly tie the hands of member countries in dealing with their large stocks of external debt.

MIDDLE POWERS: IBSA AND THE NEW SOUTH-SOUTH COOPERATION

BY GLADYS LECHINI
NACLA Report, September/October 2007

In the 1970s, the world's underdeveloped nations launched the idea of South-South cooperation. Following in the spirit of Bandung, they aimed to strengthen their capacity to negotiate with the North and to solve problems of trade and development in the new international economic order. Though the overall project met with some modest success, it ultimately failed because of its loose nature and broad scope: The fallacy of its argument was its basic assumption that all underdeveloped countries have more in common than they really do, and that all solutions can be uniformly applied with equal success.

Today, a new, more selective South-South cooperation has appeared, bringing some hope to the people of our regions. The trilateral alliance known as the India, Brazil, and South Africa Dialogue Forum, or IBSA, exemplifies the trend. From IBSA's perspective, the current international economic and financial architecture has ill-served the interests of the poor in developing countries, with economic globalization having exacerbated income inequality both within and across emerging markets. The alliance's objective is to maximize joint actions as part of a coherent strategy within international organizations like the World Trade Organization (WTO) on various issues, including public health, pharmaceutical patents, and government subsidies.

The process that led to IBSA began in the 1990s, when South African minister of trade and industry Alec Erwin had already envisioned a G7 for the South to solidify areas of common interest within the United Nations and the WTO. The idea developed during a series of international meetings attended by representatives from the three countries, and culminated with the first high-level summit in June 2003, in the run-up to the WTO ministerial in Cancún, Mexico, the following September.

Gathered in Brasília, the three ministers issued a declaration announcing their intention "to hold regular political consultations on international agenda items, as well as to exchange information on areas of mutual cooperation in order to coordinate their positions on issues of common interest." Their ultimate goal, they said, was to make the diverse processes of globalization "a positive force for change for all peoples" that "must benefit the largest number of countries."

A month before the Cancún meeting, IBSA, together with China and Argentina, began organizing an alliance among developing countries to oppose the North's agricultural protectionism. Since its inception, IBSA and China have formed the core of the Group of 22 (G22) bloc of developing countries, which led the fight against global neoliberal policies at Cancún. As thousands of protesters clashed with police outside the meeting's barricades, the G22 refused to accept a "precooked deal" that would consolidate U.S. and EU positions. Following Brazilian foreign minister Celso Amorim's maxim that "trade must be a tool not only to create wealth but also to distribute it in a more equitable way," the G22 preferred to let the negotiations break down rather than come to an agreement detrimental to its interests.

Although the G22 emerged from Cancún triumphant, it has not held together well since then. The heterogeneous group—including both strong exporting countries like Argentina and Brazil, which want to dissolve tariff barriers to their agro-products, and very protectionist ones like India, China, and Pakistan, which strive to maintain subsidies to protect their small farmers—had to be renamed the G20+ to reflect fluctuations in membership.

IBSA, however, has remained strong. The three member countries face the same problems and have similar interests. All three consider themselves "middle powers" and leaders of their respective regions, yet they have also been subject to pressures from the North. Indeed, given the associated strength of its members, IBSA has not gone unnoticed by the great powers, and its potential role has become an object of surveillance. The United States, for example, has attempted to establish privileged bilateral relations with each of these growing engines (in a hub-and-spokes model), creating commitments that could discourage present or future horizontal links among them.

We can see this in the case of South Africa, IBSA's smallest member in terms of population and GDP, but a giant in the African context, considered the continent's most powerful political and economic force. The United States remains its primary trade partner, exporting more goods to the country than to any other African nation, a relationship formalized in agreements like a generalized preferential trade agreement (which grants duty-free status to some 4,650 South African goods) and a trade and investment framework arrangement, which addresses private sector concerns requiring government interventions.

South Africa is thus entangled in a web of U.S. commercial interests that constrain its autonomy. The United States has also courted India, in an attempt to counterbalance China's regional influence, most notably in last year's United States–India Peaceful Atomic Energy Cooperation Act, under which Washington is supplying New Delhi with civilian nuclear technology, despite India's not having acceded to the Nuclear Non-Proliferation Treaty. For Brazil, which has long identified itself as South America's principal regional power, the United

States is not only a global but a hemispheric hegemon. Whether or not U.S. global dominance continues, Brazil will continue suffering the influence of its regional "big brother," as in the recent Bush-Lula agreement on ethanol and biodiesel.[1]

Other countries that may be interested in joining worry about the exclusionary nature of IBSA, since granting them membership would be an intrinsically political decision. These include, in their respective regions, Mexico and Argentina; Nigeria, Algeria, and Egypt; and China, Pakistan, and Malaysia. But until now the most obvious candidate, Russia, has shown no interest in joining any group, especially given its instability in the G8, while China has aggressively pursued its own trade interests unilaterally, though its role as a free rider at Cancún—associating with the G20 because circumstances warranted it—did not upset a setting conducive to negotiations.

BRAZIL'S BRIDGE TO AFRICA

Brazil has been the driving force behind IBSA, and its foreign policy is itself a good example of the new modalities of a more productive South-South cooperation. Engaging in the international arena by increasing its participation in multilateral institutions, Brazil widens its margins of maneuver, and in doing so has structured a network of cooperation among many of the same partners within different forums.

The IBSA countries have decided to articulate their initiatives within the framework of WTO negotiations, they say, in order to address their countries' high vulnerability to fluctuations in global commodity prices. In their negotiations, they stress the importance of establishing a predictable, rule-based, and transparent international trading system that would enable Southern countries to maximize their development through gains from enhanced exports. These concerns aside, there is an undeniable geopolitical dimension to the alliance: The IBSA nations have agreed to back each other up in their bids as regional representatives to the UN Security Council, with Brazil competing with Mexico and Argentina, South Africa with Nigeria and Egypt, and India with Pakistan and Indonesia.

Brazil's relationship with South Africa has been at the center of its negotiating strategy. By pushing forward bilateral cooperation with Pretoria, Brazil drives Argentina, its main regional partner, to negotiate through Mercosur with the Southern African Customs Union (Sacu), which led to a 2004 preferential commercial agreement with Mercosur. Brazil also pursued this strategy with India, thereby setting the stage for IBSA, and then, in a final step, brought these countries together in the G20.

In doing this, Brazil was building on years of African diplomacy dating back to the 1960s. Both political and economic considerations informed this earlier diplomatic effort. Although justified with the principle of developing South-South solidarity, Brazil's African diplomacy was part of a global strategy meant to build an international presence by diversifying external relations and building alliances with the new states in the South, thus allowing Brazil to have a say in global issues.

Even though Brazilian officials resorted to a "cultural discourse" in their diplomacy in the 1970s, recalling Brazil's African heritage—Brazil has the largest population of Afro-descendants outside of Africa—new commitments were necessary to gain the trust of African states, which always demanded that Brazil end diplomatic relations with the South African apartheid government. But Brazil did not need to resort to such a drastic action to demonstrate its anti-apartheid commitment. In 1975 Brazil became the first country to recognize Angola's independence and its government, and although it never completely broke diplomatic relations with apartheid South Africa, political and commercial relations were kept to a minimum, demonstrating Brazil's commitment to the rest of the continent. Furthermore, Brazil opened embassies, sent high-level missions, developed technical and academic cooperation, and established research centers throughout Africa. The 1970s were termed the "golden period" of Brazilian-African relations.[2]

After the end of the apartheid regime, the new South Africa offered an opportunity for mutually beneficial development and the chance to act jointly in multilateral groups. Today, in selecting South Africa as its primary African ally, the Brazilian government has gone a step beyond its traditional strategies, using Mercosur as a negotiating tool. Since Brazil had already implemented an African policy and had other partners in the southern region of Africa, it began to promote a more complex association between the Mercosur and the African trade blocs.

But the difference between the Lula government's African policy and that of its predecessors goes beyond the South Africa alliance, given its more emphatic posture toward defending national sovereignty and searching for privileged alliances. The Brazil-Africa Forum, held in the city of Fortaleza in June 2003, had the greatest impact in demonstrating the Lula administration's decision to reestablish and deepen relations with Africa. The forum, which brought together academics, politicians, diplomats, and high-level functionaries, came about after Foreign Secretary Amorim visited various African countries in May 2003, in preparation for Lula's first visit to Africa the following November, when he traveled to São Tomé and Príncipe, Angola, Mozambique, South Africa, and Namibia. The next year Lula participated in the fifth conference of heads of state from the Community of Portuguese-Speaking Countries, and in 2005 he traveled to Cameroon, Nigeria, Ghana, Guinea Bissau, and Senegal, where President Abdoulaye Wade called him "the first black president of Brazil." During the trip Lula began discussions on transferring technology to African countries so they can produce their own AIDS drugs.

Finally, in February 2006, the president went on his fourth African tour, visiting Algeria, Benin, Botswana, and South Africa, whose governments signed a series of cooperation treaties in the areas of agriculture, health, and education. Lula has now traveled to 17 African countries, more than those visited by all previous Brazilian presidents combined. Brazil has also welcomed heads of state from 16 African countries.

Of the 284 treaties that link Brazil with 37 of the 54 African nations (in technological cooperation, cultural exchanges, health, and agriculture), 112 were signed between December 2002 and December 2006. Business leaders accompanied Lula on these African tours, organizing parallel business forums to negotiate contracts. Commerce between Brazil and Africa progressively grew throughout this period, more than doubling from $5 million in 2002 to $12.6 million in 2005.[3] The most important African exports to Brazil include oil, minerals, and agricultural products, while Brazil's principal exports to Africa are sugar and its derivatives, meats, and manufactured goods.

In this context of growing commercial links, Brasília has constructed a framework agreement for creating free-trade areas with the African countries that it maintains commercial relations with, like those in the Sacu, which as mentioned established an agreement with Mercosur in 2004. The final objective is to negotiate with each country through the bilateral committees, establish preference agreements on fixed tariffs, and later come to an agreement on a free trade area linking Brazil and its African allies.

The strategy is not without its problems. When Brazil led negotiations between Mercosur and Egypt in 2004, and later with Morocco the same year, proposed regulations were exchanged, but contacts were not taken up again. This lack of substantial results in these South-South negotiations became a source of tension among Mercosur members, leading to some in the Uruguayan government to propose signing a free trade agreement with the United States, independent of Mercosur.

This would fit well into Washington's strategy, which, after the failure of the Free Trade Area of the Americas, has centered on pursuing bilateral agreements with Latin American countries as means of disrupting the process of regional integration.

IBSA'S UNCERTAIN FUTURE

These three middle powers, provided they act in concert, could have a systemic impact on global governance in the future, impeding some of the North's attempts to maintain an exclusive and elitist international order. They aim to develop a strong negotiating power through a "soft balancing" strategy, with no counter-hegemonic confrontation, as in Chávez's Bolivarian Alternative for the Americas—that is, to participate in establishing the rules of the game, which until now have only benefited the most powerful. Their conversion from rule takers into rule "conditioners," though hardly rule makers, in the international system will depend on better mutual knowledge and building confidence among the governments that comprise the group.

In addition to forming a geopolitical alliance, the IBSA countries have also identified the diverse areas of excellence in their societies, especially in the fields of biotechnology, alternative energy sources, outer space, aeronautics, information technology, and agriculture, offering a broad range of potential opportunities for trade, investment, travel, and tourism. Yet they are not natural trading partners. On the whole, India, Brazil, and South Africa produce similar products and compete for access to the same OECD markets. And even their political interests do not always converge. In contrast to India, for example, Brazil and South Africa have both renounced nuclear weapons programs and share positions advocating nonproliferation and disarmament. South Africa, because of its regional alliances within the African Union, is barred from joining Brazil and India (together with Germany and Japan) in the United Nations' Group of Four, which support each other's candidacies for permanent Security Council seats.

Given these tensions, they will have to make some sacrifices and make a strong political determination not to forsake the agreement if they are to expand both their commercial ties and their leverage in international institutions. Whether they accomplish this remains to be seen; the increasingly unstable post–Cold War international scene offers no certainties, both in terms of reaching a lasting peace and of improving our people's economic conditions.

Partners should be selected not only because of their current and future power base, but also because of their common values and interests in order to influence the global order effectively. For these middle powers, international institutions represent the opportunity to build a political space in which to create rules according to their own interests. In the process, they will face the decision between, on the one hand, tying themselves to the world's hegemon (i.e., "band wagoning" with the United States) or, on the other hand, creating more autonomous processes together with smaller states. This is the principal dilemma that the coalition will face in the future.

Neither are internal conditions very favorable, given the consequences of the neoliberal model, which, among other things, deprived the state of its capacity to ensure citizen welfare. Only by acting cohesively and in unison can they overcome common handicaps on the still unresolved, critical issues facing the

South, like securing agreements on agriculture subsidies, intellectual property, and public health.

Another prospect is the coordination among social movements of the three IBSA countries, all of which are home to an active and mobilized civil society. The democratic advances in these three countries generated a new association between the state and civil society, as a result of the actions of movements and NGOs dedicated to the struggle against human rights abuses, environmental degradation, and social inequality. After all, it was in Brazil where the peculiar institutionalization of global civil society organizing took shape in 2001 as the World Social Forum, in Porto Alegre. Proposing an alternative agenda to that of neoliberal globalization, also known as *altermundialismo* (another-world-ism), the forum was later held in Mumbai, India, and Nairobi, Kenya.

But as Khatchik Derghougassian argues, there still exist no critical links between the NGOs that favor consolidating the IBSA alliance.[4] In his study of organizations in Brazil, India, and South Africa dedicated to two issues, HIV/AIDS prevention and controlling small arms, he concludes that there are no economic nexuses between the three regions, nor any common projects between their respective civil societies. Thus the social mobilization in India, Brazil, and South Africa still reveals an important "deficit" in civil society—if there do exist vibrant social mobilizations within the three countries, forcing the state to be more responsive to its citizens, grassroots diplomacy has still not been generated in the South-South direction. This is no minor task, but one that would provide another substrate to IBSA and South-South cooperation.

Even that may depend on the willingness of these governments of the South, which have the capacity to build regional institutions, to find an effective way to challenge the prevailing imperial hierarchy, and to transform themselves into pillars of a new multipolar system. Will they be willing to go that far?

NOTES

1. Downloaded from www.iade.org.ar.
2. José Flavio Sombra Saraiva, *O lugar da Africa. A dimensão atlantica da politica externa brasileira (de 1946 a nossos dias)* (Universidade de Brasília, 1996).
3. Downloaded from www.desenvolvimento.gov.br.
4. Khatchik Derghougassian, "IBSA No-Gubernamental," paper presented at the international conference "Los poderes emergentes y la seguridad regional: el caso IBSA" (Emerging Powers and Regional Security: The IBSA Case), organized by the Universidad de San Andrés and *Le monde diplomatique*, Buenos Aires, May 30, 2006.

CHAPTER 4
ALTERNATIVE APPROACHES TO ECONOMIC "DEVELOPMENT"

ANTI-NEOLIBERAL BACKLASH: LEAVING THE WORLD BANK AND IMF BEHIND

BY ALEJANDRO REUSS
NACLA Report, July/August 2007

The backlash against neoliberalism in Latin America is now leading to confrontations between several of the region's governments and the two major international lending institutions, the World Bank and the International Monetary Fund (IMF). In the span of just a few weeks in May, President Rafael Correa announced that Ecuador was expelling the World Bank's representative from the country; President Hugo Chávez announced that Venezuela would be withdrawing from both the Bank and the IMF; and Bolivia, Nicaragua, and Venezuela all announced their intention to withdraw from the World Bank–affiliated International Centre for the Settlement of Investment Disputes (ICSID).[1] The Venezuelan government has also proposed the formation of a new regional lending institution, the Bank of the South, widely perceived as a challenge to the World Bank and the IMF.

While both the World Bank and the IMF have more than 150 member countries, the representatives of a few rich capitalist countries dominate them.[2] Both institutions tie credit to the adoption of neoliberal policies like privatizing public enterprises, reducing public employment, eliminating price controls on basic goods, weakening protections for workers and labor unions, and opening up to international trade and investment.[3] Established and funded by the World Bank, the ICSID functions as an international court in which private companies can sue the governments of member countries. While the ICSID lacks police powers to enforce its rulings, a government that does not comply faces the same possible retaliation as one that refuses World Bank or IMF lending conditions—being cut off from international credit.[4]

The recent withdrawals from the World Bank, IMF, and ICSID by Latin American governments represent a rejection of the conditions these institutions have imposed on poorer and less powerful countries. The withdrawal from ICSID in particular represents an assertion of the power of sovereign states to determine the conditions under which they will permit foreign investment—a burning issue today in Venezuela, Bolivia, and other Latin American countries. The Venezuelan government has nationalized the largest telecommunications and electricity firms by buying their stock and has asserted control over the country's oil industry by threatening to expropriate the holdings of any multinational firm that refuses to accept its new status as a minority partner.[5] Bolivia has made similar moves over its gas resources.[6]

Disputes over property rights exist in every society. In the United States, for example, conservative legal scholars argue that environmental regulation constitutes an illegal "taking" since it deprives property owners of potential benefits. Others insist that this does not violate property rights since there is no "right" to damage the environment and to harm other people. Moreover, governments throughout the world differ on what property rights they enforce. They differ over whether the government can expropriate "property" without the consent of the "owner," under what circumstances it may do so, whether it must give compensation, how "fair" compensation is determined, and even what constitutes an "expropriation." Some of the recent moves of the Venezuelan, Bolivian, and other Latin American states may run counter to, say, property rights under U.S. law—but they are, of course, sovereign countries with their own laws.

Some of the recent nationalizations also run counter to the bilateral investment treaties that hold sacrosanct the property rights of multinational corporations. Sovereign states that have entered into agreements, however, may seek to alter them or withdraw from them altogether. If it has no intention of abiding by the rulings of the ICSID, the government of a sovereign state is perfectly entitled to withdraw from it. With the tide turning against neoliberalism, the governments of Venezuela and other Latin American countries appear determined to gain greater control of their resources and to use them for social welfare and economic development projects. Might they face a cutoff of investment by multinational corporations and high finance, or the hostility of powerful governments, as a consequence? That is certainly possible. But it will be a matter of power, not of right.

NOTES

1. Hal Weitzman, "Ecuador Expels World Bank Envoy," *Financial Times* (April 27, 2007); Saul Hudson, "Venezuela to Quit IMF, World Bank," Reuters (April 30, 2007); Agencia Bolivariana de Noticias, "Paises de Alternativa Bolivariana acordan retirarse de convencion del Ciadi."
2. Alejandro Reuss, "ABCs of the World Economy: The World Bank and International Monetary Fund," *Dollars & Sense* (March/April 2000).
3. Sarah Anderson, "The IMF and World Bank's Cosmetic Makeover," *Dollars & Sense* (January/February 2001).
4. Quoted in United Nations Conference on Trade and Development, *Dispute Settlement: International Centre for Settlement of Investment Disputes, 2.9 Binding Force and Enforcement*, p. 8.
5. "Venezuela Seizes Largest Telecom," Bloomberg News, May 9, 2007; "Venezuela Buys 93% of Electric

Company in Nationalization Move," Associated Press (May 10, 2007); Reuters, "Venezuela Pulls Control From Big Oil" (May 1, 2007).

6. BBC News, "Bolivia Gas Under State Control" (May 2, 2006).

TURNING GAS INTO DEVELOPMENT IN BOLIVIA

BY AARON LUOMA AND GRETCHEN GORDON
Dollars & Sense, November/December 2006

On May 1, banners reading "Nationalized: Property of the Bolivian People" were hung over filling station entrances and strung across the gates of refineries and gas and oil fields across Bolivia. From the San Alberto field in Bolivia's southern state of Tarija, President Evo Morales stood flanked by his ministers and military before a crowd of television cameras. In a carefully orchestrated public relations event, Morales made the surprise announcement that the military was at that moment securing the country's oil and gas fields.

"This is the solution to the social and economic problems of our country," Morales proclaimed. "Once we have recovered these natural resources, this will generate work; it is the end of the looting of our natural resources by multinational oil companies."

By the time Morales won his unprecedented landslide electoral victory in December 2005, nationalization of Bolivia's oil and gas reserves had become a widespread popular demand. In a national referendum in 2004, 94% of Bolivians had voted to recover state ownership of oil and gas. After then president Carlos Mesa responded to that vote with only moderate legislative proposals, protests and blockades demanding nationalization rocked the country. Morales and his Movement Toward Socialism (MAS) party originally supported a more limited reform of the energy sector, but as the protests mounted, MAS joined the call for nationalization. When Mesa resigned, triggering early elections, nationalization became the primary electoral issue.

On paper, the Morales government's oil and gas policy falls far short of what is traditionally meant by nationalization: government expropriation of foreign property to gain total control of an industry. Instead, his administration is taking a softer approach, opening negotiations with private investors to recover a measure of control over the industry and increase government revenues from it.

The May 1 announcement drew strong reactions from both ends of the political spectrum. Gabriel Dabdoub, president of the Santa Cruz Chamber of Commerce and Industry, told *The Miami Herald*, "We're very concerned about the international repercussions. This might isolate Bolivia from the world." Spanish prime minister José Luis Rodríguez Zapatero expressed his "most profound concern," warning of "consequences for bilateral relations." At the same time, many on the Bolivian left faulted the policy for not going far enough. The Bolivian Center for Information and Documentation criticized the decree for failing to "recover the oil and gas industry that was privatized in the capitalization process."

A Cochabamba cab driver named Enrique summed up the sentiment of the majority of Bolivians in the middle: "This isn't nationalization; if it were, the multinationals wouldn't be here. But if we kick them out, they'll sue us. So we have to negotiate."

Six months on, Bolivia's government has had mixed results in implementing the decree. Slow progress in negotiations to rebuild the state oil and gas company, political scandals, and logistical problems initially gave Bolivian opposition parties ample opportunity to question the government's intentions and competence. But in October the government reached agreement on new contracts with 10 oil and gas companies, including Petrobras, the Brazilian public-private energy company, and Spanish energy giant Repsol, which together control 74% of Bolivia's gas reserves. The step garnered praise from both foreign and domestic business interests. While the government continues difficult negotiations over remaining issues with foreign energy companies, Bolivians wait to see whether Morales's "nationalization through negotiation" strategy will bring about concrete improvements in their standard of living.

HOW DID BOLIVIA GET HERE?

At more than 13,000 feet above sea level, the legendary colonial city of Potosí rests at the base of Cerro Rico ("Rich Hill"), once so full of silver it virtually bankrolled the Spanish empire for more than 300 years. Though the glory of Potosí faded as the silver market waned, to this day Bolivian children are taught that a bridge of silver stretching from Potosí to Madrid could have been built from Cerro Rico's bounty. For nearly five centuries, Bolivia has seen its abundant natural resources extracted by outsiders, while the people of Bolivia have remained the poorest in South America.

Today, natural gas is Bolivia's new silver. The country boasts 47.8 trillion cubic feet of certified gas reserves; in South America only Venezuela has more. And proven reserves could rise dramatically since only 15% to 40% of the oil- and gas-rich zone has been explored to date. Until a few years ago, many oil developers regarded natural gas as nothing more than a waste product of the oil extraction process. "The notion that gas might be a moneymaker would have struck most oil executives as absurd," writes Paul Roberts in *The End of Oil*. With oil becoming increasingly scarce, however, natural gas prices have doubled in the last six years. Gas is now seen as the bridge fuel that will help ease global demand for oil and move industry toward cleaner, non-hydrocarbon energy sources. As analysts continue to debate when oil supplies will peak, the "dash for gas" is already in full swing.

With its price rising and vast reserves to tap, natural gas has become the focus of Bolivia's politics. A keen sense of their own history drives Bolivians' demand that their gas not meet the fate of the silver, rubber, and tin before it—that the people benefit in tangible ways from the wealth beneath their feet. A leader of former state oil workers recounts the words of an Aymara woman from La Paz: "I think that if they take it all now, what will be left for my grandchildren?

"So for this reason I have to defend it," she explains.

GIVING AWAY THE STORE

On October 17, 2003, under cover of night, then president Gonzalo Sánchez de Lozada boarded a jet for Miami after Bolivians took to the streets en masse to demand his resignation. The architect of a radical economic reform in the 1990s, Sánchez de Lozada left behind a devastated economy and a capital in chaos. He also left over 60 people dead and over 400 wounded, casualties of his government's month-long crackdown on mounting protests.

U.S.-educated and known as El Gringo for his American accent, Sánchez de Lozada had worked in close collaboration with international lending institutions such as the World Bank and the International Monetary Fund to implement the economic mantra coming out of Washington: a downsized government and unfettered free markets will create a tide that will lift people out of poverty. During his first term in office (1993–97), Sánchez de Lozada privatized all of Bolivia's most strategic state industries, including telecommunications, electricity, air and rail transportation, and the government's biggest revenue producer, oil and gas.

Sánchez de Lozada claimed his plan, dubbed "capitalization," would ensure that the public would benefit from the privatization of state-owned industries. These would be converted into public-private enterprises, with Bolivians maintaining a 51% interest in the new "capitalized" firms, while foreign investors would receive a 49% share in exchange for putting forth that same value in investment. Bolivia would still have control over the industries but would be able to double their value, spurring job creation and jumpstarting the economy. Almost half a million new jobs would be created in four years, the economy would double in size in 10 years, and the dividends from the new capitalized firms would fund an ambitious pension plan for Bolivia's elderly. That was the theory, at least.

Thanks to a mix of backroom deals and grievously unrealistic economic predictions, the reality played out quite differently.

What Sánchez de Lozada's administration actually did was to divide up the assets of the state energy company YPFB (Yacimientos Petroliferos Fiscales Bolivianos) to form three public-private consortiums: two exploration and production firms and one transportation firm. Majority control of these firms—complete with over

$11 billion in reserves and infrastructure—was given, free of charge, to foreign corporations such as British Petroleum and Enron in exchange for only a promise of future investment. A new oil and gas law, a condition for an IMF loan, transferred an additional $108 billion of reserves to private control and slashed oil and gas royalties on those reserves by almost two thirds, from 50% to 18%. Then, in 1999, Sánchez de Lozada's successor Hugo Bánzer sold off Bolivia's refineries, pipelines, and gas storage facilities at bargain prices, completing the dismantling of YPFB.

In the end, capitalization turned out to be even more destructive than a classic privatization in which the state at least receives compensation for its assets. Under capitalization, Bolivia handed over its most strategic industries and resources, as well as, in the case of YPFB, its most profitable industry. The promised 51-49 split of public versus private control ended up the reverse, leaving Bolivians with no decision-making power over the capitalized firms. The foreign companies that took over Bolivia's oil and gas industry never invested in modernizing its domestic infrastructure or technical capacity, finding it more profitable to export Bolivia's natural gas as a cheap raw material to be processed in Argentina or Brazil. While capitalization brought Bolivia a swath of new foreign investors, the promised trickle-down wealth creation never came. For Bolivians, it was like giving the mechanic the keys to your car, only to see him drive off with it.

Although average annual gas production rose by 65% between the years prior to (1990–96) and following (1997–2004) capitalization, government gas revenues increased only 10% due to slashed royalty rates. Government revenue from oil and gas, which made up between 38% and 60% of state revenues in the years before capitalization, dropped to under 7% in 2002. Bolivia's finite natural resources were being depleted faster, and the country had little to show for it.

Mark Weisbrot, economist and co-director of the Washington-based Center for Economic and Policy Research (CEPR), views the results of the Washington Consensus experiment in Bolivia this way: "They clearly failed by any objective measure—income per person is less than it was 27 years ago." According to a CEPR report, Bolivia's per capita income has grown by less than 2% in total over the past 25 years, compared to 60% between 1960 and 1980. "In the short run it's the loss of revenue," explains Weisbrot. "Over the longer run it's the loss of control over the resources themselves, which is what you need . . . as a source of financing for development and as part of a development strategy."

"The majority of government revenues in Bolivia now come from donations and loans," explains Roberto Fernández, a professor of economics and history at San Simón University in Cochabamba. "We borrow money to pay salaries. What kind of government is this that doesn't even have the autonomy to say, 'I'm going to build a little school'? It has to look for who internationally can give us a loan."

Prohibited by law from running for a second consecutive term in 1997, Sánchez de Lozada regained the presidency in 2002. In October 2003, Bolivians' growing frustration and anger over the dismal state of the economy exploded on the streets, in what later became known as the Gas War. Thousands of primarily indigenous residents of El Alto, the sprawling municipality that surrounds the capital city of La Paz, came out to protest Sánchez de Lozada's plan to export cheap gas to the United States through Bolivia's historic rival, Chile. The protesters erected blockades, strangling La Paz. Sánchez de Lozada declared a national emergency and called out the military.

As a convoy of soldiers carrying cisterns of gas toward La Paz pushed through makeshift blockades of rocks and tires in the streets of El Alto, the city's overcrowded neighborhoods became a battlefield.

"They began to shoot at houses," remembers Néstor Salinas—a resident of El Alto and member of the Association of Family Members of Those Fallen in Defense of Gas—"shooting at any human being who put themselves in front of the convoy.

"Imagine children just five years old, eight-year-old girls, pregnant women, men, brothers, fathers, teenagers," he continues. "They died to defend our oil and gas."

Within days, Sánchez de Lozada fled Bolivia. As he was landing in Miami, Néstor's 29-year-old brother, David, died from a bullet wound, joining the 59 other civilians killed by government troops.

MORALES'S HYBRID ENERGY POLICY

Most Bolivians viewed Evo Morales's electoral win last year as a victory for the movement to take back control of the country's natural resources and use them to tackle Bolivia's entrenched poverty. Not an outright nationalization, Morales's oil and gas decree this May set forth a complex series of steps aimed at boosting revenues from gas and regaining some control over the industry. The decree seeks to resurrect the state oil and gas company, YPFB, to assume regulatory functions, direct oil and gas development, and participate in the entire chain of production, from exploration to commercialization.

The decree requires the three public-private energy firms created by Sánchez de Lozada in the mid-1990s, along with the two private firms that bought YPFB's refineries and pipelines at the time, to sell back to the government enough shares (at market prices) to give YPFB majority ownership. To put this in context, these firms hold only 10% of Bolivia's oil and gas reserves. The rest are held exclusively by several foreign companies, including Petrobras and Repsol.

The decree placed a temporary additional tax of 32% on production in the country's two most productive fields, bringing in $32 million a month in new revenues devoted exclusively to rebuilding YPFB. It gave oil and gas companies operating in Bolivia six months to sign new exploration and development contracts.

The decree also reasserted the government's right to establish domestic and export prices. In addition to hiking tax and royalty rates, the Morales administration aims to raise the base prices on which taxes and royalties are calculated. It is currently locked in intense negotiations with Petrobras, arguing that export prices under its existing contracts are far below current market prices. In June, the administration negotiated a 48% increase in the gas price with Argentina, bringing in an additional $110 million a year in revenues—a key achievement of the May 1 decree.

Ultimately, Morales aims to transform Bolivia from an exporter of raw materials into an industrial producer of value-added goods such as electricity, synthetic diesel, fertilizers, and plastics. "The vision is that by 2010 we could see Bolivia as a main exporter of value-added products covering the entire South American market," explains Saúl Escalera, a YPFB official. While some critics assert that small countries like Bolivia lack the capital and technology necessary for industrialization, Escalera disagrees. He notes that YPFB has already "received 20 project proposals with a total value of $12 billion from foreign firms that want to invest in Bolivia."

Many of those firms are not the predictable Western players. Gazprom, the Russian state energy giant with more than 25% of the world's gas reserves, has expressed interest in investing more than $2 billion in Bolivia, while inquires have also come from several Asian countries. In May, Venezuela's state oil company, PDVSA, inked a deal to build a gas separation plant to produce fertilizer both for Bolivia's domestic use and for export to Brazil. And an Indian firm, Jindal Steel, has a deal in the works to build a plant that will power the industrialization of Mutún, site of one of the largest iron ore deposits in the world. The $2.3 billion project is projected to generate more than 10,000 new jobs and $200 million a year in government revenue.

According to Hydrocarbons Minister Carlos Villegas, $2 billion of foreign investment has already been committed to expand gas production and export capacity, particularly to Argentina and Brazil. At an International Development Bank conference in Washington, D.C., this July, Villegas declared: "Bolivia has completed its cycle as an exporter of raw materials. The resources are there, but we will give them a new path."

BOLIVIA'S BUMPY ROAD

The efforts of YPFB to exert control over the oil and gas industry have had mixed results. Shortly after Morales's May 1 announcement, YPFB was involved in a growing corruption scandal and admitted its inability to take over fuel distribution duties as mandated by the nationalization decree. A few weeks later the government declared the nationalization process temporarily suspended due to "a lack of economic resources," creating further unease and confirming critics' concerns that YPFB lacked the capacity, competence, and cash to carry out its new role. In late August the debacle culminated with the resignation of YPFB's president, Jorge Alvarado, who had been accused of signing a diesel contract that violated the decree. It was a major setback for a president who had asserted that YPFB would be "transparent, efficient, and socially controlled."

In August, police and prosecutors searched Repsol's Bolivia offices for the second time in six months in separate smuggling and malfeasance investigations. Repsol expressed outrage, warning that these investigations were jeopardizing the company's continued investment in Bolivia. In this case as in others, the government is pursuing a problematic strategy with foreign energy companies: wielding a strong hand to expose malfeasance and discredit them while simultaneously negotiating for their continued investment in the country.

Despite these obstacles, in late August the government became more assertive in implementing the May decree. After a four-month delay, government threats of expulsion secured the additional $32 million in monthly payments to YPFB due from Repsol, Petrobras, and France's Total, providing the state company with a critical infusion of cash.

In September political problems again flared. A resolution issued by then-hydrocarbons minister Andrés Solíz Rada ordered Petrobras to hand over control of exports and domestic sales of gasoline and diesel in its two Bolivian refineries in compliance with the decree. This move backfired, however, after the Brazilian foreign minister said the measure could cause Petrobras to pull out of Bolivia, which led Vice President Álvaro García Linera to suspend Rada's resolution. Rada responded by tendering his resignation, another setback for the administration. Linera, feeling the political weight of the moment, was resolute in declaring that the nationalization process was "irrevocable" and that the government, while maintaining a posture of "negotiation and tolerance," would be "intransigent" in obligating companies to comply with the decree.

In October, however, the government reached agreement on new exploration and development contracts with 10 major companies operating in Bolivia—a major milestone. Under the new contracts, the foreign companies are to extract Bolivia's oil and gas and hand them over to YPFB, which compensates the companies for production costs, investment, and profit. The tax and royalty rates in the new contracts are variable depending on a company's level of production and whether or not they have recovered past investments. The government claims its take will range between 50% and 80%, although questions remain about how it will be calculated. YPFB president Juan Carlos Ortiz estimates that the new contracts will put annual revenue for 2006 at $1.3 billion; Morales assured the public that with the increase in exports to Argentina and the new tax rates, annual oil and gas revenue will rise to $4 billion within the next four years.

"Mission accomplished," declared Morales in a press statement at the contract signing. "We are exercising as Bolivians our property rights over natural resources, without expelling anyone and without confiscating. With this measure, within 10 to 15 years, Bolivia will no longer be this little poor country, this beggar country, this country that is always looking to international assistance."

Critics, however, question whether the government got a good deal for the country, pointing out that the contracts don't commit foreign investors to substantial future investments or provide YPFB with the physical resources to participate in all phases of the industry. And tense negotiations continue over control of the five companies which used to make up the state company, prior to capitalization. Petrobras, which owns the two formerly YPFB refineries, has shown reluctance to give up any operational control of these facilities. Considering that Bolivia supplies 50% of Brazil's gas needs and that Petrobras' transactions account for 18% of Bolivia's gross domestic product, both countries have much to lose should a deal not be reached.

OPPORTUNITIES AND OBLIGATIONS

As Bolivia struggles to work through the pitfalls of implementing Morales's decree, a clear end goal is to achieve a larger shift in power dynamics. Rather than receiving policy prescriptions from Washington or from international institutions and foreign investors, Bolivia aims to draft its own blueprint, joining a growing political shift in the region away from free-market ideology.

YPFB's Escalera describes the difference the nationalization decree has made for the state energy company. "Before, we had big plans—jobs industrialization, value added products—but didn't have the [gas]," he explains. "It was like knocking on the multinationals' door, 'Could you give me a little sugar for my tea?' If they don't want to do it, the deal is off."

"Even if they were willing to give it to me, I'd then have to go talk to Transredes [the public-private pipeline company created under capitalization] to beg for transportation," he explains, "and they would say 'forget it.' "

"Since the May 1 decree," he continues, "everything has changed. We can guarantee everything the investor wants—transportation, volume, price—now it's in my hands."

Many Bolivians hope the government's new resources and new authority will translate into concrete improvements in quality of life for the country's 9 million people, including new jobs and increased state resources for education, health care, and infrastructure. But the challenges Bolivia faces in transforming its oil and gas policy cannot be overstated. Whether the nationalization decree can be fully implemented, let alone generate concrete benefits for ordinary Bolivians, depends on multiple factors: not only getting all of the pieces in place to ensure that the anticipated surge in oil and gas revenues actually materializes, but also creating strong and effective governmental and social institutions, mitigating the social and environmental impacts of energy development, and using the new revenues effectively for national development projects.

For Salinas, whose organization is pushing for Sánchez de Lozada to return to Bolivia to stand trial for the killings during the Gas War, the Morales government also carries a moral debt.

"Our name says it clearly: 'Fallen in defense of gas,' " he explains. "This is the importance the country has to place on this issue. The families that lost [loved ones] didn't lose them for nothing, their loss made possible the social, economic, and political change that Bolivia is now living. The government now owes these families justice."

SOURCES

Ministerio de Hidrocarburos, "Estadísticas—Upstream—Producción" (July 28, 2005); Fundación Milenio (La Paz), "La nacionalización bajo la lupa," *Boletín Económico*, Análisis de Coyuntura no. 4 (August 2006), citing data from the Hydrocarbons Ministry and YPFB.

VENEZUELA'S COOPERATIVE REVOLUTION

BY BETSY BOWMAN AND BOB STONE
Dollars & Sense, July/August 2006

Zaida Rosas, a woman in her fifties with 15 grandchildren, works in the newly constructed textile co-op Venezuela Avanza in Caracas. The co-op's 209 workers are mostly formerly jobless neighborhood women. Their homes on the surrounding steep hillsides in west Caracas were almost all self-built.

Rosas works seven hours a day, five days a week, and is paid $117 a month, the uniform income all employees voted for themselves. This is much less than the minimum salary, officially set at $188 a month. This was "so we can pay back our [government start-up] loan," she explained. Venezuela Avanza *cooperativistas* have a monthly general assembly to decide policy. As in most producer co-ops, they are not paid a salary, but an advance on profits. Workers paying themselves less than the minimum wage in order to make payments to the state was, Rosas acknowledged, a bad situation. "We hope our working conditions will improve with time," she said.

To prepare the co-op's workers to collectively run a business, the new Ministry of Popular Economy (MINEP) had given them small scholarships to train in cooperativism, production, and accounting. "My family is a lot happier—I've learned to write and have my third-grade certificate," she said.

Rosas is now also part of a larger local web of cooperatives: Her factory is one of two producer co-ops, both built by a local bricklayers' cooperative, that, along with a clinic, a supermarket co-op, a school, and a community center, make up a so-called nucleus of endogenous development. These nucleos are at the core of the country's plan for fostering egalitarian economic development.

U.S. media coverage of Venezuela tends to center around the country's oil and the—not unrelated—war of words between President Hugo Chávez and the White House. Chávez, for example, likes to refer to George W. Bush as "Mr. Danger," a reference to a brutish foreigner in a classic Venezuelan novel. Somewhat more clumsily, Defense Secretary Donald Rumsfeld recently compared Chávez to Hitler. While this makes for entertaining copy, reporters have missed a major story in Venezuela—the unprecedented growth of cooperatives that has reshaped the economic lives of hundreds of thousands of Venezuelans like Rosas. On a recent visit to Caracas, we spoke with co-op members and others invested in this novel experiment to open Venezuela's economy from the bottom up.

EXPLOSION OF COOPERATIVES

Our first encounter with Venezuela's co-op movement was with Luis Guacarán, a taxi co-op member who drove us to the outskirts of Caracas. Settled into the rainy trip, we asked Guacarán what changes wrought by the Chávez government had meant for him personally. He replied that he now felt that as a citizen he had a right to share in the nation's oil wealth, which had always gone to an "oligarchy." The people needed health, education, and meaningful work; that was reason enough for Chávez to divert oil revenues in order to provide these things. Two of Guacarán's five sons are in the military, a daughter is studying petroleum engineering, another has a beauty shop. All were in vocational or professional studies.

Almost everyone we met during our visit was involved in a cooperative. The 1999 constitution requires the state to "promote and protect" co-ops. However, it was only after the passage of the Special Law on Cooperative Associations in 2001 that the totals began to skyrocket. When Chávez took office in 1998 there were 762 legally registered cooperatives with about 20,000 members. In 2001 there were almost 1,000 cooperatives. The number grew to 2,000 in 2002 and to 8,000 by 2003. In mid-2006, the National Superintendence of Cooperatives (SUNACOOP) reported that it had registered over 108,000 co-ops representing over 1.5 million members. Since mid-2003, MINEP has provided free business and self-management training, helped workers turn troubled conventional enterprises into cooperatives, and extended credit for start-ups and buyouts. The resulting movement has increasingly come to define the Bolivarian Revolution, the name Chávez has given to his efforts to reshape Venezuela's economic and political structures.

Now MINEP is trying to keep up with the explosion it set off. While pre-Chávez co-ops were mostly credit unions, the "Bolivarian" ones are much more diverse: Half are in the service sector, a third in production, with the rest divided among savings, housing, consumer, and other areas. Cooperativists work in four major sectors: 31% in commerce, restaurants, and hotels; 29% in transport, storage and communications; 18% in agriculture, hunting, and fishing; and 8.3% in industrial manufacture. Cooperativism is on the march in Venezuela on a scale and at a speed never before seen anywhere.

Most cooperatives are small. Since January 2005, however, when the government announced a policy of expropriation of closed industrial plants, MINEP has stood ready to help workers take control of some large factories facing bankruptcy. If the unused plant is deemed of "public utility," the initiation of expropriation proceedings often leads to negotiation with the owners over compensation. In one instance, owners of a shuttered Heinz tomato processing plant in Monagas state offered to sell it to the government for $600,000. After factoring in back wages, taxes, and an outstanding mortgage, the two sides reached an amicable agreement to sell the plant to the workers for $260,000, with preferential loans provided by the government. In a more typically confrontational example, displaced workers first occupied a sugar refinery in Cumanacoa and restarted it on their own. The federal government then expropriated the property and turned it over to cooperatives of the plant's workers. The owners' property rights were respected inasmuch as the government loaned the workers the money for the purchase, though the price was well below what the owners had claimed. Such expropriated factories are then often run by elected representatives of workers alongside of government appointees.

There are strings attached. "We haven't expropriated Cumanacoa and Sideroca for the workers just to help them become rich people the day after tomorrow," said Chávez. "This has not been done just for them—it is to help make everyone wealthy." Take the case of Cacao Sucre, another sugar mill closed for eight years by its private owners, leaving 120 workers unemployed in a neighborhood of grinding poverty. The state's governor put out a call for the workers to form a co-op. After receiving training in self-management, the mill co-op integrated with the 3,665-strong cane growers' co-op. In July 2005, this large cooperative became the first "Social Production Enterprise." The new designation means that the co-op is required to set aside a portion of its profits to fund health, education, and housing for the local population, and to open its food hall to the community as well.

With only 700 plants on the government's list of closed or bankrupt candidates for expropriation, cooperativization of existing large-scale facilities is limited, and so far a bit slow. Unions are identifying more underproducing enterprises. But there is a long way to go.

Cooperatives are at the center of Venezuela's new economic model. They have the potential to fulfill a number of the aims of the Bolivarian revolution, including combating unemployment, promoting durable economic development, competing peacefully with conventional capitalist firms, and advancing Chávez's still-being-defined socialism.

NOT YOUR GRANDFATHER'S WPA

Capitalism generates unemployment. Neoliberalism aggravated this tendency in Venezuela, producing a large, stable group of overlooked people who were excluded from meaningful work and consumption. If not forgotten altogether, they were blamed for their plight and made to feel superfluous. But the Bolivarian Revolution is about demanding recognition. In March of 2004 Chávez called Venezuelans to a new "mission," when MINEP inaugurated the

Misión Vuelvan Caras program—Mission About-Face. Acting "from within themselves and by their own powers" to form cooperatives, the people were to "combat unemployment and exclusion" by actually "chang[ing] the relations of production."

In Venezuela, *vuelvan caras* evokes an insurgent general's command to his troops upon being surrounded by Spaniards in the war of independence. In effect: Stop playing the role of the pursued; turn and attack the enemy frontally. The new enemy is unemployment, and the goal of full employment is to be achieved by groups—especially of the unemployed—throwing in their lot with each other and setting to work together. Vuelvan Caras teaches management, accounting, and co-op values to hundreds of thousands of scholarship students. Graduates are free to seek regular jobs or form micro-enterprises, for which credit is offered; however, co-ops get priority for technical assistance, credits, and contracts. But the original spark—the collective entrepreneurship needed for cooperativization—is to come from the people. Over 70% of the graduates of the class of 2005 formed 7,592 new co-ops.

Vuelvan Caras seems to be paying off. Unemployment reached a high of 18% in 2003 but fell to 14.5% in 2004, and 11.5% in 2005. MINEP is planning a "Vuelvan Caras II," aiming to draw in 700,000 more of the jobless. But with a population of 26 million, Venezuela's battle against structural causes of unemployment has only begun.

ECONOMIC DEVELOPMENT FROM WITHIN

Cooperatives also advance the Chávez administration's broader goal of "endogenous development." Foreign direct investment continues in Venezuela, but the government aims to avoid relying on inflows from abroad, which open a country to capitalism's usual blackmail. Endogenous development means "to be capable of producing the seed that we sow, the food that we eat, the clothes that we wear, the goods and services that we need, breaking the economic, cultural and technological dependence that has halted our development, starting with ourselves." To these ends, co-ops are ideal tools. Co-ops anchor development in Venezuela: Under the control of local worker-owners, they don't pose a threat of capital flight as capitalist firms do.

The need for endogenous development came home to Venezuelans during the 2002 oil strike carried out by Chávez's political opponents. Major distributors of the country's mostly imported food also supported the strike, halting food deliveries and exposing a gaping vulnerability. In response, the government started its own parallel supermarket chain. In just three years, Mercal had 14,000 points of sale, almost all in poor neighborhoods, selling staples at discounts of

20% to 50%. It is now the nation's largest supermarket chain and its second largest enterprise overall. The Mercal stores attract shoppers of all political stripes thanks to their low prices and high-quality merchandise. To promote "food sovereignty," Mercal has increased its proportion of domestic suppliers to over 40%, giving priority to co-ops when possible. Venezuela still imports 64% of the food it consumes, but that's down from 72% in 1998. By cutting import dependence, transport costs, and middlemen while tapping local suppliers, Mercal aims to wean itself from its $24 million-a-month subsidy.

DISPLACING CAPITALISM AND BUILDING SOCIALISM

Another reason the architects of the so-called Bolivarian Revolution are vigorously pushing the co-op model is their belief that co-ops can meet needs better than conventional capitalist firms. Freed of the burdens of supporting costly managers and profit-hungry absentee investors, co-ops have a financial buoyancy that drives labor-saving technological innovation to save labor time. "Cooperatives are the businesses of the future," says former planning and development minister Felipe Pérez-Martí. Not only are they nonexploitative, they outproduce capitalist firms, since, Pérez-Martí holds, worker-owners must seek their firm's efficiency and success. Such a claim raises eyebrows in the United States, but a growing body of research suggests that co-ops can indeed be more productive and profitable than conventional firms.

To test whether co-ops can beat capitalist firms on their own terms, a viable co-op or solidarity sector must be set up parallel to the securely dominant capitalist one. Today Venezuela is preparing this "experiment." More than 5% of the labor force now works in cooperatives, according to MINEP. While this is a much larger percentage of cooperativistas than in most countries, it is still small relative to the size of a co-op sector that would have a shot at out-competing Venezuela's capitalist sector. Chávez's supporters hope that once such a sector is launched, cooperativization will expand in a "virtuous circle" as conventional workforces, observing co-ops, demand similar control of their work. Elias Jaua, the initial minister of popular economy, says, "The private sector can understand the process and incorporate itself into the new dynamic of society, or it will be simply displaced by the new productive forces which have a better quality production, a vision based much more on solidarity than consumption." One could claim that MINEP's credits, trainings, and contracts prejudice the outcome in favor of co-ops. But Vuelvan Caras graduates are free to take jobs in the capitalist sector. And MINEP's policy of favoring employee-owned firms is not that different from U.S. laws, subsidies, and tax benefits that favor investor-owned ones.

Finally, by placing the means of production in workers' hands, the co-op movement directly builds socialism. Cooperativization, especially of idle factories occupied by their workforces, promotes "what has always been our goal: that the workers run production and that the governments are also run by the workers," according to Labor Minister Maria Cristina Iglesias. Co-ops, then, are not just means to what Chávez calls "socialism for the 21st century": They actually constitute partial realizations of it.

MANAGING THE EXPERIMENT'S RISKS

Cooperativization is key to achieving the aims of the Bolivarian Revolution. But the revolution's leaders acknowledge that a long struggle lies ahead. Traditional capitalist enterprises still dominate Venezuela's economy. And even if all of the country's current cooperativization programs succeed, will that struggle—and it will be a struggle—result in socialism? Michael Albert of *Z Magazine* grants that co-ops may be more productive, and he strongly supports Venezuela's experiment. But in the absence of plans for de-marketization, he has doubts that it will reach socialism. For the effect on cooperatives themselves of "trying to out-compete old firms in market-defined contests may [be to] entrench in them a managerial bureaucracy and a competitive rather than a social orientation," leading to a market socialist system "that still has a ruling managerial or coordinator class." Albert's concern is well founded: The history of co-ops from the Amana colonies of Iowa to the Mondragón Cooperative Corporation in the Basque country shows that even when they start out with a community-service mandate, individual co-ops, or even networks of co-ops, tend to defensively reinternalize capitalist self-seeking and become indistinguishable from their competitors when made to compete alone against an array of capitalist firms in a capitalist economy.

Disarmingly, members of Chávez's administration acknowledge these risks. Juan Carlos Loyo, deputy minister of the popular economy, noting that community service has been part of the cooperative creed since its beginning, asks for patience: "We know that we are coming from a capitalist lifestyle that is profoundly individualistic and self-centered." Marcela Maspero, a national coordinator of the new, Chavista UNT labor federation, acknowledges "the risk of converting our comrades into neoliberal capitalists." In Venezuela's unique case, however, construction of a viable co-op sector is the goal of a government with considerable financial resources, and its aim of thereby building socialism is also a popular national project. In Venezuela, success is therefore a plausible hope. A loose analogy would hold with May 1968 if both the de Gaulle government and the French Communist Party had been in favor of student-worker demands for *autogestión* or self-management.

There are problems, of course. Groups may register as "phantom co-ops" to get start-up grants, then simply walk away with the money. And since co-ops are favored in awarding government contracts, there is a significant amount of fraud. "There are cooperatives that are registered as such on paper," Jaua, the former head of MINEP, reports, "but which have a boss who is paid more, salaried workers, and unequal distribution of work and income." SUNACOOP admits that its enforcement is spotty. Many of the new cooperatives have also suffered as a result of inadequate self-management training. Government authorities are attempting to address these problems by increasing visits to local co-ops, augmenting training and support services, and decentralizing oversight to local councils.

Despite the obstacles, the new co-ops, with government support, are building a decentralized national movement with its own momentum and institutions. This May, the National Executive Cooperative Council (CENCOOP) was launched. The council is made up of five co-op members from each of Venezuela's 25 states, elected by their State Cooperative Councils, which are in turn elected by Municipal Councils composed of local cooperativists. CENCOOP will represent Venezuela at the International Cooperative Alliance—the global body embracing 700 million individual members in hundreds of thousands of cooperatives in 95 countries.

The pre-Bolivarian co-op movement at first felt left out, and criticized hasty cooperativization. But its advice was sought at each stage of the planning for CENCOOP, and it finally joined the council, sharing its valuable experience with the new movement. The new state and municipal co-op councils are part of a plan to decentralize MINEP's functions. Having helped organize CENCOOP, MINEP Superintendent Carlos Molina says his office will adopt a hands-off approach to assure the cooperative movement's increasing autonomy. Today, however, many of the new co-ops remain dependent on MINEP's support.

A MOVEMENT'S OPPONENTS

Whatever success cooperativization achieves carries its own risks, both internal and external. So far, the Chávez government has compensated capitalists for expropriations and has targeted for co-op conversion only firms that are in some sense in trouble. But at a certain point, workers in healthy firms, seeing their cooperativist neighbors enjoying newfound power in the workplace and a more equal distribution of income, may want to cooperativize their firms too. And having for years had profit extracted as a major portion of the value their labor has created—in many cases enough to cover their firm's market value many times over—won't they have grounds to demand transfer without compensation? In short, to further expand and strengthen revolutionary solidarity before new counter-revolutionary efforts take root, won't the revolution have to start a real redistribution of productive wealth—to cooperativize firms directly at the expense of Venezuela's capitalists? Sooner or later, Venezuela's cooperative experiment will have to address this question.

After joining in the World Social Forum in Caracas in last January, we caught some glimpses of the Bolivarian Revolution moving at full speed, and we've followed it since then. We are convinced that for those around the world who believe "another world is possible," the stakes of this experiment are enormous. Predictably, then, it faces genuine external threats. The short-lived coup in April 2002 and the destructive strike by oil-industry managers that December were the works of a displaced and angry elite encouraged by the United States at every step. And the campaign continues: State Department–linked groups have been pumping $5 million a year into opposition groups that backed the coup. Yet the democratizing of workplaces proceeds relentlessly, bringing ever more Venezuelans into the revolutionary process. This inclusion is itself a defense since it expands, unites, and strengthens the resistance with which Venezuelans would greet any new effort to halt or divert their revolution.

DEMOCRACY: ECONOMIC AND POLITICAL

Alongside the co-op movement, Venezuelans are engaged in building a new form of local political democracy through so-called Communal Councils. Modeled on Brazil's innovative participatory budgeting process, these councils grew out of the Land Committees Chávez created to grant land titles to the many squatters in Caracas's barrios. If a community of 100 to 200 families organizes itself and submits a local development plan, the government grants land titles. Result: Individuals get homes, and the community gets a grassroots assembly.

The councils have budgets and make decisions on a range of local matters. They delegate spokespersons to the barrio and the municipality. Today, a few thousand Communal Councils exist, but within five years the government plans to bring all Venezuelans into local counsels. In conjunction with cooperativization in the economy, the Community Council movement may portend the creation of a new decentralized, democratic polity.

SOURCES

Many valuable articles have been collected at www.venezuelanalysis.com, including C. Harnecker, "The New

Cooperative Movement in Venezuela's Bolivarian Process," *Monthly Review Zine* (May 2005); S. Wagner, "Vuelvan Caras: Venezuela's Mission for Building Socialism of the 21st Century" (July 2005); "Poverty and Unemployment Down Significantly in 2005" (October 2005); F. Perez-Marti, "The Venezuelan Model of Development: The Path of Solidarity" (June 2004); "Venezuela: Expropriations, Cooperatives and Co-management," *Green Left Weekly* (October 2005); M. Albert, "Venezuela's Path," Z-Net (November 2005); O. Sunkel, *Development From Within: Toward a Neostructuralist Approach for Latin America* (Lynne Rienner, 1993); H. Thomas, "Performance of the Mondragón Co-operatives in Spain," in D. C. Jones and J. Svejnar, eds., *Participatory and Self-Managed Firms* (Lexington Books, 1982); D. Levine and L. D'A. Tyson, "Participation, Productivity and the Firm's Environment," in A. Blinder, ed., *Paying for Productivity: A Look at the Evidence* (Brookings Institute, 1990); D. Schweickart, *After Capitalism* (Rowman & Littlefield, 2002); M. Lebowitz, "Constructing Co-management in Venezuela: Contradictions along the Path," *Monthly Review Zine* (October 2005); Z. Centeno, "Cooperativas: una vision para impulsar el desarrollo endogeno," downloaded at www.mci.gob.ve.

FROM RESISTANCE TO PRODUCTION IN ARGENTINA: WORKER-CONTROLLED BUSINESSES TAKE THE NEXT STEP

BY CHRIS TILLY AND MARIE KENNEDY
Dollars & Sense, November/December 2005

One day last June in downtown Buenos Aires, hundreds of demonstrators filled the lobby of the worker-run Hotel Bauen to demand that the Argentine government expropriate the property in favor of the workers. Upstairs in the restaurant, new wait staff described how these jobs differed from their previous restaurant positions. "Here the majority are people from outside the country, tourists," said Federico. "In my previous waiting job, I mostly saw Argentines." "I worked in a small restaurant before, so this is totally different," Patricia commented. Only then did Federico add, "Another important difference is that there's no boss here. You don't have a boss saying, 'You do this, you do that.' We all share the duties. We're all owners, so we're all involved in the decisions."

The Bauen, shut down by its owner in 2001, was occupied by former employees in 2003 and reopened by them as a cooperative in 2004, one of close to 200 bankrupt Argentine businesses "recuperated" by their employees. Although the legal status of the hotel is tenuous—it has never officially been expropriated from the previous owner—what's striking in the Bauen is the normalcy with which it functions. The staff at the front desk hand guests their keys, and uniformed maids clean the rooms. Federico and Patricia pour coffee and clear tables at the breakfast buffet—and don't necessarily think of worker ownership as the most noteworthy difference between this and other jobs.

Still, behind the routine at the Bauen, the hotel's 110 workers face a series of daunting challenges. How can they access investment funds to computerize the billing system, upgrade the aging furniture and televisions, and do long-overdue maintenance? As the carpets get stained and scuffed and the elevators function more sporadically, will the hotel be able to attract customers beyond an ideologically committed core? Given that former managers did not join the occupation, can front-line workers learn the skills needed to run a 224-room hotel? How can the cooperative effectively transmit its values to new workers like Patricia and Federico? How can it avoid getting bogged down by the factional political struggles that crisscross the movement of recuperated workplaces? Will the Bauen cooperative and its allies muster the political clout to win an expropriation decision? Can they head off threats by city inspectors to shut the hotel down? These hurdles, or ones like them, confront almost all of the recuperated businesses in Argentina.

DEINDUSTRIALIZATION AND RECUPERATION

The Argentine movement to recuperate businesses as worker cooperatives has two roots: profound deindustrialization and a wave of new social movements. President Carlos Menem, who governed from 1989 to 1999, presided over neoliberal free trade and privatization policies that undid government support for manufacturing, resulting in waves of layoffs and plant closings. As the crisis squeezed the working class in the mid-1990s, movements of unemployed workers who came to be called *piqueteros* began blocking highways, and a few groups of workers began to take over and operate closed plants.

But a much larger powder keg exploded in 2001, when investor panic and devaluation of the peso suddenly wiped out much of the assets and purchasing power of Argentina's large and, until then, prosperous middle class. In two days of massive street demonstrations, Argentina's people drove out then president Fernando de la Rua. A series of short-lived caretaker presidencies followed until, in 2003, elections brought center-left Néstor Kirchner to power. Kirchner has adopted populist rhetoric, taken a tough line with international lenders seeking to collect the country's huge debt, and allowed protest to flourish. But he has stopped short of supporting the development of a grassroots "social economy," and many in the recuperated workplace movement view him with skepticism.

Between 2001 and 2003, the combination of economic crisis and movement upsurge led business recuperations to pop up like mushrooms. Sergio Ciancaglini of LaVaca, a Buenos Aires political collective that has done much support and documentation of recuperated workplaces, marveled, "These workers invented this solution without any precedent in Argentina. They had to go up against the politicians, the bosses, the unions, the left (because they don't like cooperatives), the cooperative movement (because they've never seen a cooperative like this before)—they had to fight everybody!"

Factories make up the majority—but not all—of the cooperatives. *Sin Patrón* (Without a Boss), LaVaca's guide to Argentina's recuperated businesses, lists supermarkets, construction firms, bus companies, newspapers, hospitals, and one website designer and computer service provider, in addition to scores of factories. In almost every case, workers occupied the business when it went bankrupt, though as University of Buenos Aires economist Néstor Ortiz put it, "These were bankrupt businesses with millionaire owners" because they had been moving their profits offshore.

Although initially not all groups of workers who occupied their businesses formed cooperatives, they soon discovered that cooperativism was the only legal framework that allowed them to win government sanction. Argentina's agricultural and consumer cooperatives date back to early in the last century, and today a fifth of Argentines belong to such co-ops. Under pressure from occupying workers and their supporters, provincial governments began to stretch cooperative laws on the books to cover the newly recuperated workplaces. In many cases, the provincial government expropriated the business, compensating the former owner (minus taxes owed) and mandating long-run repayment to the government by the cooperative. But as Ernesto González of Chilavert, a recuperated printing business, noted, the long run may turn out to be very long. "We have to return the money to the government some time," he said. "It may take five to six years to fully implement the expropriation, and then we will probably have 20 to 30 years to repay—who knows? We haven't actually had to start paying anything yet. But it's not a Communist confiscation!"

Most estimates put the total number of recuperated units between 150 and 200, and the number of workers between 10,000 and 15,000. The estimates are a little fuzzy, both because new takeovers and business failures constantly alter the count, and because in the fluid situation of today's Argentina, many businesses remain in ambiguous situations. For example, the 400 workers of the giant Tandador shipyard in Buenos Aires have run the enterprise, with the approval of a series of judges, since it went into bankruptcy in 1999, but it has never been formally constituted as a recuperated business.

Despite limited economic recovery since 2001, economic misery remains widespread in Argentina. A nighttime walk through Buenos Aires reveals armies of *cartoneros*, cardboard scavengers digging through garbage bags to retrieve cardboard they can trade for a few centavos. Even so, the economy has perked up enough that owners will fight harder to hold onto their businesses; at the same time, the swell of protest has ebbed. As a result, what looked a few years ago like a rising tide of business recuperations is now looking more like a string of isolated ponds.

MAKE MONEY OR TRANSFORM SOCIETY?

Argentina's new worker-run businesses are far from a unified movement. Recuperated workplaces are grouped in at least five associations. The two most important are the similarly named National Movement of Recuperated Businesses (MNER) and National Movement of Recuperated Factories (MNFR). Each has a charismatic leader with roots in Peronism, the party named after populist leader Juan Perón. At the helm of MNER is Eduardo Murúa, a worker at Industrias

Metalúrgicas y Plásticas de Argentina (IMPA), a large recuperated aluminum products plant. Luis Caro, an attorney, heads up MNFR. Their rhetoric sounds similar. The MNER "seeks the abolition of a system that oppresses, that generates exclusion and death, that can't even incorporate the working class," says Murúa. "Each factory is a revolution!" thunders Caro.

So what's the difference? It depends whom you ask, naturally. One clear distinction is that MNER tends to confront the Kirchner government, whereas MNFR seeks a more friendly relationship. But University of Buenos Aires professor Néstor Ortiz and left Buenos Aires city councilor Daniel Betti linked the difference to a deeper division of strategy and purpose. "The MNER cooperatives don't just want to make money, but also to carry out sociocultural work, creating schools, cultural centers, the arts," declared Betti. "The MNFR businesses want to make money, and only make money."

Ortiz is more skeptical of the MNER's broader agenda. "In the 2001 era, like May '68 in France, everything seemed possible—it looked like the capitalist order had been turned upside down. Here, the former workers in the plants were often joined by young people trying to pursue a political agenda, and that wasn't healthy for the movement. The idea was that the workers' assembly had to make all the decisions, with no management. But then one sector [MNFR] saw the need to return to profitability and compete globally. This more 'right' sector hired professional and technical management—and that confronted the movement's 'social economy' paradigm." González of the Chilavert printing cooperative, which prides itself on its commitment to supporting other recuperated workplaces and running a cultural center to benefit the community, agreed that this commitment is becoming more exceptional: "Out of 200 recuperated businesses, maybe there are 10 like us."

But before concluding that the remaining enterprises have sold out to the pursuit of profit, it's worth taking a closer look at their day-to-day practice. Both IMPA, the aluminum products factory, and the Hotel Bauen pay all workers the same salary, for example, and both are run entirely by former workers; neither has hired new managers. "The training of professionals in Argentina is so hierarchical, so top-down, that if we brought them in from outside it just wouldn't work in this setting," says Pablo Piñeiro, an economist who works in the marketing department of IMPA. A stroll around the IMPA factory reveals an environmentally minded shop making windmill parts, a left-wing silkscreen collective, a community cultural center, an adult education school, and a community clinic—all operating in space loaned by IMPA. The Bauen's six meeting rooms are in use day and night, in part by paying customers but also by community and left organizations that get a solidarity price in return for the political support they have lent the Bauen's workers.

GLIMPSES OF THE SOCIAL ECONOMY

This is what Argentines call the "social economy" in practice. It's a constantly shifting combination of high ideals and pragmatic fixes. The MNER's slogan, borrowed from Brazil's Landless Workers' Movement, is "Occupy, Resist, Produce"—but the trick is finding the right balance between resistance and production. The cultural centers at Chilavert and IMPA offer workshops in ceramics, tai chi, and salsa dancing, but also a class on the history of the Argentine workers' movement, a performance recounting the history of resistance in song, and the "Struggle-Work-Culture" festival. The cultural programming represents a genuine commitment to the cultural life of the community, but also a canny way of building community support in the inevitable confrontations with the government.

Two hundred enterprises, representing a fairly random mix of industries, hardly constitute a parallel economy in a country of 40 million. But the recuperated workplaces are exploring ways to barter and otherwise build mutual economic support. Chilavert publishes books, brochures, and posters for the movement. The workers of Zanón, a recuperated ceramics manufacturer located in the province of Neuquén, have donated floor tiles to the Hotel Bauen in return for free rooms and meeting spaces when their representatives travel to Buenos Aires. In the heavily trafficked lobby of the Bauen, athletic shoe cooperative CUC (formerly an Adidas factory) displays and sells shoes. The recuperated businesses have also forged economic and political links with other outposts of the social economy. For example, the Unemployed Workers' Movement of La Matanza has started up a series of cooperative businesses: a bakery, a day care center, a sewing workshop (which produces slipcovers for an Avon subcontractor as well as high-fashion garments for sale in Japan), and a small publishing house. The publishing house prints their books at . . . you guessed it, Chilavert. And supportive academics and professionals pitch in: Hundreds of students and professors offer help with accounting and business planning, and doctors volunteer their services for Bauen workers (cooperatives stand outside the regular Argentine health plan, which is administered through unions that are absent in cooperative workplaces).

A variable mixture of principles and pragmatism also guides how the recuperated businesses run themselves. Chilavert stands at one extreme, embracing the ideal of *horizontalidad*, an Argentine term meaning participatory democracy and decision by consensus. Instead of paying all employees equally, as the Bauen and IMPA do, Chilavert sets pay based on need: Those with more dependents, or health problems, get a higher salary. The group holds monthly assemblies, and "all of us in the shop end up dealing with customers and discussing a job," Ernesto González said. At the Bauen, as well, Marcelo Ruarte, president of the Hotel Bauen cooperative, proudly said, "Since we formed the co-op, I've worked as a waiter, cleaned rooms, done laundry. We all have to pitch in to run this place." Even so, González, a trained accountant, continues to play a leading role in Chilavert's office, and Ruarte, who worked at the front desk, leads the Bauen.

At the other end of the spectrum are what González calls "the more capitalist recuperated businesses." Here, the governing council of the cooperative often plays a more traditional management role. "Not like before, but they do function as bosses. You see a boss behind the desk," he said. Worker assemblies might take place once a year, with the council making decisions in between. "There's a wage scale, and workers with more skill and responsibility make more money," González added.

González and others were quick to acknowledge that there are practical reasons why different businesses follow different management paths. He and his colleague Anita Ghilardini, a former clown who worked for several years at IMPA's cultural center and now runs the center at Chilavert, pointed out that they were lucky to inherit a very productive business, allowing more room for flexibility and even a surplus that can pay for the cultural component. He also theorized that the most socially conscious recuperated workplaces are the ones where the struggle to take over the business was most protracted and difficult. In addition, Chilavert's small size (there are 12 workers) facilitates frequent consultation, and work is organized around small projects rather than coordinated assembly lines. "In other recuperated businesses, the form of the factory imposes a certain form of management—somebody has to give orders," González observed. "But there's still a new element of discussion and consultation." And Ruarte noted that even in the highly politicized Bauen, "The old ways of looking at work have been drilled into our heads for years. Here, everybody thinks they're the 'owner.' They all want a salary of 1,000, 2,000, 3,000 pesos." Bauen employees earn 800 pesos, or about $265, a month. To put this in context, Argentina just raised its minimum wage—which only applies to the minority who are formal sector employees to 630 pesos. "As the president of the co-op, I am constantly asking for an attitude of more solidarity," says Ruarte.

The hotel cooperative tackles this problem by educating the workforce. Although Patricia, the new waitress, could not describe the difference between the MNER and the MNFR, she said she is learning a lot more about the cooperative movement from weekly worker assemblies. The cooperatives also strengthen ties of solidarity by hiring family members, friends, and political supporters when they expand—a practice that might be considered nepotism, but has a very practical basis. Patricia got the job through her aunt, a 25-year veteran at the Bauen, and Federico got it by participating in demonstrations supporting the Bauen workers. At Chilavert and IMPA, as well, workers described similar policies.

Another thing Ruarte says he constantly asks for at the Bauen is more participation by women. But in spite of the high profile of recuperated suit-maker Brukman, an all-woman shop that was featured in the recent Naomi Klein/Avi Lewis movie *The Take*, the official leaders and spokespeople of most of the recuperated workplaces are men. This is perhaps to be expected, since women in Argentina, like employed women all over the world, suffer from the double shift of work in the shop followed by housework at home. Still, Patricia said, "Women may not be the official leaders, but they are more advanced, at least in the Bauen. They are more active when it comes to confronting the government and taking part in marches." Federico agreed, "They don't get as much publicity, but they are very involved. They're more courageous."

SELLING SCREWS ISN'T EASY

The fundamental problem the cooperatives face is surviving as islands of self-management in a capitalist ocean. "If you're a factory making screws, you have to sell them on the capitalist market," Ruarte observed. "They pay you in 30 days, and it's hard to keep functioning for those 30 days." The hotel needs a $50,000 loan to repair the heating and refrigeration systems, he said. IMPA would like to add new product lines, but needs $170,000 to upgrade its machinery, according to city councilor Daniel Betti. "It's a strange reversal," he explained. "Union movements have always been based in the largest, most profitable plants, with the most militant workers. But the recuperated businesses were the most backward. They are businesses that have failed, where the owners have not invested. They are workplaces where the workers put up with everything until the business finally closed. And now, all of a sudden, they are leading the movement!"

Ruarte declared bravely that, "Without the boss, we make more money and there's more creativity." But González was less upbeat about the business dimension of worker ownership, acknowledging, "We've had to learn from our mistakes." Regardless of who is correct, most recuperated plants have great difficulty in accessing credit—whether because ownership is uncertain (as in the case of the Bauen), because they have confronted the government which controls a large pool of subsidized credit (as with IMPA), or just because lenders see their business prospects as shaky, since almost all are emerging from bankruptcy.

A pending bankruptcy law that would prioritize workers' claims and allow them to continue working during bankruptcy proceedings could greatly alter the balance of power. The House of Representatives has approved the law, and there seems to be support at the level of the Senate and the executive branch. "If this reform passes, there could be 5000 new recuperated factories," claims Sergio Ciancaglini of LaVaca.

And what if there is no change in the bankruptcy law, no sudden infusion of investment funds? Is this just one more example of workers "storming the heavens," only to fall short? When posed this question, González of Chilavert replied, "The possibility of recuperation means there is one less argument for the boss. It used to be that bosses could say, 'If you don't make these concessions, I'll close down the plant.' But now workers know they can run the factory for themselves." As if to punctuate her words, that same afternoon marchers rallied in a suburb just north of Buenos Aires to support workers newly occupying a dairy that Italy-based multinational Parmalat had closed in December. Recuperated workplaces are not likely to sweep the Argentine economy, but their example remains an important one.

DRAMA AT THE ALUMINUM PROCESSOR

Last May, philosophical divisions and other difficulties facing the recuperated workplace movement played out at IMPA, the aluminum goods producer. IMPA is something of a flagship for the movement, due to its size and history. The Buenos Aires factory was built beginning in 1928 by German owners, then nationalized by populist president Juan Perón at the end of World War II. The plant became a workers' cooperative in 1958, but over time worker involvement atrophied, and when the company fell into bankruptcy in 1998 the judge was prepared to reestablish it as a private corporation. That threat spurred the workers into action: They occupied the plant, dusted off the cooperative charter, and won an expropriation order. From fewer than 50 workers in 1998, they have rebuilt to 174 today, making them the largest recuperated business in Argentina, according to Néstor Ortíz. Still, that head-count pales next to the more than 1,000 who toiled in the plant at its peak, and today vast areas of the factory stand idle. IMPA pounds out aluminum belts, containers, tubes, and packaging foils.

IMPA is the home of Murúa, leader of the "left" MNER. But according to workers at IMPA and elsewhere, Murúa was spending too much time building a political movement and not enough time taking care of his home base. "Worker assemblies weren't happening, there was no communication," said Ruarte. "That's bad. Also, there was theft from the factory—and some people say workers were involved." Piñeiro added, "Our requests to hold assemblies were denied, and when an assembly finally happened, we learned that there were economic problems we hadn't been told about." As dissatisfaction rippled through the workforce, Murúa's rival Caro—at the prompting of the government, according to City Councilor Betti—linked up with a group of disgruntled workers, brought some of his own men, and occupied the factory, locking out Murúa and his allies and shutting down the plant. The case came before a judge, who mandated an assembly where a new leadership would be elected.

When the assembly was held, the majority of the workers voted for a slate independent of *both* Murúa and Caro. "They overthrew their oligarchy, their monarchy," commented Ruarte. Was it a vote for business as usual, for warmer relations with the government? "The factions are not so clear here, but we wanted to negotiate with the government more than Murúa did," said IMPA's Piñeiro. "The factions matter at the level of the leaders, but the workers want to work. Our attitude toward the government is one of pressure *and* support." Ruarte expressed a similar pragmatic outlook: "When people ask us, 'Who are you with?', our answer is that we're not with anybody. We're not anybody's tool. If we get involved in politics, we won't be doing our best to run the business." And Ciancaglini of LaVaca argued, "If you set aside the leaders and the speeches and go inside the factories, you can't tell the difference between the MNER and the MNFR. In general, the recuperated workplaces are very autonomous and make their own decisions."

RESOURCES

Sin Patrón, available at www.lavaca.org; Andrés Gaudin, "Occupying, Resisting, Producing," *Dollars & Sense*, March/April 2004; Marina Sitrin, ed., *Horizontalidad en/in Argentina* (bilingual extract) and *Horizontalidad: voces de poder popular en Argentina* (full version, Spanish), both available from www.akpress.com; *Página 12* (progressive Buenos Aires daily newspaper), www.pagina12.com.ar; *El Correo de Económicas* (progressive Listserv on economic topics based at the University of Buenos Aires), www.labelgrano.org.ar/Varios/correo.htm.

KEEPING FAIR TRADE FAIR IN MEXICO

BY HOPE BASTIAN
NACLA Report, May/June 2006

Sam's Club, a nationwide wholesale chain with more than 500 locations across the United States, recently joined a growing roster of large corporations that sell fair-trade products. The company announced last September that it would begin carrying the Brazilian Marques de Paiva brand of fair-trade-certified coffee. Nestlé, which is one of four major coffee roasters that collectively buy almost half of the world's annual coffee output, soon followed suit, launching its own fair-trade coffee. Indeed, transnational corporations have started tapping into the fair-trade market, taking advantage of U.S. and European consumers' willingness to pay more for products they believe guarantee producers in poor countries better prices for their goods.

On the surface, the crossover of fair-trade products from a small specialty market to the mainstream would seem a welcome development for small-scale coffee producers in places such as Mexico—the world's top supplier of fair-trade and certified-organic coffee. But some Mexican farmers see things quite differently: They say the prices offered by the fair-trade market are no longer enough for them to cover the costs of production and take care of their families.

Francisco Cruz Sánchez and Ofelio Ángeles Ortega have been producing organic coffee for 20 years as members of Yeni Navan, a cooperative of about 1,100 small coffee producers in the southern Mexican state of Oaxaca. The cooperative has a simple office on the outskirts of Oaxaca City. One of the walls of the office has a colorful mural of women in traditional dress from different regions of the state. Next to the painting is a large map with the locations of the 44 indigenous communities where Yeni Navan's producers live. Francisco Cruz Sánchez points out his hometown, Santa Cruz Yagavila, a settlement of 800 people up in the Sierra Norte Mountains, seven hours away from the city by bus. He complains that this year the harvest wasn't very good there. "We just got too much rain at the wrong time," he says shrugging his shoulders. "We lost a lot of the harvest because of that and competition from the coyotes."

Ángeles Ortega, now serving as the president of Yeni Navan, grew up in a coffee-producing family in El Ocote Tataltepec, a remote village in the mountains of Oaxaca. "I was just a little boy back then, I wasn't thinking about coffee prices yet, but I remember my parents talking about how the prices were falling," says Ángeles Ortega. "My father didn't know what to do. The way the prices were, he wasn't making any money growing coffee."

In Mexico, fair-trade coffee first started to take root in the mid 1980s as coffee prices in the country began a slow and erratic decline. Well-founded rumors spread throughout Oaxaca that the state-owned Mexican Coffee Institute (INMECAFE), which provided small producers with credits, technical assistance, stable prices and export markets, would soon be shut down as part of the agricultural sector reforms preceding the North American Free Trade Agreement (NAFTA). Ángeles Ortega's family became involved with Yeni Navan after hearing from the local priest about a cooperative of organic coffee producers that was forming in order to seek out new markets and better prices.

Since 1962, the International Coffee Agreement (ICA), an accord between coffee-producing and importing countries, had established quotas to regulate the global coffee supply and maintain the market price of coffee. But at the end of the Cold War, the United States pulled out of the agreement and quotas could no longer be enforced, leaving supply and prices to the vicissitudes of the market. Coffee production in Vietnam and Brazil skyrocketed, creating a coffee glut and a dramatic crash in the price of coffee worldwide. The dismantling of INMECAFE the same year left small producers in Mexico vulnerable to price fluctuations just at the time when they most needed to be protected.

Because they were organized, Yeni Navan members escaped the worst of the crisis. By 1991, with help from the Union of Indigenous Campesinos of the Isthmus Region (UCIRI)—another growers' cooperative with experience selling coffee directly to European importers—Yeni Navan found its first clients in Europe. Before, with the dissolution of INMECAFE, the farmers had little choice but to sell their harvest to local middlemen, called coyotes, who would buy the coffee at rock-bottom prices and then sell it abroad for a profit. But through the budding fair-trade market, cooperatives like Yeni Navan began directly linking up with European importers that promised to offer "fair" prices.

The consolidation of the fair-trade market gained a boost in 1992 when a loose network of European fair-trade advocacy organizations joined together to form TransFair International, which later became the Fairtrade Labeling Organizations International (FLO). Grouping together 20 national fair-trade organizations, FLO sets standards that producers and companies must adhere to for their products to be sold with the fair-trade label. It also administers a certification program and registry of fair-trade companies and producers.

FLO's fair-trade standards require that coffee buyers establish long-term, stable relationships with the producer cooperatives, pay FLO-established minimum prices and provide cooperatives with pre-shipment financing if requested. Through the Standards Committee—a body with representation from member organizations, producer organizations and traders—FLO sets minimum prices and conditions.

According to FLO's website, minimum prices are determined by calculating the cost of sustainable production and living costs in each region where coffee is grown. There are currently two minimum prices for coffee: one for coffee from Central America, Mexico, Africa and Asia and a second for coffee from South America and the Caribbean. FLO's Producer Business Unit or any of the 20 national fair-trade organizations can make requests for changes in standards and pricing. All fair-trade producers within the FLO system are grouped into regional organizations like the Latin American and Caribbean Coordinator for Small Producers of Fair Trade (CLAC). These regional organizations also hold seats on FLO's board of directors where they can petition for changes in standards and prices.

RISING COSTS, STAGNANT PRICES

In 1995, the fair-trade price for 100 pounds of washed arabica coffee beans was set at $120, supplemented by a $5 "social premium," and if the coffee was certified organic, the price went up another $15. When these prices were established, Cruz Sánchez says they were fair: "In those years the price was very good, very high, because here in Mexico the costs of production and processing were lower."

At the time, the fair-trade market was a lifeline to many small producers. Those without access to this specialty market found themselves facing a limited range of equally unappealing options: migrating to find work, taking on loans with exorbitant monthly interest rates, or planting other crops—in some cases, illegal ones—to make ends meet.

"As producers of organic fair-trade coffee we always received 16 pesos, 17 pesos, up to 18 pesos per kilo of coffee," Cruz Sánchez recalls. "A conventional, independent producer who was not part of any organization would only receive seven or eight pesos. So back then you saw the difference, we would get almost double the price."

When the free market price for coffee beans slightly improved with the 1996 harvest season, organic fair-trade farmers found that although they were producing a more expensive and labor-intensive organic crop, they were only receiving marginally higher prices than non-fair-trade producers. These farmers began asking FLO to adjust its minimum prices to reflect the rising costs of production and in 1999, the base price was raised by one dollar to $121 per 100 pounds of green arabica beans; the organic and social premiums stayed the same.

But the small price hike has not helped farmers offset rising production costs, nor have prices been adjusted for inflation, which rises by an average of about 6% a year. Increasing shipping costs, labor costs, and certification costs have also cut into the small profit margins that the fair-trade market once promised producers. Ten years ago, for instance, it cost the cooperative 4,000 pesos to transport and fill a container at its warehouse with beans for export. Today, the same process costs the cooperative 10,000 pesos.

"Year after year the costs of production have increased, but the base price has stayed at $121 for 100 pounds [plus the $5 social premium]," says Cruz Sánchez. "Now, due to the high costs we pay, it is no longer such a good price."

Taurino Reyes Santiago, director of Certimex, a Mexican certification body contracted by FLO to perform inspections, agrees. "The prices [for fair-trade coffee] have not changed, the price structure is the same, but then each year the costs of living continue to rise and rise and rise," he says. "Maybe the costs of production are still covered, but the costs of living and the basic necessities that the producer has are no longer covered."

In the last five years, immigration has increased from Mexico's coffee-growing regions, forcing more producing families to depend on contract labor to replace that of family members who have left to find work in the United States or other parts of Mexico. Organic coffee farmers have been hit especially hard by the increases in labor costs. Instead of simply applying chemicals, for example, organic farmers must pass through the fields two or three times to harvest beans at their optimal ripeness. And keeping the organic coffee bushes healthy requires the near constant care of fieldworkers. In some areas of Oaxaca, daily wages for laborers have doubled in five years.

"No one here wants to work for less than 120 to 150 pesos a day. Whereas in other regions it may cost 60 to 40 pesos, in the regions where there is a lot of emigration the labor costs go up 100%," observes Reyes, the Certimex director. Many producers cannot afford to pay the extra labor. As a result, cooperatives report that the volume of coffee beans they were able to buy from their members decreased in the 2004–05 harvest because beans were left on the bushes for lack of money to contract the necessary labor.

MAINSTREAMING FAIR TRADE

The inspection process represents another huge cost for cooperatives that sell fair-trade and organic certified coffee. Yeni Navan's coffee must go through three inspection and certification processes before it gains access to the fair-trade and organic markets. The first and most rigorous process is the cooperative's own internal inspections of members' fields and processing and storage areas to be sure that organic standards are being strictly followed. Any member who fails the internal inspection will not be allowed to sell their coffee to the cooperative. After the internal inspections are completed, Yeni Navan contracts Certimex to audit the cooperative's internal certification and controls procedures. Certimex inspects a sample of members, meaning a second trip to land parcels and process and storage facilities to confirm that organic standards are being met. Once this inspection is complete, the cooperative's coffee is certified organic by Certimex and Naturland—a certifier recognized by the European Union. But before the coffee can be sold on the fair-trade market, a third inspection is carried out under the auspices of FLO—in this case, subcontracted to Certimex.

In the most recent harvest, the internal and external inspection processes cost the cooperative $15,938. Yeni Navan spent another $9,637 in fees and dues to fair-trade and international organic certifying organizations like FLO, Naturland, the International Federation of Organic Agriculture Movements and CLAC.

With the extra investment of time and money that come with being a member of a cooperative, many Oaxacan farmers have simply found that producing fair-trade organic coffee no longer enables them to make ends meet. Indeed, says Ángeles Ortega, 210 small producers have left the cooperative in the last year. Reyes also admits the harsh reality: "You're not going to see a significant difference in the lives or incomes of farmers when production is so low and the needs for resources, investments and costs of production are so high."

In the most recent harvest, slight improvements in coffee prices on the world market led some of the newer Yeni Navan members to sidestep the cooperative and sell their coffee to the coyotes. Although coyotes pay less than the cooperatives, they are also much less demanding about quality. This means that growers can economize on labor by picking both ripe and unripe beans and get away with selling inferior quality beans the cooperative would never buy. Another incentive is that coyotes pay cash.

Without the extra labor costs, getting a decent price for their coffee on the free market might help in the short term, but prices will inevitably drop again, likely sending these producers back to the cooperative. But with increasing costs, stagnant prices and more and more producers leaving the cooperative, Yeni Navan's production levels have fallen precipitously. Last season, the cooperative saw its production decrease by 60% and it was unable to fulfill several of its contracts with importers. If these shortfalls continue, Yeni Navan's fair-weather members may not have a cooperative to come back to when the free market coffee prices take their next dive.

Many small producers wish FLO would raise the minimum prices to reflect increases in the costs of production and costs of living over the last 10 years. Even within FLO there are some like Guillermo Denaux, regional coordinator for Mexico and Central America and coffee product officer, who recognizes that the fair-trade price is sometimes not enough, but feels trapped between the demands of buyers and traders in different parts of the world.

"There are some buyers who actually find the minimum price too high. If the price were lower, the volumes would actually be higher and having more volume in sales within the fair-trade system would have a more positive impact for producers," says Denaux. "But of course we have heard from a lot of producers, especially the ones in Mexico, that with the actual minimum price right now it's quite difficult to cover the costs of production."

In the end, the fair-trade market is still subject to the mechanics of the free market. "This price has been here since FLO's existence, and even though there is a lot of pressure to change it, I think that since it is so difficult to find a common agreed point between buyers and sellers there has been little movement," says Denaux.

FLO's minimum prices have been a recurring topic of discussion at the producers' regional CLAC meetings and the quarterly meetings of Mexican fair-trade producers. But Cruz Sánchez and other farmers fear that changes in FLO are taking the international organization in an entirely different direction—furthering the trend toward even lower pricing. "I think that FLO is now becoming a better friend of the transnational corporations," he says. For him, recent developments, such as Nestlé's entrance into the fair-trade market, indicate that the fair-trade movement is moving further away from its roots. And as fair-trade goes mainstream, Cruz Sánchez worries about huge coffee plantations' efforts to gain admission to FLO. If they succeed, he predicts, "It's going to be a disaster, a big threat for small producers."

CHAPTER 5
SOCIAL MOVEMENTS

OAXACA'S DANGEROUS TEACHERS

BY DAVID BACON
Dollars & Sense, September/October 2006

At 8:30 a.m. on October 21, 2002, Oaxaca state police arrested a dangerous schoolteacher.

Romauldo Juan Gutiérrez Cortez was pulled over as he was driving to his school in the rural Mixteca region. Police took him to Oaxaca de Juárez, the state capital, where he was held for days on false charges. Gutiérrez is the state coordinator for the Binational Front of Indigenous Organizations (the Frente), which had organized a loud, embarrassing protest during a visit to Oaxaca by Mexican president Vicente Fox not long before. Oaxaca governor José Murat was out for revenge.

As Gutiérrez languished in jail, Oaxacan migrant farmworkers north of the border in California's central valley picketed the Mexican consulate, held press conferences, and clogged Murat's phone lines with calls and faxes. In Oaxaca itself, other Frente members organized similar protests. After a week, the governor succumbed to the pressure: Gutiérrez was released.

Since then, the Frente has organized many other binational campaigns. Cooperation across the border is today one of the most important tools Oaxacans have for defending human rights in their home state.

Thousands of indigenous people migrate from Oaxaca's hillside villages to the United States every year—among Mexican states, Oaxaca has the second-highest concentration of indigenous residents. They leave in part because of a repressive political system that thwarts economic development in Mexico's poor rural areas. Lack of development in turn pushes people off the land. From there, they find their way to other parts of Mexico or the United States, where they often live in poverty even as they send money home. This economic reality was the central issue in this year's heated presidential election, which was marred by charges of vote fraud.

The people who have been driven from Oaxaca to the United States by economic crisis have carried a tradition of militant social movements with them. By organizing across the border, the Frente and other Oaxacan organizations increase their power. Binational pressure freed Gutiérrez from Murat's jail, where local efforts alone might not have succeeded. Many other human rights violations in Oaxaca over the last decade have resulted in cross-border resistance, and the Frente was at the heart of many of these protests.

Winning political change in Mexico itself is central to the Frente's activity. For Oaxaca's indigenous residents, greater democracy and respect for human rights are the keys to eventually achieving a government committed to increasing rural family income. That in turn might make it possible for people to make a living at home, instead of heading to California for survival.

MIGRATION: A CONSEQUENCE OF ECONOMIC REFORMS

"Migration is a necessity, not a choice," Gutiérrez explains. "There is no work here. You can't tell a child to study to be a doctor if there is no work for doctors in Mexico. It is a very daunting task for a Mexican teacher to convince students to get an education and stay in the country. It is disheartening to see a student go through many hardships to get an education here in Mexico and become a professional, and then later in the United States do manual labor. Sometimes those with an education are working side by side with others who do not even know how to read."

Lack of economic opportunity in Oaxaca's villages is a result of Mexican economic development policies. For more than two decades, under pressure from the World Bank, the International Monetary Fund, and conditions placed on U.S. bank loans and bailouts, the government has encouraged foreign investment, while cutting expenditures intended to raise rural incomes. Prices have risen dramatically since the government cut subsidies for necessities like gasoline, electricity, bus fares, tortillas, and milk.

The government also closed the CONASUPO stores, which bought corn at subsidized prices from farmers to help them stay on the land and sold tortillas, milk, and food to the urban poor. The North American Free Trade Agreement's subsidies to U.S. farmers have forced Mexican agricultural prices down. The end of the *ejido* land reform system has allowed the reconcentration of land ownership and rural wealth. The sale of government enterprises to private investors led to layoffs and the destruction of unions. Foreign investors may now own land and factories anywhere in Mexico, without Mexican partners.

The Mexican government estimates that 37.7%, or 40 million, of its 106 million citizens live in poverty, with 25 million, or 23.6%, living in extreme poverty. According to a representative of EDUCA, a Oaxacan education and development organization, 75% of the state's 3.4 million residents live in extreme poverty. It is the second-poorest state in Mexico, after Chiapas.

Meanwhile, Fox boasts that Mexicans in the United States—often working for poverty wages—are sending home over $18 billion a year. "Migration helps pacify people," Gutiérrez says. "Poverty is a ticking time bomb, but as long as there is money coming in from family in the United States, there is peace. To curb migration our country has to have a better employment plan. We must push our government to think about the working class."

The economic reforms of the last two decades are deeply unpopular, and people like Oaxaca's teachers would change them if they could. But those who have benefited from them have a big stake in suppressing any dissent or advocacy of political and economic alternatives. Governor Murat's campaign to stifle change by silencing Gutiérrez is only a small part of Oaxaca's long history of human rights violations.

TEACHING RESISTANCE

Oaxaca has many dangerous teachers like Gutiérrez. In the 1970s and 1980s, more than a hundred of Oaxaca's teachers were killed in the struggle for control of their union, Section 22 of the National Union of Education Workers. Today Section 22 is one of Mexico's most militant unions, and in many villages teachers are also community leaders and repositories of Mexico's most progressive traditions.

On one recent afternoon, Gutiérrez stood at the back of a classroom in rural Santiago Juxtlahuaca, dapper in a pressed white shirt and chinos. Two boys and two girls, wearing new tennis shoes undoubtedly sent by family members working in the north, stood at the blackboard, giving a report and carefully gauging his reaction. As they recounted the history of Mexico's expropriation of oil in 1936, a smile curved beneath Gutiérrez's pencil mustache. The expropriation was a high point in Mexican revolutionary nationalism. "Education is a very noble field, which I love," Gutiérrez says. "But today it means confronting the government. You have to be ready to fight for the people and their children, and not just in the classroom."

Not just in the classroom, but throughout Oaxaca and also the United States. Today over 60,000 Oaxacans labor in California's San Joaquin Valley alone. Many times that number are dispersed in communities throughout the United States. In the countryside of the Mixteca, village after village has been emptied of working-age residents.

Gutiérrez's role in the Binational Front of Indigenous Organizations illustrates his understanding of the need to challenge human rights violations on both sides of the border. If Mexico's indigenous migrants succeed, they may be able to help force a change in the political structure at home, and thereby influence the migration of Mexican citizens abroad.

SUPPRESSING THE NEWS

Today, though, Oaxaca's political system is still controlled by Mexico's old ruling Party of the Institutionalized Revolution (PRI). The PRI lost its control over the national government to the National Action Party (PAN) in 2000. While the PAN has more direct ties to Mexico's growing corporate class, and received the bulk of that class's campaign money in the 2006 election, both parties pursue the same neoliberal economic policies that line party leaders' pockets and those of their corporate allies. Efforts to change this system bring down their wrath, as Gutiérrez discovered.

"Before my arrest I thought we had a decent justice system," he says. "I knew it wasn't perfect, but I thought it worked." In prison, Gutiérrez met members of a local union who had been there for months, along with other political prisoners. "There are over 2,000 complaints of political oppression in the state that have not been investigated," Gutiérrez charges. His own case adds one more.

The news outlets that expose these abuses also find themselves in the government's crosshairs. *Noticias,* an independent newspaper founded in 1978, learned this the hard way. In 2004, the paper exposed public works fraud in the Murat administration. And in that fall's gubernatorial election, *Noticias* supported the left-wing candidate of the Party of the Democratic Revolution (PRD). The PRD lost amid charges of vote rigging. On December 1, the same day Murat's PRI successor, Ulises Ruiz, took office, hooligans broke into *Noticias'* building and threatened the reporters.

More provocations followed, and six months later state police and dozens of thugs belonging to the Revolutionary Confederation of Workers and Peasants (CROC) surrounded *Noticias'* offices. CROC is a labor federation founded by the PRI in the early 1950s. Though in some areas it functions as a normal union, the PRI often uses it to protect employers from labor unrest and to intimidate the party's opponents.

Amnesty International reports that 102 of *Noticias'* 130 employees belonged to CROC, but their relationship with the union had been strained, and CROC leadership called a strike "against the express wishes of the *Noticias* workforce." The Ruiz administration ordered it to stop publishing. Thirty-one workers decided to defend the office, where they were barricaded in for days and not permitted visitors, or even food and water.

CROC's secretary for labor and conflict, Ulises Bravo, told *The Miami Herald* that the strike was "completely labor-related and [had] nothing to do with a political agenda. *Noticias* . . . tried to make this into a political issue because that gets them publicity and sells more papers."

Oaxaca's other newspapers stayed out of the fray. *The Miami Herald*'s Jonathan Clark reports that "privately, editors and reporters say they fear reprisals from the government for reporting on the issue. Editors reluctantly admit they need the government's publicity money to survive financially, and reporters say they fear that they will be harassed or fired for what they write."

Facing a news blockade in Oaxaca, the journalists hit the phones. From inside the besieged newsroom, reporter César Morales got on the air in Fresno,

California. He was interviewed by Rufino Domínguez, a Frente coordinator, and journalist Eduardo Stanley, cohosts of a bilingual program for Mixtec migrants on community radio station KFCF. Morales described "an assault by more than a hundred plain-clothes police, and thugs brought in to beat us." He called for help, and letters and faxes from California deluged Oaxaca.

In this case, binational pressure was not enough. The PRI eventually evicted the journalists and closed the paper's offices. *Noticias* is still distributed in Oaxaca, but it is written, edited, and printed elsewhere. Nevertheless, Oaxacans in California had developed a new ability to use media in their binational campaigns.

THE FRENTE'S CROSS-BORDER SOCIAL MOVEMENT

Oaxacans abroad don't just protest conditions at home. The Frente defends worker rights in California fields, has convinced the state's courts to provide indigenous language interpreters, and helps keep alive the traditions that are the cultural glue binding together Mixtec, Zapotec, Triqui, and Chatino communities.

The Frente was, in fact, founded in California. Leaders like Domínguez have a long history organizing strikes and other movements in Mexico. When they arrived in California in 1987, they started the group with meetings in the San Joaquin Valley, Los Angeles, and San Diego. At first it was called the Mixtec/Zapotec Binational Front, because organizers wanted to unite Mixtec and Zapotec immigrants, two of the largest indigenous groups in Oaxaca.

Soon it had to change its name. Triquis and other indigenous Oaxacans wanted to participate, so the organization became the Indigenous Oaxacan Binational Front. Then Purepechas from Michoacán and indigenous people from other Mexican states also joined, and it became the Binational Front of Indigenous Organizations. Through all the changes, its binational character has only grown stronger.

Oaxacans have formed many other organizations during their long migration through Mexico and the United States. Most of these organizations are composed of members from a single town, and many of them are not as political as the Frente. The Frente is also different in that it unites people speaking different languages, from different indigenous groups, in order to promote community and workplace struggles for social justice.

Racism against indigenous people in Mexico has required them to develop a history of community resistance, and to fight for their own cultural identity. Centolia Maldonado, one of the Frente's leaders in Oaxaca, recalls her bitter experience as a migrant in northern Mexico. "They called us 'Oaxaquitas'—Indians," she remembers. "The people from the north were always valued more. There is terrible discrimination when people migrate."

In 1992, the Frente used the celebrations of the 500-year anniversary of the arrival of Christopher Columbus in the Americas as a platform to dramatize its call for indigenous rights. Domínguez says the protest countered "people who say that Christopher Columbus was welcomed when he came. They never talk about the massacres or the genocide that occurred in our villages, on the whole of the American continent. We wanted to tell the other side of the story."

The Frente's response to the Zapatista uprising on January 1, 1994, strengthened its commitment to cross-border action. The Frente pressured the Mexican government to refrain from using massive military force in Chiapas. From Fresno, California, across the border to Baja California and Oaxaca, Frente activists went on hunger strikes and demonstrated in front of consulates and government offices. That action, Domínguez says, "helped us realize that when there's movement in Oaxaca, there's got to be movement in the United States to make an impression on the Mexican government."

Participatory democracy is important in indigenous village life, and the Frente honors this tradition in its binational assemblies, where members discuss its political positions in detail. As a result, those political positions take into account the transnational nature of members' problems. The Frente opposes U.S. proposals for guest worker programs, arguing that they treat migrants only as temporary workers, not as people who belong to and are creating communities. Instead, the Frente calls for the legalization of undocumented migrants in the United States.

It also demands that the Mexican government fulfill the right of Mexican citizens living in the United States to vote in their country's elections. The Fox administration agreed to create a system to handle those votes in the 2006 election, but there were so many restrictions that only about 40,000 of the estimated 12 million Mexican citizens in the United States were able to cast ballots.

ATTACKS ON HUMAN RIGHTS ESCALATE DURING AN ELECTION YEAR

In the late 1990s, the Frente in Oaxaca began an alliance with the PRD. Domínguez explains, "Mexican electoral laws don't permit a social organization to run independent candidates, so we have to make an alliance. Within the PRD there are divisions and internal problems, but it's all we have." Within this alliance, the Frente keeps its independence. "We should have a relationship with political parties without losing our identity and being dependent on politicians," Domínguez says.

In the recent presidential campaign, the Frente supported the PRD candidate, former Mexico City mayor Andrés Manuel López Obrador. Frente activist Leoncio Vásquez said the country faced a clear choice in political direction. "López Obrador declared openly that he'd put poor people first," Vásquez explained. "He's against corruption and corporations who violate workers' and human rights." Raising rural income was the centerpiece of López Obrador's proposals on migration. He was particularly critical of Fox's support for the Bush guest-worker proposal.

During the campaign, attacks on human rights in Oaxaca escalated. On May 19, Moises Cruz Sánchez, a PRD activist in the Mixtec town of San Juan Mixtepec, was gunned down in front of his wife and children as he left a local restaurant. The two gunmen fled, and police couldn't seem to find them.

That month in Fresno the Frente organized demonstrations against a planned visit by Ruiz to California. Response to the protests revealed increasing cooperation between U.S. and Mexican authorities. After receiving a copy of a letter sent to the Mexican consulate to protest Ruiz's visit, Detective Dean Williamson of the Fresno Police paid a surprise visit to the Frente's office on Tulare Street. "It's an official procedure," said Williamson, "in which we're trying to clarify possible threats affecting public security."

Then violence escalated again in Oaxaca. In early May, the state's teachers struck for higher salaries and an end to human rights violations. Thousands of teachers occupied the main square in the state capital. Over 120,000 Oaxaca residents joined them in the largest rally in the state's history. On June 11, Ruiz promised business owners he would use a heavy hand to put down the protest. At four in the morning on June 14, helicopters began hovering over the tents of the sleeping teachers. As parents woke their children, billowing clouds of tear gas filled the cobblestone streets. Hundreds of police charged in. Within minutes, scores were beaten, and one pregnant woman miscarried. But Ruiz underestimated the teachers. They retook the square at the end of the day, and the following morning 300,000 people marched through Oaxaca demanding Ruiz's resignation.

In the following weeks, the protestors formed the Oaxaca Popular People's Assembly (APPO). Doctors and nurses joined, shutting down clinics. The government responded with increased violence. A state university student was killed in the street, and José Jiménez Colmanares, husband of a striking teacher, was gunned down during a protest march. Gunmen fired on the Channel 9 radio station after it had been occupied by demonstrators. Two reporters from *Noticias*, which recently opened another editorial office in the Oaxacan capital, were also shot at.

The APPO has many active indigenous members, some of whom also belong to the Frente. In the Mixteca, protestors occupied the Huajuapan de León city hall. Ruiz issued arrest orders for 50 leaders, including three Frente statewide officials.

On July 2, Mexicans went to the polls. The results gave a microscopic 200,000-vote majority to PAN candidate Felipe Calderón. Demands for a recount and accusations of fraud were immediate.

A million people rallied in Mexico City's main square on July 16, and two million on July 30, to demand a recount. The PRD and its candidate refuse to accept the results without one—a contrast to 1988, when leftist candidate Cuauhtémoc Cárdenas conceded although it appeared that fraud robbed him of victory.

Whether the PRD will get the recount it demands is still unclear. Regardless, millions of Mexicans see a clear difference in political direction between the current political establishment and the PRD and the social forces that support it.

Pointing to attacks on striking steel workers in Michoacán and Sonora, the stationing of tanks outside the Mexican Congress, and the raging conflict in Oaxaca, Domínguez says that "a tiny group is trying to hold onto power by increasingly violent and illegal means."

But many Mexicans are challenging the lack of human rights that keeps that establishment in power. The Frente is an important part of that movement. "Indigenous people are always on the bottom in Oaxaca," Vásquez says. "The rich use their economic resources to maintain a government that puts them first. Big corporations control what's going on in Mexico, and those who criticize the government get harassed constantly, with arbitrary arrest and even assassination. That's one of the reasons why people from our communities have been forced to leave to find a means of survival elsewhere."

TIME OF THE SNAILS: AUTONOMY AND RESISTANCE IN CHIAPAS

BY RICHARD STAHLER-SHOLK
NACLA Report, March/April 2005

The people of Nuevo San Isidro watched warily as a helicopter appeared over the horizon, circled in over their seven thatched huts and landed somewhere on the far side of the Lacantún River. This Tzotzil indigenous community had migrated to the remote jungle near the Mexican-Guatemalan border in February 2001. They came from Chavajebal in Chiapas' central highlands, a region of land scarcity and paramilitary violence, and wanted simply to work the land peacefully. But in October 2004, when government agents came in and promised to help them relocate elsewhere in exchange for government aid, their small community was divided: Six of the original 13 families started taking the aid and seven refused. Those who refused identified with the Zapatista Army of National Liberation (EZLN) and moved a few hundred yards upriver, establishing formal affiliation with the Zapatista Autonomous Rebel Municipality of "Freedom for the Mayan Peoples," part of one of the Zapatista regional Juntas de Buen Gobierno (Juntas of Good Government) called "Towards Hope." They now referred to the pro-government side of the village as the *priístas*, an old habit from the 71 years during which the Institutional Revolutionary Party (PRI) ruled Mexico.

While the Mexican government tries to uproot communities, freeing up more land and resources for the global market, the Zapatistas have continued to resist by constructing autonomous government. They began by building on community structures of local self-governance continually created since the 1950s by migrants from the highlands and other regions to Las Cañadas, the jungle canyons of the agricultural frontier of eastern Chiapas.[1] When government troops encircled this region in a military offensive in December 1994, the EZLN declared the existence of 38 autonomous municipalities, including many in the highlands and other areas outside Las Cañadas.[2] In July 2000, the EZLN grouped the Zapatista Autonomous Rebel Municipalities into regional autonomous government structures administered by five Juntas of Good Government based in governing centers called Caracoles (snails or conch shells, an ancient Mayan symbol).

The helicopter that circled over the newly divided community of Nuevo San Isidro had brought 19 government agents. The wary Zapatista side gathered on the riverbank to see their pro-government neighbors ferry their benefactors across the river by *cayuco* in groups of four. Some time after the last cayuco had crossed, as the villagers continued talking among themselves at the riverside, an agrarian reform official appeared in the clearing escorted by two *priístas*. She was a wiry, thirty-something woman named Alejandra, sporting close-cropped brown hair with frosted highlights. With the overly chipper air of a kindergarten teacher, she greeted the assembled crowd and launched into a speech about how she and her colleagues were here to help; they were going to have a meeting at the pro-government cluster of huts, and they wanted to invite everyone on this side to come and hear a proposal about "how to make the best use of the land."

Gregorio (not his real name), who spoke the best Spanish, responded. "We are not with the government," he began, pointing to a hand-lettered sign nailed to a tree at the riverbank that read "Zapatista Army of National Liberation. Entry by government officials is prohibited." He continued, "We are a Zapatista community. We are in resistance. We don't want government people here."

Alejandra started to protest that she had only come to invite them to a meeting, and that it was about giving them land. "We already know that the government's word is pure lies," Gregorio replied. "Look what happened to the people in Santa Cruz. You promised them aid for three years and it ended after three months." Alejandra broke in again: "I recognize that some mistakes have been made. But I'm here to make sure the promises are kept. You can pick out the land you want. Look, these people have already chosen their land!"

Gregorio kept his composure. "This is the same government that is responsible for the massacre at Acteal in 1997," he said, "45 men, women and children massacred. The government also killed people from this community, on June 10, 1998, in Chavajebal. Why do they send soldiers from village to village to kill? Then they come with promises that are pure lies." He switched back and forth from Spanish to Tzotzil for the benefit of the *priísta* escorts.

Alejandra, visibly agitated but maintaining her forced smile, responded: "No, I agree, that wasn't right. I have nothing to do with what the soldiers do, I disagree with it, in fact, I have denounced it myself. But look, I just came to invite you to a meeting, so you can hear the proposal yourselves." Gregorio effectively ended the conversation: "If you want to invite us to a meeting you can present yourselves at Caracol Number One, to the Zapatista Junta of Good Government, and see what response they give you. I'll take you there myself right now if you want." Alejandra backpedaled. "No, no, I already know where it is. Anyway, that's all we came for. If you want to come, we'll be meeting over there." She said goodbye with a huge smile and a wave as she whirled around to disappear with her entourage.

The villagers lingered by the riverbank, chuckling that Alejandra was afraid to take her proposal to the Zapatista regional autonomous authorities.

But there was an underlying sense that the stakes were rising, and that the community would be even more isolated if their neighbors were spirited off to faraway lands.

Since the government's initial military response to the 1994 Zapatista uprising, the counterinsurgency has shifted emphasis toward state-sponsored paramilitary groups composed mainly of rootless young indigenous men who lack land and are given arms and money to attack communities of Zapatista supporters.[3] This allows the government to portray the killing in Chiapas as inter-communal violence, and its own troops as a stabilizing force. The most intense military / paramilitary operations have shifted over the years from the jungle canyons of east-central Chiapas, to the northern zone, then to the central highlands and now to this southeastern slice of jungle where the government had demarcated the vast "Montes Azules Biosphere Reserve" nearly 30 years before. The government has been waging a campaign to evict settlers from Montes Azules over the last two years, particularly targeting Zapatista settlements of indigenous people who have recently taken refuge here.[4]

Officially, the government invokes a conservationist rationale for evicting settlers from the biosphere reserve. Yet, the Echeverría administration in 1972 had conceded 1.5 million acres, including much of what in 1978 was designated the Montes Azules reserve, to a group of 66 indigenous families it had inaccurately labeled the "Lacandón Community." The government gave them trinkets in exchange for exclusive lumber concessions to strip valuable hardwood from the forest. Over the decades, various communities of Tzeltal and Ch'ol people living within the overlapping Montes Azules and Lacandón Community boundaries also received recognition of their land rights under agrarian reforms. In the midst of all these overlapping concessions, the government only initiated evictions when communities of Zapatista supporters began to settle the southern fringe of the jungle reserve.

Another clue to the newfound interest in Montes Azules may be found in President Vicente Fox's much-publicized "Plan Puebla-Panamá" (PPP), a grand scheme to attract billions of dollars of investment to southern Mexico and Central America.[5] The PPP envisions port and railway facilities for expanded maquiladora plants and dams for hydroelectric power for the anticipated industrial boom. Part of the attraction of the region for foreign capital is the rich biodiversity found in this stretch of jungle. An exposé by local NGOs has already halted one bio-prospecting project by the U.S.-funded "ICBG Maya" consortium.[6]

Not far from the settlement in Nuevo San Isidro is the mysterious Chajul "ecotourism station," which locals say is a base for bio-piracy, run by former Secretary of Environment, turned entrepreneur, Julia Carabias. Her pseudo-NGO, ENDESU, began building another station in 2002 at Río Tzendales, where a billboard proclaimed a "conservation" project to be supported by the Ford Motor Company. In mid-2004 the legislative framework for bio-prospecting was drafted in a proposed "Law for the Conservation of Biodiversity and Environmental Protection for the State of Chiapas," denounced by human rights groups as a violation of indigenous rights to autonomous control of resources in their territories.[7]

Since the 1980s, the neoliberal agenda in Mexico has been implemented with the help of a series of programs designed to create new clientelistic mechanisms to divide and co-opt discontent. The prototype was the National Solidarity Program (PRONASOL), which selectively doled out benefits through local committees to compensate for the social impact of economic austerity (which far exceeded the payouts). A similar program called PROCEDE undermines the management of communal landholdings by offering individual titles to those who opt out of the collective agrarian *ejidos*. Resistance to the counter-reform is weakened as state resources are drained from this social property sector and the cheap products of U.S. agribusiness flood the Mexican market. Another program, PROCAMPO, gave direct per-hectare compensation payments to producers as price supports for peasant agriculture were being dismantled.

The Zapatista movement had its roots in independent rural organizing initiatives that demanded rights rather than clientelistic privileges. The Zapatistas insisted not only on individual citizenship rights within a democratic national framework, but also collective ethnic rights for indigenous peoples, a departure from the atomizing ideology of neoliberalism.[8]

The Zapatistas also continued pressing at the negotiating table for recognition of indigenous rights and culture, something the government formally conceded with the signing of the San Andrés Accords in February 1996. Implementing legislation, however, was never passed, so the Zapatistas inaugurated a second phase of the autonomy movement by proceeding to implement it themselves. The Zapatista communities boycotted the municipal elections of October 1996, and instead elected parallel authorities through indigenous *usos y costumbres* (traditional customs and practices). Since they lacked official recognition and resources, the autonomous municipalities were supported through five Zapatista multiservice centers called Aguascalientes. For the most part, however, the municipalities relied on local resources to launch production and social service projects, drawing on the indigenous tradition of a community labor tax in which each family contributed a quota of person-days.[9]

Following the collapse of the San Andrés process, the Zapatistas began a third phase by further institutionalizing their de facto municipal governments, often expelling the official government authorities. The federal government launched a series of joint police-military raids in April and May 1998, dismantling the two autonomous municipalities of Ricardo Flores Magón and Tierra y Libertad. The Chiapas state government, meanwhile, approved a redistricting scheme creating seven new municipalities aimed at undermining Zapatista autonomy claims.

The fourth and most recent phase of the movement began in July 2003, when the Zapatistas launched a regional structure of autonomous government in Chiapas. Each autonomous municipality now sends rotating representatives to one of five regional Juntas de Buen Gobierno based in the Caracoles that replaced the old Aguascalientes. In a preliminary self-evaluation of the Juntas after one year, the Zapatistas celebrated advances in social-service provision, as well as the experience gained by community members serving one- to two-week shifts in the regional governments.[10] Yet they recognized problems of inefficiency and discontinuity caused by the frequent rotation; as well as serious under-representation of women in governing councils that are distant from their communities. There was also uneven ability to attend to dispersed settlements far from the Caracoles. In October 2004, one of the Zapatista Juntas de Buen Gobierno decided to consolidate eight beleaguered, isolated communities from Montes Azules, including Nuevo San Isidro, in order to better integrate them into the resistance offered by their new regional structures of government.[11]

As the Zapatista autonomy movement evolves, it offers potential alternatives to the neoliberal model, but autonomy is not without its dilemmas. One model of autonomy that predates the 1994 emergence of the EZLN in Chiapas is based on the concept of the Pluriethnic Autonomous Region (RAP).[12] The RAP model envisions autonomy as decentralization, and creates an additional representative layer for an indigenous territory within the existing structures of national government. A variant of this model can be seen in the North and South Atlantic autonomous regions of Nicaragua. In essence, this created a fourth level of government, in addition to the federal, state and local. In the Nicaraguan case, implementation of a 1987 autonomy statute fell short of expectations due to problems of representation and the under-funding of the autonomous government structures.

Skeptics of the RAP model cite the danger of regional "bossism," and the concern that it merely replicates the top-down structure of existing political institutions without developing new leadership capacity rooted in local communities. Some interpretations of a comparable experience in Ecuador suggest that a territorially bounded definition of autonomy might create a kind of self-policed homeland, limiting options for indigenous people whose subsistence and cultural identity depend increasingly on complex patterns of mobility.[13] The Zapatistas themselves, while preferring to build autonomy from the community level upward, nevertheless remained open to a pluralism of autonomy models.

Another dilemma is presented by a version of autonomy without resources, i.e., the potential for the neoliberal state to pass off responsibility for the unprofitable provision of public goods to "autonomous," but underfunded units. The market paradigm tends to privatize gains while socializing costs and risks. The apparent recognition of autonomous spaces in society could create new mechanisms for division and cooptation, as social sectors and regions compete with each other for a share of the shrinking pie. This could leave them vulnerable to clientelistic politicians or even paternalistic NGOs moving into the breach.

A third potential trap is what an analyst in the Guatemalan context called "managed neoliberal multiculturalism."[14] It is noteworthy, for example, that the 1991 agrarian counter-reform, which modified Article 27 of the Constitution and eroded the communal agrarian ejido, was coupled with reforms to Article 4 that for the first time explicitly recognized the multiethnic character of the Mexican nation.[15] Both reforms were imposed from above without grassroots consultation, and taken together, they reflect the neoliberal model's recognition of a plurality of indigenous identities, as long as those identities do not become the basis for collective organization around substantive rights. This allows entrepreneurial ecotourism and bio-prospecting ventures in the Lacandón jungle to pick and choose partners among the "diverse" indigenous peoples, while celebrating the Disneyesque concept of a multiethnic "Selva Maya."

The limits of working within the neoliberal legal framework of individual property guarantees and corporate prerogatives are illustrated by the struggle over the San Andrés Accords. After the March 2001 Zapatista caravan to Mexico City demanding implementation of the Accords, the legislature passed a sham "indigenous rights law" that actually reneged on key provisions of the agreements.[16] The original Article 4 of the indigenous rights law drafted by the congressional peace commission, COCOPA, affirmed that "indigenous peoples have the right to free determination and, as expression of that, to autonomy." Its replacement begins with the affirmation that "the Mexican Nation is one and indivisible," and adds that "the right of indigenous peoples to free determination will be exercised in a constitutional framework of autonomy that assures national unity. The recognition of indigenous peoples and communities will be done in the constitutions and laws of the federative entities."

Rights of indigenous communities to elect their own authorities, in the revised version, would only be granted "within a framework that respects the federal pact and the sovereignty of the states." In other words, the right to have rights will be at the discretion of the existing authorities. Crucial language guaranteeing indigenous peoples access and use of resources in their territories was replaced. Access would be decided "with respect for the forms and modes of property and land tenancy established in this Constitution and relevant law, as well as rights acquired by third parties or by members of the community, to the use and preferential enjoyment of the natural resources of the places inhabited and occupied by the communities, except those corresponding to strategic areas."

Article 26 of the original COCOPA law requiring "the necessary mechanisms so that development plans and programs take into account the indigenous peoples and communities in their cultural needs and specificities" was eliminated along with a clause that "the State will guarantee them their equitable access to the distribution of the national wealth." Indigenous identity was to be recognized, but stripped of collective rights.

When this "indigenous rights" legislation passed the Congress in a "fast-track" deal between the National Action Party (PAN) and the PRI, it was denounced by indigenous rights groups and rejected in all the states with large indigenous populations but ratified in enough states to pass. The Supreme Court rejected all 320 constitutional challenges to the law, claiming it had no jurisdiction over such matters, and the law took effect.

Meanwhile, since their inauguration in August 2003, the Zapatista Juntas de Buen Gobierno have been offering to serve both Zapatista and non-Zapatistas, and the Fox administration has had to reluctantly concede that they are probably not unconstitutional. To overcome the dilemma of autonomy without resources and the danger of losing decision-making control to outside NGO funders, the *Juntas* have set up mechanisms for reviewing NGO development proposals and taking a 10% tax to redistribute to communities within each region.[17]

The Juntas do not preclude other authority structures or autonomy models, but they do exert a greater discipline over who gets to claim the "Zapatista" label within a given region. This, in effect, means greater control over the movement by the Zapatista communities themselves, represented in the Juntas, rather than the insurgent structures of the EZLN. In some of the Caracoles, there are already signs of local acceptance of the legitimacy of the Juntas, even by non-Zapatistas, who turn to them for dispute resolution and other governance functions. But the October 2004 Montes Azules evacuation and regrouping of communities of Zapatista supporters illustrates the continued conflictive negotiation of space between the state as broker for global capital and the rebels representing community autonomy.

NOTES

1. Xóchitl Leyva Solano, "Regional, Communal, and Organizational Transformations in Las Cañadas," in Jan Rus, Rosalva Aída Hernández Castillo, and Shannan L. Mattiace, eds., *Mayan Lives, Mayan Utopias: The Indigenous Peoples of Chiapas and the Zapatista Rebellion* (Rowman & Littlefield, 2003), 161–84. The other chapters of this book provide an excellent picture of the many facets of the Zapatista autonomy movement.
2. The Zapatistas based the right of self-government on Mexico's 1917 revolutionary Constitution. For the text, see EZLN, "Third Declaration of the Lacandón Jungle" (January 1995).

3. See José Francisco Gallardo et al., *Always Near, Always Far: The Armed Forces in Mexico* (San Francisco: Global Exchange, 2000), chapters 9-10; "The Wars Within: Counterinsurgency in Chiapas and Colombia," *NACLA Report on the Americas* 31, no. 5 (March/April 1998).

4. Maderas del Pueblo del Sureste, "Breve historia de la llamada 'Comunidad Lacandona' " (San Cristóbal de Las Casas, Chiapas: December 2002); "¡No al desalojo!: el caso de la Reserva Montes Azules en la Selva Lacandona, Chiapas" (San Cristóbal de Las Casas, Chiapas: April 2003); CIEPAC (Centro de Investigaciones Económicas y Políticas de Acción Comunitaria), "Nuevos desalojos en los Montes Azules," *Chiapas al Día* no. 393 (February 3, 2004).

5. CIEPAC, "El Plan Puebla Panamá (PPP)" (March 2001), available at www.ciepac.org.

6. Andrés Barreda, "Biopiracy, Bioprospecting, and Resistance: Four Cases in Mexico," in Timothy A. Wise, Hilda Salazar, and Laura Carlsen, eds., *Confronting Globalization: Economic Integration and Popular Resistance in Mexico* (Kumarian Press, 2003), 101–25; "Mexico Biopiracy Project Cancelled," ETC Group (November 9, 2001), available at www.etcgroup.org.

7. CIEPAC, "El Pukuj Runs Loose in Montes Azules," *Chiapas al Día* no. 409 (April 29, 2004), and "La Red de Derechos Humanos de Chiapas rechaza el proyecto de ley de biodiversidad para el Estado de Chiapas por ignorar a los pueblos indígenas," *Chiapas al Día* no. 418 (June 30, 2004).

8. See Neil Harvey, "Resisting Neoliberalism, Constructing Citizenship: Indigenous Movements in Chiapas," in Wayne A. Cornelius, Todd A. Eisenstadt, and Jane Hindley, eds., *Subnational Politics and Democratization in Mexico* (La Jolla, California: U.C.-San Diego Center for U.S.-Mexico Studies, 1999), 239–65. For a comparative discussion of this reframing of indigenous rights in the region, see Deborah Yashar, "Democracy, Indigenous Movements, and the Postliberal Challenge in Latin America," *World Politics* 52, no. 1 (1999): 76-104.

9. For examples of implementation of community-level autonomy, see Richard Stahler-Sholk, "Massacre in Chiapas," *Latin American Perspectives* 25, no. 4 (July 1998): 63–75; Jeanne Simonelli and Duncan Earle, "Disencumbering Development: Alleviating Poverty Through Autonomy in Chiapas," in Robyn Eversole, ed., *Here to Help: NGOs Combating Poverty in Latin America* (Armonk, NY: M.E. Sharpe, 2003), 174–219; and June Nash, "Indigenous Development Alternatives," *Urban Anthropology and Studies of Cultural Systems and World Economic Development* 32, no. 1 (spring 2003): 57–98.

10. Subcomandante Insurgente Marcos, "Leer un video" (August 2004).

11. Hermann Bellinghausen, "Comenzó la reubicación de poblados zapatistas en el sur de Montes Azules," *La Jornada* (October 29, 2004), and "Reubicaciones de la SRA propician confrontaciones en la selva lacandona," *La Jornada* (September 15, 2004).

12. For a balanced assessment of the RAP model in Chiapas, see Shannan L. Mattiace, *To See With Two Eyes: Peasant Activism and Indian Autonomy in Chiapas, Mexico* (University of New Mexico Press, 2003). For a positive presentation of the territorial decentralization model including the Nicaraguan case, see Héctor Díaz Polanco, *Autonomía regional: la autodeterminación de los pueblos indios* (Mexico City: Siglo XXI, 1991). For a critical view of this model from a Zapatista adviser, see Gustavo Esteva, "The Meaning and Scope of the Struggle for Autonomy," in Rus et al., eds., *Mayan Lives, Mayan Utopias*, 243–69. On the political prospects of autonomy claims, see Donna Lee Van Cott, "Explaining Ethnic Autonomy Regimes in Latin America," *Studies in Comparative International Development* 35, no. 4 (winter 2001): 30–58.

13. Rudi Colloredo-Mansfeld, "Autonomy and Interdependence in Native Movements: Towards a Pragmatic Politics in the Ecuadorian Andes," *Identities: Global Studies in Culture and Power* 9, no. 2 (April–June 2002): 173–95. For interesting analysis of the changing definitions of indigenous community in Chiapas in the context of globalization, see Jan Rus, "Local Adaptation to Global Change: The Reordering of Native Society in Highland Chiapas, Mexico 1974–1994," *European Review of Latin American and Caribbean Studies*, no. 58 (June 1995): 71–89.

14. Charles R. Hale, "Does Multiculturalism Menace? Governance, Cultural Rights and the Politics of Identity in

Guatemala," *Journal of Latin American Studies* 34, part 3 (August 2002): 485–524.

15. On the impact of the agrarian counter-reform in Chiapas, see Neil Harvey, "Rural Reforms and the Question of Autonomy in Chiapas," in Wayne A. Cornelius and David Myhre, eds., *The Transformation of Rural Mexico: Reforming the Ejido Sector* (La Jolla, CA: UCSD Center for U.S.-Mexico Studies, 1998).

16. For a textual comparison of the initial November 1996 compromise language for an indigenous rights law drafted by the congressional peace commission (COCOPA), the executive's December 1996 modifications, and the bill introduced in April 2001, see EZLN, "Reformas a la Iniciativa de Ley de Derechos y Cultura Indígena." See also Luis Hernández Navarro and Laura Carlsen, "Indigenous Rights: The Battle for Constitutional Reform in Mexico," in Kevin J. Middlebrook, ed., *Dilemmas of Political Change in Mexico* (London: Institute of Latin American Studies, 2004), 440–65.

17. Subcomandante Insurgente Marcos, "Chiapas: la treceava estela," seven-part communiqué (July 2003). English translation in *¡Ya Basta! Ten Years of the Zapatista Uprising* (AK Press, 2004), 589–625.

BRAZIL'S LANDLESS HOLD THEIR GROUND

BY HARRY E. VANDEN
NACLA Report, March/April 2005

Over the past few decades, there have been various forms of popular protest in Latin America against the austerity measures and conservative economic policies that have come to be called "neoliberalism." These protests have taken diverse forms: the Zapatista rebellion in Mexico, the neopopulist Fifth Republic Movement (MVR) led by Hugo Chávez in Venezuela, the national indigenous movement led by the National Indigenous Confederation of Ecuador (CONAIE), the regime-changing popular mobilizations in Argentina and Bolivia, and the Landless Rural Workers' Movement in Brazil (Movimento dos Trabalhadores Rurais Sem Terra, MST), which is the subject of this article.

Such movements are also a recent and vociferous manifestation of the specter of mass popular mobilization that has haunted the Latin American elite since colonial times. At present, a great many people—especially the poor—seem to feel that the much touted return to democracy, the celebration of civil society and the incorporation of Latin America into the globalization process has left them marginalized both economically and politically. The reactions in Mexico, Brazil, Ecuador, Venezuela, Argentina, and Bolivia have been strong and significant and, in varying ways, make one wonder if the dominant political project is working for common people. It is also quite possible that it is the democratization and celebration of civil society that allow—some would say encourage—the political mobilization that is manifest in the widespread emergence of forceful mass-based social and political movements.

There is a growing consensus that the traditional politicians' new political enterprise is leaving behind the great majorities and, effectively, further marginalizing specific groups within those majorities. Indicators of the growing malaise are many: general alienation from the traditional political process, increased crime, surging abstention rates in select electoral contests, as suggested by the low turnout in Argentina in 2001.[1] The 1998 national elections in Brazil saw a similar phenomenon, with 40% of the electorate either abstaining or casting blank or annulled ballots.[2] Changing attitudes have often led to the abandonment of traditional political parties for new, more amorphous, ad hoc parties like Chávez's MVR in Venezuela. They have also produced an upsurge of new sociopolitical movements and mass organizations along with a plethora of national strikes, demonstrations, and protests such as those that washed across Argentina at the end of 2001 and the beginning of 2002.

Mass communication systems and easy, relatively affordable access to the Internet have combined with higher levels of literacy and much greater political freedom under the democratization process.[3] This has occurred just as ideas of grassroots democracy, popular participation, and even elements of liberation theology and Christian-Base Community organizing have been widely disseminated. There is growing belief that economic equality should exist and that systems working against such equality need to be changed. Unlike the radical revolutionary movements of the last few decades, these new movements do not advocate the radical restructuring of the state through violent revolution. Rather, their primary focus is to work through the existing political system by pushing it to its limits to achieve necessary change and restructuring.[4]

The end of authoritarian rule and the expansive democratization of the late 1980s created new political dynamics in many Latin American nations. Political spaces began to open up in what came to be labeled "civil society," and new forms of political action followed. The projection of an elitist armed vanguard as the spearhead of necessary change began to fade in the face of unarmed political and social mobilizations. The assertion of popular power reminiscent of mobilizations by the pre-coup Peasant Leagues in northeastern Brazil began to bubble up in new and varied forms.

By the time neoliberal economic policy became more widespread in the 1990s, it was becoming evident that the extant political systems in much of Latin America were unable to meet the needs of the vast majorities. Indeed, in the eyes of most Latin American popular sectors, the structural adjustments and neoliberal reforms advocated by international financial institutions like the IMF threatened their security and well-being. Their insecurity and dissatisfaction drove them to seek new forms of protest and different political structures that might better address their needs since traditional parties and governments seemed increasingly unable to respond.

As the 1990s progressed, dissatisfaction with traditional political leaders and parties became more widespread along with doubts about the legitimacy of the political system itself. Traditional personalism, clientelism, corruption, and avarice became subjects of ridicule and anger, if not rage. The effects of neoliberalism and continued classism and racism amid ever stronger calls for equality were inescapable. With growing questions about the system's relevance and legitimacy, these demands were not exclusively addressed to the political system per se but to society more generally. Nor did the populace in most nations look to armed struggles and revolutionary movements to remedy their problems (Colombia is the significant exception here). They sought something different. Groups were looking for new political structures that allowed for their participation. There was a search for new structures that would respond to the perceived—though not always clearly articulated—demands emerging from the popular sectors.

The MST itself was formed as a response to long-standing economic, social and political conditions in Brazil. Land, wealth, and power have been allocated in extremely unequal ways since the conquest in the early 1500s. Land has remained highly concentrated, and as late as 1996, 1% of landowners owned 45% of the land.[5] Conversely, as of 2001, there were some 4.5 million landless rural workers in Brazil. Wealth has remained equally concentrated. The Brazilian Institute of Government Statistics reported in 2001 that the upper 10% of the population received an average income that was 19 times greater than that of the lowest 40%.[6]

The plantation agriculture that dominated the colonial period and the early republican era became the standard for Brazilian society. The wealthy few owned the land, reaped the profits, and decided the political destiny of the many. The institution of slavery provided most of the labor for the early plantation system and thus further entrenched polarized social relations between the wealthy landowning elite and the disenfranchised toiling masses laboring in the fields. Land remained in relatively few hands, and agricultural laborers continued to be poorly paid and poorly treated.

The commercialization and mechanization of agriculture beginning in the 1970s made much of the existing rural labor force superfluous. As this process continued and became more tightly linked to the increasing globalization of production, large commercial or family estates fired rural laborers, expelled sharecroppers from the land they farmed, and acquired the land of farmers who owned small plots. This resulted in growing rural unemployment and the growth of rural landless families, many of whom had to migrate to cities, swelling the numbers of the urban poor. Others opted for the government-sponsored Amazon colonization program, whereby the government transplanted entire families to the Amazon region where they cut down the rainforest for planting. Few found decent jobs in the city, and the easily eroded rainforest subsoil allowed for little sustained agriculture, worsening their collective plight.

The immediate origins of the MST go back to the bitter struggle to survive under the agricultural policies implemented by the military government that ruled Brazil from 1964 to 1985. The landless rural workers in the southern Brazilian state of Rio Grande do Sul began to organize to demand land in the early 1980s. Other landless people soon picked up their cry in the neighboring states of Paraná and Santa Catarina.[7] They built on a long tradition of rural resistance and rebellion that extends back to the establishments of *quilombos* (large inland settlements of runaway slaves) and to the famous rebellion of the poor peasants of Canudos in the 1890s. In more recent times it included the well-known Peasant Leagues of Brazil's impoverished northeast in the 1950s and early 1960s and the Grass Wars in Rio Grande do Sul and other southern states in the 1970s.[8]

When the MST was founded in southern Brazil in 1984 as a response to rural poverty and the lack of access to land, similar conditions existed in many Brazilian states. Indeed, there were landless workers and peasants throughout the nation, and the MST soon spread from Rio Grande do Sul and Paraná in the south to states like Pernambuco in the northeast and Pará in the Amazon region. It rapidly became a national organization with coordinated policies and strong local participatory structures characterized by frequent state and national meetings based on direct representation. By 2001 there were active MST organizations in 23 of the 26 states.[9]

Today the MST is arguably the largest and most powerful social movement in Latin America. The ranks of those associated with it exceed 200,000 and perhaps even double that number. It has a high mobilization capacity at the local, state, and even national level. In 1997, for instance, the organization was able to mobilize 100,000 people for a march on Brasília.

Its members views are well articulated. They have a clear understanding of the increased commercialization of agriculture and its consequences for the way production is organized, if not rural life more generally. Similarly, they are fully conscious of how globalization is strengthening these trends and threatening their livelihoods. In small classes, meetings, and assemblies, and through their newspaper, *Jornal Dos Trabalhadores Sem Terra*; their magazine, *Revista Sem Terra*; and numerous pamphlets, they inform their base through a well-planned program of political education. They even establish schools in their encampments, settlements, and cooperatives to make sure the next generation has a clear idea of the politics in play.[10] The next generation of leaders attends their national school ITERRA, where they get a strong political and popular orientation, well-grounded instruction in political and organizational theory, and practical skills such as accounting and administration.

The MST also facilitates the organic development of highly participatory grassroots organizing rooted in groups of about 10 families, which constitute a "base nucleus" in each neighborhood. Local general assemblies convene frequently and all members of the family units are encouraged to participate. Frequently held regional, state, and even national assemblies in turn incorporate representatives of these local-level units.[11] Leadership is collective at all levels, including nationally, where some 102 militants make up the National Coordinating Council.[12]

Their political culture and decision-making processes clearly break from the authoritarian tradition. The movement has been heavily influenced by liberation theology and the participatory democratic culture generated by the use and study of Paulo Freire's approach to self-taught, critical education. Indeed, the strongly participatory nature of the organization and the collective nature of leadership and decision-making have made for a political culture that challenges traditional authoritarian notions and vertical decision-making structures.[13]

One of the characteristics of recent social movements like the MST is a broad national vision. The Sem Terra envision a thoroughgoing land reform and complete restructuring of agrarian production in all of Brazil, as suggested by their pamphlet prepared for their fourth national congress in 2000, "Agrarian Reform for a Brazil Without Latifundios."[14] The MST believes that it is impossible to develop the nation, construct a democratic society, or alleviate poverty and social inequality in the countryside without eliminating the *latifundio*. But they go on to say that agrarian reform is only viable if it is part of a popular project that would transform Brazil's economic and social structures.[15]

Like many of Latin America's recent social and political movements, the Sem Terra are well aware of how their struggle is linked to international conditions. Thus, they begin by challenging the positive vision of neoliberalism presented by global media.[16] In a draft document on the "Fundamental Principles for the Social and Economic Transformation of Rural Brazil," they note that "the political unity of the Brazilian dominant classes under Fernando Henrique Cardoso's administration (1994–2000) has consolidated the implementation of neoliberalism [in Brazil]," and that these neoliberal policies have led to the increased concentration of land and wealth in the hands of the few and the further impoverishment of Brazilian society. "Popular movements," the document goes on to say, "must challenge this neoliberal conceptualization of our economy and society."[17]

Mass political mobilization is another fundamental organizational principle as seen in their massive mobilizations for land takeovers and street demonstrations.[18] This strategy is widely communicated to those affiliated with the organization. A pamphlet disseminated by the organization, "Brazil Needs a Popular Project," calls for popular mobilizations, noting that "all the changes in the history of humanity only happened when the people were mobilized," and that in Brazil, "all the social and political changes that happened were won when the people mobilized and struggled."[19]

As has been the case in other Latin American countries, traditional politics and political parties have proven unable and/or unwilling to address the deteriorating economic conditions of marginalized groups who suffer the negative effects of economic globalization. In turn, the social movements have responded with grassroots organization and the development of a new repertoire of action that breaks with old forms of political activity. Developing organization and group actions, sometimes with the outside assistance of progressive organizations concerned with social justice, have tied individual members together in a strongly forged group identity.

In the case of Brazil and the Sem Terra, this outside role was played by the Lutheran Church and even more so by the Pastoral Land Commission of the Catholic Church. Although these organizations assisted the MST along with some segments of the Workers' Party (PT), the organization never lost its autonomy. It was decided from the onset that this was to be an organization for the Landless Workers, to be run by the Landless Workers and for their benefit as they defined it.

They have taken over large estates and public lands; constructed black plastic-covered encampments along the side of the road to call attention to their demands for land; and have marched and staged confrontations when necessary. They even occupied the family farm of Cardoso shortly before the 2002 election to draw attention to his land-owning interests and the consequent bias they attributed to him. At times they are brutally repressed, imprisoned, and even assassinated, yet still, they persevere, forcing the distribution of land to their people and others without land. Their ability to mobilize as many as 12,000 people for a single land takeover or 100,000 for a national march suggests the strength of their organizational abilities and how well they communicate and coordinate at the national level. They also garner a great deal of national support, having created a consensus throughout the country that land distribution is a problem and that some substantial reforms are necessary.[20]

The Landless remain keenly attuned to, and consider themselves part of, the international struggle over globalization. They have helped organize and participated in the World Social Forum of Porto Alegre, and have sent representatives to demonstrations and protests throughout the world. Struggles that were once local and isolated are now international and linked.[21] International communications networks, including cellular phones and, especially, e-mail, have greatly facilitated the globalization of awareness about local struggles and the support and solidarity they receive. Combined with dramatic actions like massive land takeovers, the MST has generated considerable support at both the national and international level and has helped transform local struggles into national events, redefining local problems as national problems that require national attention and resources.

The interaction between the MST and the PT is also instructive. Relations between the two organizations are generally excellent at the local level with overlapping membership, but the national leaderships have remained separate and not always as cordial. The MST has maintained a militant line in regard to the need to take over unused land and assert their agenda, whereas much of the PT leadership has wanted to be more conciliatory. Thus, the Sem Terra generally support the PT in most local campaigns and backed Luiz Inácio Lula da Silva in his successful campaign for the presidency. They helped achieve significant regime change in Brazil: Lula was elected with an unprecedented

61% of the vote in the 2002 runoff.

Indeed, realizing the PT's historic challenge to neoliberal policies and elitist rule, the landless turned out heavily in the election to join some 80% of registered voters who participated in both rounds of voting. Once the election was over, the MST did not demand to be part of the government. Rather, they continued to press the government for a comprehensive land reform program and a redistribution of both land and wealth. There would be no return to "politics as usual." The PT would pursue its Zero Hunger program and other social and economic initiatives and the MST would press the PT government for the structural reforms—like comprehensive agrarian reform—that it considered necessary. By 2004, the MST displayed considerable dissatisfaction with what it considered the relative inaction of the government in regard to land reform, and it was threatening to once again engage in massive land takeovers. At the same time, the Lula government was facing increasing pressure from international financial institutions and national economic interests for moderate policies. By functioning in civil society and not becoming part of the government, however, the MST was free to pursue its original demands for land reform and socio-economic transformation.

Like the MST, many of the region's social movements have grown and have become increasingly politicized. They have come to represent a clear response to the neoliberal economic policies that have been forced on Latin American nations by international financial institutions, the U.S. government and national economic elites. In the 20 years since Brazil's military left government, the MST has embedded itself in civil society, taking advantage of the considerable political space that has opened up with the institutionalization of nominal democracy. Currently, the leftist PT is in control of the national and many state and municipal governments and has promised reform and structural change. Though they may lack the political will to implement many of their promised policies like land reform, they are not totally opposed to the policies being advocated by the MST. If nothing else, the changed political situation makes repression unlikely and allows for considerable political space in which social movements like the MST can maneuver.

As they engage in grassroots organization and massive local and national mobilizations, the MST and social movements elsewhere have challenged the patterns of policy-making in Brazil and many other Latin American countries. Their growth and militancy have generated a whole new repertoire of actions that include national mobilizations so massive that they can topple governments—as in Bolivia—or force them to change their policies. They have left the traditional parties far behind as they forge new political horizons and create a nonauthoritarian, participatory political culture. Such movements are using existing political space to maximum effect. In the process they are substantially strengthening participatory democratic practice.

They have vigorously resisted the corporate-led economic globalization process that has been heralded as the panacea to underdevelopment and poverty. Indeed, the economic realities that the masses of people all over Latin America are living, provide a potent empirical antidote to the universal prescription to globalize. The formulation of highly political social movements and the participatory democracy they practice provide a new and promising response to global neoliberalism. Further, these responses represent a substantial change from previous forms of political action, and they are transforming the conduct of politics in Brazil and Latin America.

NOTES

1. Susan Kaufman Purcell, "Electoral Lessons," *América Economica* (December 6, 2001): 40.
2. Banco de Datos Políticos das Américas, "Brazil: Eleções Presidencias de 1998,", accessed April 19, 2002.
3. See United Nations Development Program, *Human Development Report 1999* (Oxford University Press), 3–9.
4. CONAIE's very brief participation in a would-be junta that held the Ecuadoran Congress building overnight in January 2000 is the exception. See Jennifer N. Collins, "A Sense of Possibility: Ecuador's Indigenous Movement Takes Center Stage," *NACLA Report on the Americas* 35, no. 5 (March/April 2002): 40–46.
5. James Petras, "The Rural Landless Workers' Movement," *Z Magazine* (March 2000): 35.
6. Brazilian Institute of Statistics, Statistical Report 2001, as cited in "Pais termina anos 90 tão desigual como começou," *Folha de São Paulo* (April 5, 2001).
7. See João Pedro Stedile, "Memories of Struggle in the MST," *NACLA Report on the Americas* 38, no. 5 (March/April 2005): 24; and João Pedro Stedile and Bernardo Mançano Fernandes, *Brava gente: a trajectorai do MST e a luta pela terra no Brasil* (São Paulo: Fundacão Perseo Abramo, 1999). In English, see Angus Wright and Wendy Wolford, *To Inherit the Earth: The Landless Movement and the Struggle for a New Brazil* (Food First Books, 2003), and Sue Bradford and Jan Rocha, *Cutting the Wire: Tthe Story of Landless Movement in Brazil* (London: Latin American Bureau, 2002).
8. See Elide Rugai Bastos, *As ligas camponesas* (Petópolis: Vozes, 1984).
9. See Bradford and Rocha, *Cutting The Wire*, and interview with Geraldo Fontes, member of the National Coordinating Council, São Paulo, September 17, 2003.
10. In field research in Rio Grande do Sul State in 2001, the author observed a mixed-grade class in one of the *campamentos* learning about *trasgenicos*—genetically engineered crops, their hazards, and the corporations that control them. The MST produces educational material and guides, as well as training and orientation, on how to develop schools and popular education. See "O que queremos com as escolas dos asentamientos," *Caderno de Formacão* no. 18 (March 1999); and "Como fazemos a escola de educacão fundamental," *Cuaderno de Educacão* no. 9 (MST, Education Sector, 1999).
11. The neighborhood organization of 10 families could be the base unit (*nucleo de base*) in a larger cooperative or settlement, or even a temporary encampment. Each group then sends two representatives to a ruling council in each settlement, cooperative or encampment. General meetings in which all can participate are also held. These organizations in turn send representatives to the regional and state congresses. Special meetings are held to pick the representatives to the National Encounters (every two years) and National Congresses (every five years). As per Geraldo Fontes, member of the National Coordinating Council, in interview in São Paulo, September 17, 2003.
12. Geraldo Flores, interview, September 17, 2003.
13. See "O MST e a cultura," *Caderno de Formacão* no. 34 (São Paulo: Ademar Bogo, 2000), and Carlos Rodrigues

Brandão, "História do menino que lia o mundo," *Fazendo História* no. 7 (Veranópolis: ITERRA, 2001).

14. *Reforma agraria, por um Brasil sem latifundio* (São Paulo: Movimiento dos Trabalhadores Rurais Sem Terra-MST, 2000).

15. Ibid., p. 4.

16. See, for instance, the political education pamphlet that the MST uses to explain neoliberalism to its affiliates: "O Neoliberalism, ou o mecanismo para fabricar mais pobres entre os pobres," *Notebook* no. 5 (São Paulo: Consulta Popular, 1993).

17. The Landless Rural Workers Movement (MST), "Fundamental Principles for the Social and Economic Transformation of Rural Brazil," Translated by Wilder Robles, *Journal of Peasant Studies* 28, no. 2 (January 2001): 153–54.

18. See Stedile, "Memories of Struggle in the MST," p. 24

19. "MST, O Brasil precisa de um projeto popular," *Cuartilla* no. 11 (São Paulo: Secretaria Operative de Consulta Popular, 2000): 1–29.

20. It should, however, be noted that much of the press was not always sympathetic and condemned their land takeovers as illegal actions. The rural landowners also did all in their power to stop their actions and discredit them in the public eye.

21. See Donatella de la Porta and Sidney Tarrow, eds., *Transnational Protest & Global Activism* (Roman and Littlefield, 2005).

BOLIVIAN WOMEN'S ORGANIZATIONS IN THE MAS ERA

BY KARIN MONASTERIOS P.
NACLA Report, March/April 2007

Throughout the 1990s, the Bolivian women's movement was ideologically polarized between a liberal, NGO-based "gender technocracy" and the anarcha-feminism embodied in the Mujeres Creando (Women Creating) movement. Between them stood the great majority of the country's female population—a huge contingent of women of indigenous descent living in a colonized condition. Neither the technocratic nor the anarchist tendency considered them the subject of political representation.

Today, the correlation of forces that predominated until recently is beginning to change. This is largely the result of the starring role played by women's grassroots organizations in the social mobilizations that destabilized the neoliberal order. That upheaval launched a new period in Bolivia's political history, one best characterized as the era of "indigenous nationalism." Since the inauguration of Bolivia's first indigenous president, Evo Morales, these indigenous women's groups (both rural and urban) have come to be perceived as the legitimate representatives of large women's majorities. At the same time, the women's movement has significantly realigned its political stances vis-à-vis the challenges of decolonization and radical democratization represented in the platform of Morales' party, the Movimiento al Socialismo (Movement Toward Socialism, MAS).

THE NGO MOVEMENT: GENDER TECHNOCRACY

The term *gender technocracy* was coined by autonomous Latin American feminists as a useful concept to differentiate the elite of professional women associated with NGOs working on gender-related issues from what they considered an authentic feminist movement, struggling from a fundamentally anti-patriarchal position. Bolivia's gender technocracy was born in the mid-1980s, when international cooperation funds for development projects with a "gender approach" became available. This signaled the export of the liberal version of northern-hemisphere feminism—hegemonic since its institutionalization in the United Nations—to peripheral countries through bi- and multilateral development cooperation programs. In fact, the regulating discourse of "gender and development" was made possible thanks to the cooperation agencies' solid institutional resources and their capacity to permeate state policies in peripheral countries. This partly explains why gender technocracy's discourse has been unable to this day to address grassroots women's consciousness, and even less to address the state from the "bottom up," with demands that represent the majority of women's interests and aspirations as women.

As NGOs arrived on the political scene, a new form of mediation developed between civil society and the state. Grassroots organizations increasingly became the "beneficiaries" of NGO projects, while NGOs began to identify themselves as "representatives" of civil society to the state and cooperation agencies. This was the case of NGOs such as Fundación San Gabriel and Caritas Bolivia, which operated food aid programs. Other NGOs, such as Fundación Tierra, Instituto Politécnico Tupak Katari, and El Centro de Promoción de la Mujer Gregoria Apaza (CPMGA), also appeared in this period.[1]

Gender technocracy was organized along two axes: a state regulating body and the women's NGOs that worked closely with it. Together they played a key role in framing the discourse of gender inequality as—solely—a matter of state management. That is why women's NGOs increasingly took on a quasi-public-sector role, a development that took place in the context of "democratization" after the fall of the 1970s military regimes. This helped legitimize what was in fact a co-optation of the movements by the neoliberal state.

The main characteristic of the women's NGO movement is that it builds its demands on the principles of UN conventions, rather than on a dialogue with Bolivian women about their needs. Gender technocracy thus differs from the rest of women's organizations because its main goal has not been to confront specific relations of gender subordination in Bolivia, but rather to mitigate the poor life conditions of marginal women through short-term programs that follow UN dictates. "Influencing state policies from a gender and development perspective"— as the mission statements of practically all the gender NGOs put it—has been the real goal, yet the question of where this influence, and its legitimacy, would come from was never debated, either by the gender technocracy or by the cooperation agencies; no such debate was required as long as the technocracy was thought of as "representing" women's interests and demands.

By accommodating the political style of each administration, the technocratic NGOs ended up endorsing the government's social programs, beginning with the structural-adjustment package implemented in 1985. Most of them also offered near unconditional support for the popular participation project launched by President Gonzalo Sánchez de Lozada in 1995, which obliged social organizations to reorganize on a territorial basis, in close relationship with municipal-level political party structures, thus removing their autonomy and denaturalizing them. This was also the case with microenterprise policies, which decreased the value of labor power (that is, they depressed salaries), particularly that of the female workforce.

Finally, we have the problem of reducing women's political participation to a matter of power quotas within formal political structures. Within the framework of Sánchez de Lozada's reforms, the gender technocracy launched an aggressive campaign to require that 30% of all candidates in national and municipal elections be women. The quota worked to consolidate male leadership within the political parties' patriarchal structures, rather than to actually promote the representation of women's interests. Elite urban women linked to the leadership of right-wing parties mainly benefited. Indigenous women's leadership, in contrast, emerged from social movements that have become political parties, including the MAS and the Movimiento Indígena Pachacuti.[2]

Thus, the class nature of gender technocracy reveals itself in two basic dimensions: First, as part of the NGO conglomerate, it has played an important role in legitamizing neoliberal policies. Second, it has maintained a strategic alliance with the neoliberal state and international cooperation agencies—an alliance key to its survival—obligating gender NGOs to define their roles very little in relation to civil society and women, or to women's interests, needs and aspirations.

There is, however, a third aspect of gender technocracy's class nature that has only lately manifested, and is now possible to name, in the current context of changing correlation of forces between mestizo and colonized society—a context that typifies the MAS era. (By "colonized society," I refer to the population of predominantly indigenous heritage, which according to the last census of 2002, represents 62.2% of Bolivia's population.) I will develop this point further in the last section of this article.

During the neoliberal period, the political parties gave birth to new women's political organizations that were closely aligned with the gender technocracy, such as the Foro Político de Mujeres (Women's Political Forum), the Asociación de Mujeres Parlamentarias (Association of Congresswomen), and the Asociación de Concejalas de Bolivia (Association of Councilwomen of Bolivia). These groups' aim was to promote the rights of women elected to public offices. They typically reproduced the ethnic and class divisions of traditional political parties.

THE MUJERES CREANDO MOVEMENT AND THE FEMINIST ASSEMBLY

At the other end of the spectrum of the women's movement, we find the anarcha-feminist movement Mujeres Creando, situated generally within the autonomous Latin American feminist camp. Autonomy here is defined in terms of the state and political parties (according to the principle of "no to co-optation") and NGOs ("no to mediation"). Consistent with this autonomist position, the movement has followed an independent and unique path with regard to the processes of political reconfiguration and policy making. Its actions derive from a politics of the everyday-private, and they seek to make an impact both at the macro-level of structural problems, and at the level of the microphysics of power, in which collective subjectivities are structured and power and domination find a privileged space of reproduction and legitimacy. The movement is remarkable for its strategy, based on deconstructing symbols and languages of patriarchal domination in a context of internal colonialism. Its weapons range from graffiti, television shows, and the press to silent theater, poetry, and workshops.

The movement was key in sustaining two of the most important colonized women's mobilizations: the women coca growers' march of 1995 and the microcredit women debtors' mobilization of 1999. In both cases Café Carcajada, the headquarters of Mujeres Creando, served as a space to strategize and as a lodge for women who arrived from different parts of the country.[3] Though small in membership, this movement has a far ideological reach and remains the only one in Bolivia that advances its political demands from a standpoint of gender subalternity. Mujeres Creando has contributed greatly to naming patriarchy as a specific form of domination that Bolivian society at large cannot yet recognize in its true dimensions.

Having rejected any kind of long-lasting alliances and stable structure, the movement must now work with other sectors of mobilized women. The Feminist Assembly, founded in 2004, has been working to join forces with the women of indigenous and peri-urban organizations; it proposes to be a parallel to the Constituent Assembly.

THE BARTOLINA SISA NATIONAL FEDERATION OF PEASANT WOMEN

From nonfeminist positions and at the margin of the gender-and-development discourse, there exist important women's organizations within the major contemporary social movements. The most salient are the Federación Nacional de Mujeres Campesinas Bartolina Sisa (the Bartolina Sisa National Federation of Bolivian Peasant Women, or FNMCB-BS by its Spanish acronym) and the neighborhood councils. Although the latter comprises both men and women, its members are mostly women; both are made up of indigenous-descended women to a greater or lesser degree.

Born in the late 1970s within the Confederación Sindical Única de Trabajadores Campesinos de Bolivia (the Sole Trade Union Confederation of Peasant Workers of Bolivia, or CSUTCB), the Bartolina Sisa Federation stands out as the only organization of indigenous women in the country. It is also the most important women's organization, not only because as part of the indigenous and peasant movement it has made the most radical demands on the colonialist state, but also because it represents the largest section of the women's movement, with a membership that reaches over 100,000 women and a trade-union structure that reaches from the national executive directors to community-level producer's associations.

Since its creation, the Federation has been torn between an autonomist and an integrationist trend—in reference to the CSUTCB's sexist ideology and patriarchal structures—a conflict that has taken its political toll and resulted in a significant loss in membership from which the group has recovered only in recent years. The Federation might well have separated from the CSUTCB, had it not been for its deliberate choice in 2004 to "stay with its brothers in the struggle for decolonization," as some Federation executives said in a recent interview with the author.

This women's organization is in the vanguard of the indigenous movement, being one of the nine organizations that founded the Pacto de Unidad (Covenant for Unity) in June 2006. The FNMCB-BS brings together peasant women from different sectors of agricultural production and is based on a solid organizational structure throughout Bolivia's nine departments (national territories analogous to states in the U.S. or provinces in Canada).

Having been an anti-systemic organization under previous political regimes, the FNMCB-BS is now entering a conciliatory phase vis-à-vis the state. This partly results from government initiatives to establish a direct dialogue with social movements and their grassroots organizations. Policies in this direction are currently being developed by the Presidential Ministry and the recently created Vice Ministry of Coordination With Social Movements.

THE NEIGHBORHOOD COUNCILS MOVEMENT

Besides the indigenous movement, the second outstanding movement in Bolivia's contemporary history is that of the neighborhood councils. The councils represent that intermediary social category standing between the urban and the rural, comprising a large sector of indigenous people who are becoming urbanized. Having emerged from the territorial restructuring policies of neoliberal reforms, the councils have ironically taken a leading role in building demands for radical social change through a "politics of basic needs" that is closely connected to a powerful discourse of nationalization. This began with the Water War of 2000 and was later reasserted in the October 2003 uprising known as the Gas War. Together with the peasant and indigenous movement, the neighborhood councils in the western cities of La Paz and El Alto played a key role in the wave of mobilizations that both put an end to the neoliberal administrations of Sánchez de Lozada and

Carlos Mesa and resulted in the popular demand for early elections and Morales's victory in January 2006.

The confluence of the neighborhood movement's basic-needs politics with the demands for indigenous sovereignty (such as refounding the state through a constituent assembly, new territorial divisions and redistributing land) has resulted in a new kind of nationalism that imagines an indigenous form of citizenship built on reappropriating natural resources for the benefit of Bolivians. It is precisely in the two key elements of nationalization and indigenous identity that the two movements, neighborhood and indigenous, find common ground for decolonization.[4] Both the women of the neighborhood councils and of the FNMCB-BS speak from the standpoint of the ethnic subaltern. Using a discourse of decolonization, they advocate an "indigenous" subject vis-à-vis a state that has reproduced colonial social relations between a mestizo society and an indigenous one. This is changing who gets to represent women's interests and demands, with that role rapidly shifting to women's grassroots organizations, while the NGO technocracy is losing its legitimacy.

THE IMPACT OF THE MAS GOVERNMENT ON WOMEN'S ORGANIZATIONS

Morales's rise to power has no doubt had a strong impact on Bolivian society. A realignment of forces is under way, as distinct social sectors respond differently to a process of decolonization that implies a qualitative change in relations between mestizo and colonized society. This is related not only to changes in the correlation of forces among the traditionally dominant classes, but also with nationalization, land redistribution, and—for the technocratic political class—the loss of monopoly over the institutions and its concurrent loss of prestige. In this framework, the loss of symbolic and material power in some social sectors becomes evident. For the women's movement this means a real change in the correlation of forces between mestizo women's organizations and indigenous-based (urban and/or rural) women's organizations. It is a critical moment for the technocratic middle class, particularly the NGOs, partly because their legitimacy is being seriously questioned, but also because they have resisted—rather than adjusted to—the new state of affairs. NGOs refuse to accept that decolonization implies at least the partial renouncement of the mediating role they have played between the state and civil society. However, their greatest fear probably lies in the possibility of finding themselves on an equal footing with their beneficiaries, with a government that favors direct dialogue with grassroots organizations.

Some NGOs are attempting to reorganize clearly counterrevolutionary projects. This is the case of We Bet for Bolivia, a project that was initially created during the transitional phase of the Mesa administration to stamp the Constituent Assembly with a "constitutional" agenda that radically differed from social movements' "foundational" proposals. Put together by four traditional NGOs, We Bet for Bolivia has now relaunched with the new aim of gaining "social control over the revenues of nationalized hydrocarbons" with the support of the Revenue Watch Institute, a U.S. organization.[5] These programs signal that NGOs will not easily renounce their mediating role, even if they have to seek legitimacy from external circuits.

Beyond today's potential opportunities for women's grassroots organizations, there remains the issue of linking the national-decolonizing project advocated by these organizations with the patriarchal emancipation project proposed from relatively isolated—but not irrelevant—feminist positions, such as those of Mujeres Creando, the Feminist Assembly and, with significant differences, the author of this text herself. Women's organizations in Bolivia are still conservative, and it is not clear up to what point they will adopt a double claim of gender and ethnic subordination, although this may well be possible within the FNMCB-BS. To a great extent this will depend on the ability of the women in these movements to think critically about the gender dimension of power and democracy. It will also depend on the efforts and initiatives of the (few) feminists who work in this milieu, and—largely—on whether grassroots organizations such as the FNMCB-BS, the neighborhood councils, and new groups will gain access to real resources.

There is no doubt that women's organizations' autonomy within social movements is a fundamental issue. If efforts do not converge in this direction, their participation will remain critical for mobilizing, but invisible in terms of decision making and political leadership. Strategic gender needs will be indefinitely postponed as long debates on the topic fail to address the issue of internal colonialism and its reproduction mechanisms.[6] There is still much work to be done in order to achieve this articulation. What is clear is that emancipation from patriarchy in Bolivia is not unrelated to emancipation from internal colonialism, since it is precisely in its fabric where gender identity and ethnic subordination are simultaneously constituted. Indeed, this topic remains largely unexplored.

This article is an updated version of "The Women's Movement," which originally appeared in the October 2004 issue of Barataria, *a quarterly journal based in La Paz.*

NOTES

1   The CPMGA and Fundación La Paz are specifically women's NGOs, while the others include a gender component in their development projects. As a church institution, Caritas is the oldest.

2.   See Karin Monasterios P. and Luis Tapia, *Partidos y participación política de las mujeres de El Alto* (La Paz: Centro de Promoción de la Mujer Gregoria Apaza, 2001).

3. A thorough account of Mujeres Creando's mobilization strategies and its philosophical positions can be found in a paper I presented at the XXIV International Congress of the Latin American Studies Association (2003). The paper, titled "La tecnocracia de género y el feminismo autónomo de Mujeres Creando: Los extravíos de la representación de las mujeres en Bolivia y los desafíos de la acción directa," represents the first attempt from academia to theorize the work of Mujeres Creando.

4. For further discussions on this topic, see Álvaro García Linera, "La crisis de estado y las sublevaciones indígena-plebeyas," in Alvaro García Linera, Raúl Prada, and Luis Tapia, eds., *Memorias de Octubre* (La Paz: Muela del Diablo, 2004).

5. I am referring to Fundación Tierra, CPMGA, Acción Cultural Loyola, and the Centro de Investigación y Promoción del Campesinado. The last two are closely tied to the Catholic Church in Bolivia.

6. Strategic gender needs are those that allow women to challenge their subordination within the gendered division of labor and gendered structures of power more generally, and range from equal rights legislation to reproductive choice. See Maxine Molyneux, "Mobilisation Without Emancipation? Women's Interests, State and Revolution in Nicaragua," in David Slater, ed., *New Social Movements and the State in Latin America* (Amsterdam: CEDLA, 1985), 233–59.

OUT IN PUBLIC: GAY AND LESBIAN ACTIVISM IN NICARAGUA

BY FLORENCE E. BABB
NACLA Report, May/June 2004

2000: I return to Nicaragua after being away for two years to find the capital city transformed with a new city center boasting hotels, shopping malls and multiplex cinemas. The movie *Boys Don't Cry* is playing and its story of sexual transgression in the U.S. Midwest is meeting a favorable response, at least among those I talk to in the progressive community. Rita, a longtime AIDS activist and self-proclaimed "dyke," tells me she wishes all the legislators in the country would see it and expand their notion of citizen rights to include sexual minorities.

2002: "I'm neither in the closet nor on the balcony" is the way that Carlos, a Nicaraguan in his early thirties, describes himself to me during Gay Pride week in June. We are sitting with a couple of other men in the local gay bar they run, waiting for a panel discussion to begin on HIV and safer sex practices. While Carlos is quite comfortable with his sexuality as a gay man and has a middle-class awareness of the globalized identity that "gay" confers, like many others in Managua's LGBT (lesbian, gay, bisexual, transgender) population he does not feel a need to proclaim his identity loudly.

2003: At a weekly Sunday service of the gay Metropolitan Church in Managua, the young pastor named Alberto speaks of "God's love for everyone, rich and poor, gay, straight, lesbian, and bisexual." The dozen assembled men—including several I know as renowned drag queens, here wearing street clothes—and a couple of women pass a candle from one person to the next, saying, "God loves you as you are." They take communion and Alberto gives thanks to the *jornada*, in reference to Gay Pride week, for allowing the LGBT community to speak out about human rights. They conclude their mass with guitar music and flirtatious dancing on the patio. A few days later, some of these same individuals are present when I give a talk based on my research on lesbian and gay politics and culture in Nicaragua. The venue is Puntos de Encuentro (Gathering Points), Nicaragua's largest feminist nongovernmental organization (NGO), and I am addressing the small community of activists and their allies. The audience includes women and men who work in other NGOs such as Xochiquetzal, which offers services relating to health, sexuality, and AIDS. After I finish, a lively conversation ensues about whether there is truly something that can be called a "movement" in the country. Later, a reporter asks whether I would say that it is "normal" to be homosexual and whether human rights should extend to the homosexual population. I don my anthropological hat for the occasion and assure the well-meaning man that homosexuals are normal and deserving of full rights to social inclusion.

These are a few of the many private and public responses to an increasingly vocal and visible gay and lesbian presence that I have encountered in Nicaragua since 1989. As a foreign researcher and observer of the public emergence of an LGBT community and social movement since the Sandinistas lost the 1990 elections, I had expected to find some resistance to my participation in the charged discussion. What I have found, to my surprise, is a passion for debating the local, national, and transnational aspects of gay culture and politics with as broad and international a group as possible.

To understand the current context, however, one needs to look back at the changes that have occurred over the last 25 years. The revolutionary Sandinista National Liberation Front (FSLN) government (1979–90) provided an opportunity for disenfranchised women and men to become players in the social drama transforming much of the country in the 1980s. Along with agrarian, health, education, and legal reform, gender equality became part of the agenda. And the new constitution of 1987 included women's rights under the rubric of protecting the family as the basic unit of society.

The inclusive vision of the Sandinistas did not extend, however, to a non-heteronormative conception of the Nicaraguan family and society. When lesbians and gay men began organizing in the second half of the 1980s, the Sandinistas were not prepared to extend their revolutionary vision to this new constituency by supporting their call for social recognition and civil rights. As in other socialist-oriented societies, homosexuality was regarded as part of the "decadent" bourgeois past, and it met a chilly response from party militants, despite the fact that well-regarded Sandinistas were among those quietly organizing in Managua. Although same-sex relations, particularly among men, were well known in urban Nicaragua, in 1987, FSLN security agents called in and detained a number of gay men and lesbians whose more political sexual identification was viewed as a deviation.

If the silencing of the nascent gay movement in Nicaragua was effective, this changed by 1989, when some 50 Nicaraguan gay rights activists and their international supporters marched openly to the Plaza de la Revolución for the 10th anniversary celebration of the Sandinista victory, capturing national and international attention. They wore black T-shirts with hand-painted pink triangles, symbolic of gay pride internationally. Although the FSLN initially clamped down on gay organizing, this public appearance of activists, who were both Sandinista and gay, marked the beginning of a more open and outspoken movement along with a more tolerant public reception.

The Sandinista loss in the 1990 election signaled the entry of a centrist government eager to reclaim U.S. support, peacetime relations, and an end to the economic embargo. The consequent neoliberal climate favored the return of some Nicaraguans who had left the country during the years of revolutionary government. Among these were a number of gay "Miami boys" who established businesses that included gay-friendly bars and cultural venues. At the same time, Nicaraguan and internationalist activists began establishing NGOs to meet needs the state was no longer willing or able to address. Whereas the Sandinista Health Ministry was by the end of the 1980s promoting AIDS education and making condoms widely available, such proactive services became the providence of NGOs in the subsequent decade. Centers operated by lesbian and gay activists, often feminist in orientation, provided not only services but also a base for a gay community to form.

Not coincidentally, the NGOs were catalyzing agents for the first Gay Pride celebrations in the country. The year 1991 marked the separation of many feminists from the Nicaraguan Women's Association (AMNLAE) and also the first public Gay Pride event. Several hundred people, both gay and straight, gathered at a popular cultural center for a film showing of the gay-themed *Torch Song Trilogy* followed by a panel discussion of homosexuality and human rights. The audience responded with passionate testimonies of experiences in family and society, endorsing a call for greater tolerance and understanding. In the years since then, Gay Pride has received more attention, with weeks of activities for its commemoration.

Lesbian and gay activism was galvanized the following year by the reactivation of a draconian sodomy law. The government of Violeta Barrios de Chamorro set out to regulate sexual behavior, sanctioning as "natural" and legal only those sexual practices related to procreation. The law criminalized sexual activity "between persons of the same sex" conducted in a "scandalous way." More than 25 groups joined together to launch the Campaign for a Sexuality Free of Prejudice. Despite years of protest, however, the law remains on the books. Although it is rarely enforced, many believe that the law fuels continuing intolerance.

Throughout the 1990s, gay activism continued to find expression in small groups of individuals and in NGOs, health clinics, and cultural venues. The Central American University offered its first course in sexuality studies, and gay bars and clubs offered space for same-sex individuals to socialize. The NGO Xochiquetzal began publishing the magazine *Fuera del closet* (Out of the Closet) in 1993, which offers a mix of poetry, art and informative articles. Women were often the ones putting a public face on lesbian and gay issues, notably when Mary Bolt González wrote the first book on gay identity in Nicaragua, *Sencillamente diferentes* (Simply Different), published in 1996, focusing on lesbian self-esteem.

Lesbians are certainly prominent in the organized activity of the fledgling movement, but they are far less in evidence in the social spaces that are by and large available to gay men in the larger society. This is not surprising given the continued separation of genders in *la casa* and *la calle* (home and street). The neoliberal turn has presented new opportunities for men, particularly those of the middle class, who have the economic means to enjoy gay bars and other venues. Women, in contrast, are scarce until Gay Pride brings together more diverse crowds for a host of events ranging from academic panels to readings of erotic poetry. Annual gatherings such as a contest to select the Goddess Xochiquetzal are intended to help democratize the social space, but a majority who compete are men in drag. The 2003 competition saw the first woman contestant to enter and win.

The former pastor of the Metropolitan Church, Armando, related to me places where gay men regularly meet in Managua, including bars, movie theaters, house parties and even the Metrocentro Mall, which he called "Metro Gay." In contrast, he said lesbians have few places to meet and socialize, and he described their parties as *fiestas de traje* (potluck dinners). Lesbians themselves frequently cite their family responsibilities, including care of children, and lack of financial resources to enter what they perceive as male spaces. A number of those lesbians working in NGOs also have very full professional lives and close circles of friendship, but little available time to spare. As a result, there is occasional tension between gay men and lesbians over the women's perceived dominance in NGOs and men's perceived advantages as consumers under the new market conditions of globalization.

The transnationalization of lesbian and gay politics and culture is on display in Nicaragua. The adoption of the Gay Pride annual celebration on or around June 28 in honor of the 1969 Stonewall rebellion in New York City as practiced in the United States and other countries is one sign of global connection. Other material, ideological, and linguistic markers also suggest Nicaraguans' desire to affiliate with the international gay movement. Pink triangles, red ribbons, rainbows, and the acronym LGBT—or LGBTT, which not only recognizes lesbians, gay men, bisexuals, and transgendered individuals, but also transvestites—are all in evidence. The tropes of the "closet" and "coming out" are widespread now, as many lesbians and gay men seek greater public visibility.

In contrast to the past, when male same-sex partners were often described as "active" (penetrative) and "passive" (penetrated), with the latter category stigmatized, today the terms used to describe "gays" and "lesbians" are heard more frequently and in a more positive light. Also common is more open discussion of AIDS and human rights, as Nicaraguans participate actively in the global discourse surrounding these issues. On the cultural front, the popular television program, *Sexto sentido* (Sixth Sense), brings a sympathetic gay character to viewers throughout the country. In all these ways, lesbian and gay issues have received growing public attention in recent years. Although not always favorable, this attention contributes to an increasing awareness of sexual diversity among the broader Nicaraguan population.

In a similar way to the women's movement of a decade or two ago, the gay and lesbian movement today reveals how far some nations are willing to go in accommodating cultural difference and extending citizenship rights to all. In Nicaragua, the mass women's movement produced a feminist leadership that became instrumental in charting the direction of lesbian and gay culture and politics. This has been one of the most striking aspects of the nascent movement— the degree to which women have assumed prominent roles through participation in NGOs and social activism. Indeed, to understand contemporary sexual politics in the country, it is crucial to consider women's stake in the course of local and national change. Moreover, the association of Nicaraguan gay politics with transnational currents is most clearly apparent through the involvement of women, as well as men, in a host of projects across Central America and beyond.

During Gay Pride week in 2002, the lesbian-feminist leadership of Xochiquetzal called together 13 lesbians and 13 gay men for a day long meeting held in a lesbian-owned bar. They formed a Managua "cell" in hope of inspiring more cells to organize around the country, which could eventually coalesce into a national movement. Among the advances were agreements to endorse lesbian and gay rights, to support others to "come out" and to move cautiously toward forming alliances internationally. While the initiative to build a national lesbian and gay movement has yet to bear fruit, the event stimulated a good deal of productive discussion. The participants took the collective thinking of the group back to their various individual organizations and put it to practical use.

For now, lesbian and gay groups and NGOs often find that more is gained by creating and claiming ties with international counterparts and movements than by remaining focused at local or national levels. In the face of continued homophobia and internal political differences, identification and solidarity with international groups may be desirable. Furthermore, most organizations depend on international financial support, often from Europe, and funding agencies expect to find programs and services that mirror the activities of their own countries' gay rights movement. As a result, competition over scarce funding is often fierce among feminist and gay organizations. Arguably, the competition for resources among NGOs and other groups substantially impedes the formation of stronger ties of solidarity at the national level. Even those who are the beneficiaries of such international support are often harsh critics of the consequences of the state relinquishing responsibility for many social projects now taken on by NGOs. As Nicaraguan feminist and left intellectual Sofía Montenegro put it, "NGOs are cheap for the state and good for capitalism, but the social movements have become NGO-ized."

While globalization presents opportunities for individuals and social movements to expand sexual expression and sexual rights, neoliberalism has benefited some far more than others as sexual subjects and citizens, particularly men and cultural elites. Women and members of the popular classes in general have experienced diminished possibilities and greater hardship in the post-Sandinista years, even if they have also found new ways of organizing collectively.

The mass mobilization of the population brought about by the Nicaraguan Revolution provided an opportunity for young women and men to explore and redefine their sexuality. During their years in power, the Sandinistas began to provide a space for more open discussion of gender and sexual relations and of personal life and politics, though they were ambivalent about the new desires expressed as a result of those spaces. In the post-Sandinista neoliberal era, the FSLN leadership has faced its own crisis, signaling that there is much left unresolved in Nicaragua's *machista* political culture. Thus it is all the more remarkable that lesbians and gay men in this small Central American nation have been at the forefront in charting a politics of sexuality in Latin America.

PUERTO RICO'S SOCIAL MOVEMENTS: DECOLONIZING STEP-BY-STEP

BY MICHAEL GONZÁLEZ-CRUZ
NACLA Report, November/December 2007

During Puerto Rico's May 2006 fiscal crisis, the people watched as the Estado Libre Asociado (ELA), or U.S. commonwealth government, fell apart as a model of both economic and political development. After the governor shut down most public operations, leaving about 80,000 employees temporarily laid off, the island's congress approved a 7% sales tax that enabled the island government to keep up payments to its bondholders, payments that amount to $3.6 billion annually. The major corporations were left free from contributing to this stabilizing of the ELA's functioning, since in proportional terms, workers in Puerto Rico pay more taxes than the banks, and the colonial constitution obliges the government to pay bondholders before public salaries.

The two Puerto Rican political parties, it became clear, have become little more than brokers, buying and selling influence to the highest bidder. Once voters cast their ballots, they don't return to participate in the party organization and are uninvolved in defining the party's goals and agenda. These colonial parties pursue only their narrow interests, acting as service providers to the great private banking, real estate, and insurance interests, and keeping Wall Street ratings agencies like Moody's and Standard & Poor's happy.

Unions have been little better at representing popular interests. During the crisis, the labor movement split into three camps, including unions co-opted by the colonial regime that supported the sales tax; independent progressive unions like the Federation of Teachers and others, that demanded a tax on capital, both island-based and foreign; and public sector unions under the AFL-CIO that opposed the tax but remained largely immobile as spectators during mass actions.

With the crisis, the working class, especially the public sector, was confronted with three questions: How viable is the ELA, since it depends on foreign investment? Will unions play a role as the true workers' representatives or continue to act merely as intermediaries for the employer state? And what kind of organization is necessary to push for popular demands?

The words of Filiberto Ojeda Ríos, leader of the clandestine Ejercito Popular Boricua–Macheteros, inspired many on this issue. In August 2005, a month before FBI snipers killed him, Ojeda predicted in his last radio interview that Puerto Rico would face an inflationary crisis, and that the parties would not only protect their narrow interests but even take advantage of the opportunity afforded by the crisis, as indeed they did: Along with the sales tax, Governor Vilá's proposals included privatizing certain dimensions of the Education Department, as well as electricity, water, and other basic services.[1]

When Ojeda died—on September 23, the 137th anniversary of the legendary rebellion against Spanish rule known as El Grito de Lares—he had spent 15 years hiding from U.S. authorities after being convicted for participating in a 1983 armed bank robbery. For many young pro-independence activists in Puerto Rico and the diaspora, his death amounted to a targeted assassination, and he quickly became a potent national icon, especially as the colonial fiscal crisis wracked Puerto Rico nine months after his death.

Not since the late 1990s has there been as strong a popular decolonizing sentiment in Puerto Rico. The most important precedents, in which many of today's young activists cut their teeth, were struggles that gave way to popular victories: the clemency granted to 12 of 15 Puerto Rican political prisoners and prisoners of war, and the withdrawal of the U.S. Navy from the island municipality of Vieques.

A week before President Clinton pardoned the prisoners in 1999, about 100,000 Puerto Ricans marched in the rain from the Barrio Obrero in Santurce to San Juan, where they gathered at the Federal Courthouse, many of them holding signs with images of the prisoners. Nationalist militants from a previous generation like Rafael Cancel Miranda and Lolita Lebrón (who participated in the legendary 1954 attack on the U.S. Congress and was later pardoned by President Carter) were present, along with the leadership of the Puerto Rican Independence Party, Illinois congressman Luis Gutiérrez, Aníbal Acevedo Vilá (now governor, elected in 2004), and an ecumenical religious contingent.

Clinton's pardon brought international attention to almost 15 years of work done by the National Committee for the Liberation of the Political Prisoners and Prisoners of War, headquartered in Chicago, and the educational campaign of the Unitary Committee Against Repression, as well as the groups Ofensiva 92 and the Comité Pro Derechos Humanos in San Juan. The prisoners' release proved that when progressive, pro-independence forces unite, the movement for national liberation can advance.

The political work to liberate the prisoners grew during the struggle against the U.S. Navy. For many, Vieques (76% of whose land was appropriated by the Navy in 1941) encapsulated the problem of Puerto Rico's colonial status. It had been a site of conflict before, first when the residents who lost their land and were harassed by the troops launched their own struggle, and again in the late 1970s, when independence organizations joined the Vieques community and attempted to break the military perimeter. In 1979, the nationalist activist Ángel Rodríguez Cristóbal died in a Florida federal prison after the U.S. Military Police arrested him along with other socialist, religious, and community activists on a Vieques beach.

But it was the death in 1999 of David Sanes, a young man accidentally killed in a U.S. bombing exercise, that united the progressive forces in Vieques. In addition to this kind of bombing exercise, the Navy also used artillery coated with depleted uranium, which contaminated the island's flora and marine life. After the young man's death, the Comité Pro Rescate y Desarrollo de Vieques, led by the teacher Ismael Guadalupe, began a campaign that gained the support of many Puerto Ricans both within and beyond the island. By the end of April 2000, about 500 demonstrators had occupied the Vieques military zone, among them unionists, clergy, and students. Before the eyes of the international press, the FBI invaded the camps on March 4 on the orders of admiral Kevin Green, arresting hundreds of nonviolent activists. After the arrests, thousands of activists continued to sporadically interrupt military maneuvers in the firing range, and in total some 2,000 people were arrested during this Grito de Vieques.

As a result of these efforts of the social movements, President Bush closed the training camp. The freeing of the prisoners in 1999 and the triumph of the battle of Vieques in 2003 demonstrated that the Puerto Rican national liberation movement still continues its struggle. The 2005 assassination of Ojeda and the fiscal crisis that followed forced the movement to continue innovating and to expand its terrain.

EDUCATION FOR LIBERATION

During the Vieques struggle, the activist-attorney Alberto Marquéz noted, "The use and abuse of repressive forces create great indignation among sectors that at first were uncommitted to that struggle. Imagine, for example, young people, not pro-independence, but whose daily bread consists of violence, the violence of the ghetto, of the *caserío* (housing project), drug violence, police violence, persecution, they see the TV footage of repression against those who peacefully protest. Well, look, they identify, they identify."

This sentiment reflects much of the post-Vieques organizing, which has been centered among students. In his final interview, Ojeda had expressed a similar idea. Because neither the colonial political parties nor the unions are capable of mobilizing the poor and working classes, Puerto Rico's independence movement needed to focus its efforts on organizing them, instead of working narrowly on the status issue. "An educational movement must be forged to promote independence," he said.[2]

In mid-2005, after reflecting on the history of the Puerto Rican independence movement, a group of students and professors at the University of Puerto Rico concluded that the most urgent task in advancing decolonization consists in popular education. Their initiative, La Nueva Escuela (the New School, lne.alternativalne. org), focuses on educating both children and adults in communities that the colonial regime has impoverished and marginalized for more than a century. Offering a bank of talent, from sociologists, psychologists, and social workers to lawyers, teachers, and students, Nueva Escuela attempts to help communities challenge the power of the privileged classes and colonial authorities. "In the face of anxiety and cynicism that the government officials, the major media, and traditional, oppressive education, La Nueva Escuela rises as an alternative of hope and struggle," says the group's invitation to its June National Assembly, held in Santurce.

Nueva Escuela began by publishing a magazine called *AlterNativa*. The first edition, which explains Ojeda's political vision and denounces the FBI's repressive campaign, sold out in a month. The subsequent two issues covered various subjects, including the economy, alternative media, human rights, community work, and the environment. But the real heart of Nueva Escuela's initiative has been holding public educational events and establishing committees throughout urban communities, including public housing projects in San Juan, Mayagüez, Guánica, and Toa Baja, as well as rural communities.

Its major priority has been to develop a campaign in response to a policy instituted in 1993 under Governor Pedro Rosselló known as *mano dura contra el crimen* (iron fist against crime). This policy obliged the Puerto Rican National Guard to join the state police in raids on public housing projects, giving way to a series of operations, most infamously the 1996 Operation Centurion, which practically amounted to the military occupation of 76 of Puerto Rico's 329 public housing complexes. The authorities used helicopters, heavy arms, and armored vehicles to round up residents and take up positions in all the communities, laying siege to poor, marginal communities and systematically violating their human rights.

In October 2006, Ramón Torres, an activist from the Candelaria housing project in Mayagüez, invited Nueva Escuela to advise the community on citizens' rights, after a series of raids in which security forces physically, emotionally, and verbally abused residents, searching them and their belongings, vehicles, and homes without court approval. They even strip-searched women and children in public. Moreover, the indiscriminate nighttime use of tear gas in buildings had also terrorized children and the elderly, many of whom now suffer from respiratory disease.

Considering the gravity of the situation, Nueva Escuela developed a complete educational plan that included talks by a volunteer lawyer on civil rights and workshops for youth and children on how to confront illegal police actions. This had the objective of forcing the FBI and other colonial agencies to respect the civil and human rights of all the citizens of Puerto Rico, wherever they may live. Nueva

Escuela promoted the organization of Candelaria Pa'lante, a residents' collective that fights for their rights with the support of the Puerto Rican Independence Party and a local legal clinic.

Nueva Escuela's attention thus focuses on communities' immediate needs, which are always connected to Puerto Rico's colonial reality. Beyond this, the thematic axes of the educational-organizing campaign have included national liberation and decolonization, developing a sustainable economy, human rights, alternative media, popular education, and community organizing. Among the most frequent activities are community movies, theater workshops, and summer camps, educating for a new *patria*. Nueva Escuela additionally offers political-training camps for youth, who participate in workshops and seminars, while also enjoying the beauty of their island's natural environment.

Recovering historical memory has also been a major part of the group's activity. In October 2006, Nueva Escuela published a document on the 1950 Nationalist insurrection led by Pedro Albizu Campos in Mayagüez, in which a group of combatants confronted the police and were chased into Barrio Dulces Labios, a poor, urban community, where they were overwhelmed. The youth of Nueva Escuela went knocking on doors in Dulces Labios, sharing this history with the residents and inviting them to commemorate their community's heroes. During the weekend, a hundred residents came together with Nueva Escuela to listen to Ezequiel Lugo, a veteran of the insurrection, tell of the fight against the police at the corner of Calle San Juan and Echagüe.

Another resident shared his memories, telling of Dominga Cruz, a woman from Dulces Labios who survived the Ponce massacre of 1937, in which the colonial police killed about 20 unarmed Nationalists. Following this exchange, the community organized an event dedicated to women revolutionaries. About 300 residents participated in this "Rumba Pa' Dominga." As pro-independence literature circulated, they offered their memories of Cruz and promised to keep up the struggle. In this way, Nueva Escuela unites the community, recovering its values and promoting popular organization on the margins of the colonial political system. Nueva Escuela now has a small house that serves as its work center in Barrio Dulces Labios, where workshops on history and culture, as well as social services, are offered.

The collective has also developed work in the Residencial Manuel A. Pérez in San Juan. In this public housing complex, residents and fine arts students from the University of Puerto Rico painted a three-story-high mural depicting Ojeda Ríos. The piece denounces the injustices of the classist, racist penal system, linking the class struggle to that of national liberation. The Public Housing administration threatened to censor the mural, and José Tito Román, a resident of the community and student leader, invited Nueva Escuela to offer a talk on the revolutionary vision and mission of Ojeda and the Macheteros. Nueva Escuela and the Youth of 98, a guerrilla theater group, brought the community together using reggaeton music, videos, and a presentation by Ojeda's widow on the Machetero leader's political thought. Out of this event, the Manuela Pérez Collective was organized, through which the community defends its freedom of expression, and aims to improve its quality of life.

After developing this organizing effort, repression against the community and Nueva Escuela grew, and both have appealed to the courts to defend their rights. For the moment, they have successfully defended the mural of Ojeda and another titled *Being Poor Is Not a Crime*, which also denounces police brutality. In September 2006, the lawyer Carlos Torres, a member of the Nueva Escuela collective, was threatened while he was on his way to court in Bayamón, and in August 2007 Roberto Viqueira, a marine biologist, was arrested and illegally searched as he was conducting research in the Bosque Seco (dry forest) of Guánica. Other Nueva Escuela members have been harassed by the FBI, but because some of them are public workers, they are reluctant to denounce the FBI's intimidation. For this reason, the collective does not disclose the exact number of its members or their identities.

But Nueva Escuela's most salient accomplishment has been the creation of a democratically organized collective linked to poor and working communities. While stagnation and division remain the rule among the political parties and the unions, this kind of issues-based educational organizing may be the key to revitalizing the independence movement in the 21st century.

NOTES

1. José Elías Torres, ed., *Filiberto Ojeda Ríos: su propuesta, su visión* (San Juan: Editorial Callejón, 2006).
2. The entire interview was broadcast by WPAB 550 in Ponce, Puerto Rico. For more information, see Ibid.

CHAPTER 6
MIGRATION

THE MIGRANTS WILL BE HEARD: A CONVERSATION WITH RUBÉN MARTÍNEZ

BY DEIDRE MCFADYEN
NACLA Report, March/April 2007

A Los Angeles native of Mexican and Salvadoran descent, Rubén Martínez is one of the United States' most trenchant writers on immigration and the migrant experience. His books, including *Crossing Over: A Mexican Family on the Migrant Trail* (2002); *The New Americans* (2004), a companion volume to the PBS series of the same name; and *The Other Side: Notes From the New LA, Mexico City and Beyond* (1992), combine essay and reportage on migrant life. He is at work on a new book, *American Monsoon: The New War for the West.* Martínez is an associate editor at Pacific News Service and a professor of literature and writing at Loyola Marymount University in Los Angeles. He has appeared as a guest commentator and essayist on *Frontline, Nightline,* and *All Things Considered.* His honors include a Freedom of Information Award from the ACLU, a Greater Press Club of Los Angeles Award of Excellence and an Emmy for hosting the PBS series *Life & Times.* On the occasion of NACLA's 40th anniversary, Deidre McFadyen spoke with Martínez about the resurgent immigrant rights movement.

Do you think that the mass demonstrations and actions in 2006 have sparked a new "civil rights movement" around immigrant rights?

The migrant marches were undoubtedly historic and unprecedented. Although there have been sporadic incidents of undocumented immigrants organizing to defend, or in this case to expand, their rights, it had never, never been on this scale. The movement was beautifully organic, catapulting past the traditional leadership—faith-based immigrants' rights advocates, some progressives in labor—which always had its heart in the right place but had not done well in the awkward task of being the "voice of the voiceless" (an unfortunately patronizing mainstay of the American left).

What do you say to those who compare the immigrant rights movement to the civil rights movements of the 1950s and 1960s? Is that a fair comparison?

Comparisons to the civil rights movement were made by some in the media and by some self-serving, self-appointed "leaders" who grabbed the microphones in the chaos of the moment. The comparison is superficial, and I think insulting to the memory, and ongoing energy of, the actual civil rights movement, a fundamental progressive American narrative that will not, and should not, be displaced. Simply, African Americans in the Jim Crow South and Latin American immigrants scattered across the country today have fundamentally different experiences. No matter how bad conditions can get for undocumented workers, they are not chattel, period. This new movement is possible to an extent because of the example of what came before, but it flows from a different social and economic model—globalization—and at least for the moment the imagined and implied goals are specific to immigrant laborers. It remains to be seen if this community can imagine a narrative that speaks beyond itself, like the civil rights movement did in the mid-1960s.

While immigrants and advocates from many ethnic and racial backgrounds have participated, the immigrant rights movement has been viewed as mostly a Latino (largely Mexican) movement. How do you see the role of Mexicans within this movement? Will this movement lead to greater political power for Latinos in the United States? Is there a rift between African Americans and Latinos around this issue that needs to be addressed by both sectors?

You're pointing to the real problems exposed by the mass demonstrations—contradictions that were invisible when the immigrant communities were, well, invisible. So the movement is beautifully organic, and organically troubled. The fact that the movement is by and large understood as a Mexican phenomenon is practically unavoidable because of sheer demographics—the vast majority of immigrants from Latin America living here are from Mexico, casting a long shadow over the nevertheless substantial numbers of Central Americans (most of whom are from El Salvador and Guatemala).

So Mexicans play a de facto hegemonic role and are seemingly aware of their position in that they're always reminding us of their Mexican-ness. That red-green-white flag has been fairly ubiquitous. It was also over a decade ago during the precursor to this year's movement, the marches against then governor Pete Wilson and the anti-immigrant ballot initiative he supported. Then as well as now, it was something of a political liability, although in the end, save for hardcore nativist activists and their brethren at Fox and Lou Dobbs at CNN, the reception to the marches was largely sympathetic. That is, except in one important regard: The marches have certainly not helped deal with long-simmering tensions between black and brown in America. Those tensions are a daily fact of life here in Los Angeles, where competition between the communities exists in virtually every public realm—municipal politics, the labor economy, the housing market, street gangs, the prison system, public schools. Mexicans have not helped their cause, and have not furthered better relations with African Americans, with their nationalist posturing, which can be understood as a simple defensive reaction to nativist racism.

This is a very young movement. This is a movement led by people who were long ignored in our public life and then suddenly thrust into it by the nativist reaction. I don't think many immigrants imagined themselves as having much in common with any particular group in America. But now that this community has "come out"—in a way it was first "outed" by the nativists and then outed itself in the marches—it must begin the process of imagining itself not on the margins but at the center. In places like Los Angeles, that is precisely where immigrants are.

What would it mean for the movement to imagine itself at the center? What sort of shared vision can you see the movement promoting?

I'm referring not just to demographics but to social and cultural and even political position. In the end, the nativist reaction came too late; what the Minutemen seek, mass deportation, is largely impossible because it cannot be done without measures that most Americans would not abide. Immigrants are at the center of our lives in symbolic and literal ways. The fact that the typical middle-class urban family with two working parents is likely to have a Mexican or Central American woman spending more time with the children than the parents do—that is an economic relationship, a relationship of power and also one of incredible intimacy. Media are becoming more and more Hispanicized. Top radio markets in many urban centers conduct their business in Spanish. (That was very much on display during the marches last spring; without the enormously popular drive-time Spanish-language DJs who called people out from the shadows, there would not have been a mass movement.) Urban space is being realigned according to the culture and economy of the newcomers. Just as the European immigrants of the late 19th and early 20th centuries made their Little Italys and Little Warsaws, so today we have a tremendously energetic, and entrepreneurial, street life. There is even a growing presence on network primetime TV, a space that has only recently begun to tentatively welcome the color brown. The concept behind the comedy hit *Ugly Betty* is a translation of a Colombian *telenovela*. Last year, Matt Santos, a Mexican American character played by Jimmy Smits, won the presidential election just as *The West Wing* wrapped up. In real life, Antonio Villaraigosa, the favorite son of East Los Angeles, the most mythologized Latino barrio in the country, was elected mayor of the second-largest city in the country, and there is talk that he might become the first viable Latino presidential candidate in our history.

Across the country, in cities and small towns, immigrant and native breach the gap imagined by those who insist on using difference to divide. "Mixed race" relationships, and the children that result from them, are on the rise. America will change the immigrant. The immigrant will change America. Forget the ludicrous rhetoric of *reconquista*—this is a profound, sublime process. America has undergone it before, and it is again.

Would you say more about how immigrants inhabit the center in Los Angeles?

I have returned to my hometown of Los Angeles after nearly a decade away, and it is a model in many ways of the immigrant city that is taking its first real steps to integrate its immigrants. The labor movement is more powerful here today than perhaps at any other time in the city's history, making real-world gains like living wages for workers in the immigrant-heavy service sector. The local school district has gone on a building spree, finally dealing with the gross overcrowding of immigrant classrooms. There are communities across the country taking such steps.

I think in the end there are more communities moving in a progressive direction than places like Hazelton, Pennsylvania, which enacted astoundingly aggressive immigration legislation. The progressive story isn't as sexy as the nativist one, sadly, which is why we've heard so much more about the Minutemen hunting migrants than we have about the Samaritan groups that have been in the desert much longer and offer succor to those same migrants. The headlines just don't correspond to the reality in our communities.

While the draconian Sensenbrenner bill stalled, not only did broader immigration reform fail—the only piece of legislation to pass the Congress in 2006 was to extend the border wall—but in places like Arizona, Georgia, and Texas, we see efforts to strip whatever basic rights that immigrants and their American-born children now have. What are the prospects for comprehensive immigration reform (i.e., legalization, worker rights, family reunification, and backlog reduction) with the new Congress?

The 2006 midterm election is cause for cautious optimism for immigrants' rights—it basically stopped nativist momentum in its tracks. But it hasn't rolled back any of the federal, state, and local legislation, some of it extraordinarily vicious (and patently unconstitutional, such as turning landlords into immigration agents).

I say "cause for cautious optimism" because the fact that Congress is in Democratic hands does not automatically augur any amelioration. It was, after all, the Democratic Party that brought us the building blocks of today's wall—Operation Gatekeeper and other operations that built insurmountable barriers at various high-density crossing points on the line that essentially pushed migrants onto deadly paths in the Southwestern deserts.

At this point, the movement needs to move away from responding to the nativists to pushing their natural liberal and progressive allies, who now have a modicum of power.

What role do you see unions playing in the efforts to win legalization for millions

of undocumented workers?

Whatever gains the unions have made in the last couple of decades is directly attributable to immigrants, documented and not, energizing the rank and file, much as labor was fueled by an earlier wave of European immigrants in the early 1900s. And it is in the labor movement that immigrants have their best opportunity to speak to the broadest possible constituency, bypassing the culture wars altogether and tackling that most prickly of issues in American politics—class. The nationalist imaginary I referred to earlier is partly responsible for keeping immigrants from fully regarding themselves as capable of leadership beyond their own ranks, but there is a tremendous opportunity for a revived labor movement to provide leadership in the vacuum created by globalization. Through labor, immigrants could finally reach out to communities that should be allies—working-class folks of every color.

Should unions accept a guest-worker program to deal with future flows of immigrants once legalization happens, or should they draw the line on this issue and reject temporary worker visas?

It's a conundrum. Realpolitik would seem to dictate that guest worker is a necessary step to affording some kind of rational program to the cross-border situation, given the much nastier possibilities out there. On the other hand, the old arguments about how guest workers harm "native" workers remain relevant—globalization thrives on displacing workers. But what if labor took cross-border organizing more seriously, gave some real meaning to all those unions that have "international" in their names? Shouldn't labor be helping frame the debate, rather than fumbling around for the lesser evils?

What is your reading of the diversity and cleavages in the "pro-immigration reform" camp? And the cleavages in the movement itself, particularly those that surfaced between the March mobilization (which had the support of a broad coalition that included the Catholic Church, the National Council of La Raza [NCLR], Antonio Villaraigosa and other Democrats) and the May 1 demonstrations (which many sectors linked to the Democratic Party refused to endorse, and in which the left wing of the movement had a much more central role)?

Above all, this was a grassroots movement. Activists of all stripes like to invoke that cliché, of course, but this is one of the few cases that merits the moniker. And it was a long time in the making. The idea of this kind of mobilization—unique in that the undocumented represented themselves—had been around for years. I remember sitting in a Mexican bar on Whittier Boulevard in East Los Angeles sometime around

1991 and hearing a crew of day laborers talk about what would happen if all the *mojados* (wetbacks) got together and walked off their jobs. Music groups like Los Tigres del Norte had imagined such in their *corridos* as well.

And this movement occurred at the grass roots because, frankly, the leadership had utterly failed. Latino elected officials were among the least likely to approach the issue, seeing it as certain political death. The handful of progressive activists who stuck by the migrants were just too marginal to draw more than occasional attention to the issue (and failed to strike upon a media-savvy strategy like that of the Minutemen). It's true that Cardinal Roger Mahony (leader of the immigrant-heavy, largest Catholic parish in the country) made an impassioned statement at the beginning of the year basically saying the church would conduct massive civil disobedience. But if Mahony had really wanted to be a leader on the issue, he would have made the statement years ago.

Once the massive marches began—we must remember that the numbers that turned out were due mostly to Spanish-language popular media—the leadership scrambled to take credit for and to direct the movement. I think both the mainstream players (the church, unions, Villaraigosa, the NCLR, etc.) and the more left-wing elements were equally distant from the millions on the streets. The day laborer from Jalisco, the nanny from Guatemala City—had the NCLR or Refuse & Resist ever reached out to them before? I don't think the split between the center and the left of the political class means much in the end. What counts is the will of the migrants to continue to represent themselves, and the role of Spanish-language popular media in organizing them.

What about the diversity and divisions within the "anti-immigrant" movement, which includes some within the "fair trade" camp? After all, many pro-labor Democrats voted for the wall and stepped-up border enforcement, arguing that they were protecting the U.S. working class.

I hate to sound dogmatic and schematic here, but for me there is a clear ethical border on this issue, and I can't differentiate between a "green" paranoid about population growth and some nauseating "populist" Democrat. Of course there are issues to discuss in terms of the impact of migrants on wages, and the possible displacement of workers in some sectors of the economy. But the border is deadly, period. It's an immoral, hypocritical line. For me that is the primordial issue, and any discussion that doesn't deal with the bodies of the dead is also immoral and hypocritical.

That said, many of those stirred by the Minutemen are decidedly working-class, and it is fairly obvious that their passion is essentially class-based (and unfortunately marinated in traditional borderlands racism). It would be wonderful if labor could find a way to help cross the border between working-class whites and their migrant brethren. But there are less and less working-class whites in labor these days. The only institution that could possibly help bridge the divide is evangelical Christianity (the one space where migrants and working-class whites have something in common!), but the leadership there remained utterly silent on the issue—they couldn't deal with the obvious contradiction of a Bible full of rhetoric about "welcoming the stranger" on the one hand and arch-conservative neo-Christian attitudes on the other. So it doesn't look like that dream coalition will arrive anytime soon.

But it might not have to. The alliance between working-class migrants and middle-class liberals and elements from the right wing, including George W. Bush himself, looks like it might suffice for some movement on the issue—some basic reform package before 2008. How good or bad that legislation is will depend on many factors, but one thing is clear: The migrants will be heard. For the first time, they are truly a part of the debate.

The immigrant rights movement leapt on the political stage with those massive nationwide rallies in the spring of 2006, but the rallies called since then have drawn far fewer participants. What will it take for the movement to sustain its momentum?

I think the movement stumbled on its own success. The massive turnouts stunned everyone, including the migrants themselves, and it was difficult for anyone to imagine exactly what direction the movement was supposed to take—prolonged work stoppages, focus on electoral and legislative politics, César Chávez–style performances, simply continue marching, etc. The hesitation was understandable; this is a juridically vulnerable population, after all, and tactics like civil disobedience suddenly become a complicated choice. It also appears that ultimately the consensus was to pull the punch and allow mainstream liberal political forces to do their job of organizing in an election year. Lord knows there were people in Democratic leadership circles worried about repercussions at the polls if the movement took any missteps (such as violence at a march) or just wore on people's nerves. Now the question is whether or not the Democratic Party can exercise true political leadership on the issue and enact meaningful reform.

Federal immigration officials raided six plants owned by Swift & Company, the world's second-largest beef and pork processor on December 12, 2006. Nearly 1,300 people—almost 10% of Swift's workforce—were hauled off. What is the significance of this raid? If raids on this scale continue, will they weaken the movement or invigorate it?

Here it appears that the Bush administration is pushing in different directions simultaneously: sending a message to labor that it should sign on fully to a guest-worker initiative on the one hand, and throwing some red meat to the nativists on the other. The symbolism of the act was terrible in the migrant community, by the way: December 12 is one of the holiest days of the year for Latin American Catholics, the Virgin of Guadalupe's feast day. I would be surprised if there were many more of these massive raids, but it was a particularly vulgar act. If raids of this sort indeed were to continue, there'd soon be chaos in the migrant communities, and I think it's impossible to predict how the movement would respond to such an extreme scenario. The most obvious radical tactic would be for citizens to serve as shields for noncitizens.

But in terms of the balance sheet, 2006 was largely positive in terms of immigration politics. The marches will go into the history books as a unique moment in the life of the "foreigner" in America. They were the culmination of a long social and political process, one that will come to be seen undoubtedly as a watershed like the earlier great waves of migration in the mid-19th and early-20th centuries.

I really do think much of the reaction to the immigrant is a delayed response—part of the "native" population has been startled awake to realize that a momentous change is taking place, and the response is clearly one of fear. It is fear we hear on AM talk radio and in the racist screeds of writers like Samuel Huntington. And fear, of course, can be a dangerous thing. By contrast, in the migrant communities there is ambition and hope. People weren't looking over their shoulders for the *migra* at the marches. They felt secure in the rightness of the cause and in the strength of their numbers, and they felt secure that they had a right to protest, whether they had papers or not. Perhaps they felt, for the first time, truly American.

DREAMS AND BORDERS: LOOKING AT IMMIGRATION FROM THE MEXICAN SIDE

BY CHRIS TILLY AND MARIE KENNEDY
Dollars & Sense, January/February 2007

The raid came on a Friday night. Law enforcement officials swooped down on hundreds of undocumented immigrants who had not made it far past the border. That's when "the American dream," as so many migrants call it without irony, ended for over 100 of them who were detained, some hospitalized with major injuries. It was the third major raid on migrants in this location in a month's time.

"Everybody was running as fast as they could because the authorities were hitting them to force them to climb onto the pickup trucks," reported Teresa García, one of the ones who ended up in the hospital. "I slipped and fell; people were stepping on me and then I lost consciousness." One woman, she added, "was pregnant, maybe five months, and I was able to see them pulling her and hitting her to arrest her. It was very violent, there was a lot of yelling."

This sounds like an all too familiar experience for Mexicans trying to cross into Arizona, California, or Texas. Except this raid did not take place in any of those states, but in Mexico's southernmost state of Chiapas. And those detained were not Mexicans, but Guatemalans, Hondurans, Salvadorans, Nicaraguans, and one Cuban.

Welcome to Mexico's other immigration problem. In the words of Isabel Vericat, a filmmaker working on a documentary spotlighting illegal immigration across Mexico's southern border, "The northern border of Mexico begins in the south." An estimated 350,000 undocumented immigrants—a majority Central American, but also including many from South America—crossed from Guatemala and Belize in 2005. They came not to seek a living in Mexico's sputtering economy, but to find a way to *el norte*. Of the 350,000, it is estimated that about 40,000 made it to their objective. Another 10,000 ended up staying in Mexico. The rest were detained and deported.

Between Mexico's northern border problem and its southern border problem, the country is caught in a difficult squeeze. The government of Felipe Calderón complains that its U.S. counterpart does not sufficiently take into account the needs nor respect the human rights of Mexican immigrants. But at the same time, Mexican authorities are implicated in brutal repression against migrants from farther south—at the behest of the U.S. government.

SURVIVAL STRATEGY

The number of Mexican-born people (documented and undocumented) in the United States is estimated at over 11 million, with about half a million crossing each year. The Banco de México (Mexico's central bank) claims that the real numbers are substantially higher than these official statistics, citing as evidence the fact that the population in a number of Mexican states has stopped growing despite no drop in the birth rate.

Migration's impact on communities, particularly declining rural ones, is enormous. The family saga of our friend Angelina, a market woman in Michoacán's capital city of Morelia who lives in an agricultural town about one hour to the north, offers a window into that impact. Her aging father has gone to *el otro lado* repeatedly to work in agriculture, injuring himself on the job there in 2004. Her husband was crippled there in a car accident. One sister crossed illegally, only to be deported. Four other siblings are working in Texas and Rhode Island. Her son just went to join relatives in Ohio and do *yarda work*, Spanglish for landscaping. Millions of families across Mexico have similar stories.

Border wall or not, immigration reform or not, nobody in Mexico expects this to change soon. (The only noticeable changes in recent years have been increasing rates of immigration of women from Mexico's more remote southern states, and of unaccompanied children, many of them looking for their parents.) The Banco de México projected in February that even if Mexico achieves a 5% annual economic growth rate (higher than it has seen since 2000), the pay differential will continue drawing migrants to the north "for two or three decades." Héctor Rangel, the president of the board of Mexican bank BBVA Bancomer, remarked not long afterward that Mexico has been "unable to create the number of jobs necessary to hold on to our population."

NAFTA has been a bust for most Mexicans. The current example of trucking is indicative. In early 2007, with much fanfare, the Mexican government announced that Mexican truck drivers could now haul their loads into the United States. But a couple of weeks into the pilot program, the Mexican trucking association demanded that the agreement be scrapped and a new one negotiated. With long delays at the border plus fines for "safety" infractions, the operators say the current agreement is worthless.

But the problem goes well beyond trucking. Mexico's average wage level is only marginally beyond where it stood in 1994 when NAFTA went into effect, and slow economic growth has driven millions into informal sector jobs, ranging from selling on street corners to sewing in the home. The maquiladora (export assembly) industry grew in the 1990s, but has since shrunk as transnational corporations shifted their sourcing to Central America or China to take advantage of even lower wages. Meanwhile, U.S. agricultural imports such as poultry have swept the Mexican market, putting hundreds of thousands of small producers out of business. The deadline for removing all remaining restrictions on U.S. corn, beans, and wheat—with their low prices thanks to U.S. government subsidies—comes in 2008. Looking ahead with dread, Mexican peasant associations and their allies have called for re-negotiating NAFTA, but the government remains staunchly pro-free-trade. Perhaps the only "bright" spot, according to researcher Huberto Juárez of the Autonomous University of Puebla, is that as Mexican wages stagnate and Chinese wages rise, Mexico's wage levels are becoming cost-competitive with China's in some manufacturing sectors.

In this context, the remittances sent home by Mexico's millions of migrants are vital not only for their families' economic survival, but also for the country's. Migration is Mexico's second largest source of export earnings (in this case, via the export of labor), yielding $24 billion in 2006, second only to petroleum. But like Mexico's oil, which is projected to run out in 20 years or so, remittances can form a deceptive cushion that allows the government to shirk its job-creation responsibilities—temporarily. What's more, the northward flow drains Mexico of human resources that could potentially be put to better use. (A sociologist from the Autonomous University of Zacatecas recently suggested, only half in jest, that if Mexico sends 500,000 migrants to the United States each year, it should seek to bring in an equal number from Central America to keep the economy running.) Raúl Delgado, director of the International Network on Migration and Development, criticizes governments of immigrant-sending countries for relying too heavily on remittances at the expense of carrying out well-rounded development policies "following alternative strategies" and "fighting to transform the asymmetrical and unjust relations that characterize the current global order."

THE SOUTHERN BORDER

If the pay difference is a magnet drawing Mexican migrants, it is an even stronger magnet for people struggling to survive in the poorer Central American countries, which over the last 20 to 30 years have been ravaged by civil wars, hurricanes, free trade, and the global coffee glut. Deals between corrupt border guards and *polleros* (traffickers whom migrants pay to escort them across) make it easy to cross the border itself. But once in southern Mexico, immigrants from Central America or farther south are easy prey for those same polleros and police, along with *maras* (Salvadoran gangs active in the border area), Mexican organized crime, and freelance robbers and con men. Migrants with money can pay to travel north by car or even plane. But most have no choice other than the train.

The train in question starts in Arriaga, Chiapas, 180 miles north of the border. (It began at the border until Hurricane Stan devastated a long stretch of it in 2005.) Migrants must walk for 10 dangerous days to reach Arriaga. If they succeed, they climb onto train cars, holding on any way they can. The rail voyage to the northern border takes another 10 to 12 days.

That's if everything goes right. But usually it doesn't. In the 180-mile gauntlet from the border to Arriaga, in addition to deportation, migrants run the risk of extortion, robbery, assault, rape, and even murder. According to first-hand accounts from migrants collected by filmmaker Vericat, the perpetrators are often the uniformed police who are charged with enforcing immigration law. Thousands of women, mostly young Central American mothers, many under 18, with one or more children to support, have been lured or forced into prostitution in the Soconusco border region of Chiapas when the option of going farther north evaporated. Vericat reports that Soconusco has become the third largest center of prostitution in the world, behind only border regions in Brazil and Thailand.

And getting on the train does not mean they are home free, either. The train ride is exhausting and dangerous. Mounting or dismounting—or falling—from the moving train can cause serious injury or death. Police raids are frequent. The February 10, 2007, raid we described above targeted the train in Arriaga; reportedly there were 500 migrants aboard. In that raid, one woman fell under the train and lost a foot. The travelers must sometimes get off to get food, water, or a little sleep in some place where they don't have to hold on for dear life. Apizaco, in the central state of Tlaxcala where we spent the first half of 2007, marks the halfway point in the journey. The Casa del Migrante in Apizaco, a charitable organization that provides assistance with no questions asked, reports that migrants are often out of money and desperate. Confused, some of them make the tragic error of re-boarding the train heading south instead of north.

And of course, at the U.S. border they face another set of obstacles. Even once on the job in the United States, they are not safe, as we have seen in recent Immigrant and Customs Enforcement actions like the March raid in New Bedford, Massachusetts, that nabbed hundreds of undocumented Central Americans. But many of those who are deported keep trying, again and again.

THE IMMIGRATION DEBATES IN MEXICO

The policy discussion of immigration in Mexico is split. Looking north, everybody agrees that the United States should allow more Mexicans to enter legally and that the border wall is a barbarity. Everybody recognizes the hypocrisy of the wealthy northern neighbor that depends on large numbers of Mexican laborers but insists on selectively enforcing a law that is completely out of step with reality. The only disagreement is between the Calderón administration, which is pressing the Bush administration in the most cautious of ways, and critics who call on the government to stand up more forcefully for opportunities for Mexicans.

The debate about the southern border is much more wide-open. Legislators from the center-to-right PRI and PAN parties, which make up a majority in Congress, have called for stronger sanctions against undocumented immigrants from the south in phrases that could have come from U.S. Republicans. But the government of Calderón (from the PAN) has announced plans to decriminalize illegal immigration (that is, deport them but don't fine them, in order to decrease the incentives for extortion by officials) and to expand legal immigration channels, increasing the number of Guatemalans permitted to enter for agricultural work and issuing visas of up to five years for professional workers. At the same time, they have promised the U.S. government to tighten up the "porous" southern border, by means they have yet to specify. And Mexico's federal agents continue to deal out violent treatment to migrants.

Meanwhile, a chain of Casas del Migrante located at strategic points in the migration from the south, such as Arriaga and Apizaco, offer temporary shelter, food, counseling, and small amounts of cash, defying legal restrictions. And many ordinary Mexicans offer the immigrants from the south a meal or place to sleep. In one highly publicized case, María Concepción, who lives in a community along the south-north train route where it passes through the central state of Querétaro, was recently sentenced to two years in prison for human trafficking after being caught feeding supper to six migrants from Honduras in 2005. The government claimed to have witnesses who testified that Concepción worked for pay with a network of traffickers. Concepción and her family members insist she was just offering charity, and that everybody in the community "would give them a taco or some water," in the words of her daughter. Because they have concluded that for the government "it's a crime even to give them a glass of water, now we don't even give them a glass of water." Still, other communities such as La Patrona in the state of Veracruz— spotlighted in the recent film *De Nadie* (About No One)—still pull together to help passing migrants.

But for most Mexicans, unlike the issue of the northern border, the issue of the southern border remains a bit remote. Arturo, a neighbor of ours in Tlaxcala who runs a laundromat, commented, "Mexico is just a trampoline for the Central Americans, because there's nothing for them here, no jobs." Still, with the growing volume of migrants and increasing media coverage, there is growing consciousness of the human rights issues involved. On a visit to the hospital, Arturo had met a Guatemalan who had fallen under the train in Apizaco. "The police picked him up and beat him. He was at the hospital, under armed guard, and once he was better they were going to deport him. That's not fair, that's a violation of human rights! If the man wants to work, let him try to get a job."

BURNING QUESTIONS

The week leading up to Easter is a time of school vacations and colorful celebrations all across Mexico—not a time when many are thinking about the grim issues of immigration. But the night before Easter we saw the issues flare up—literally—at the 2007 Holy Saturday festivities in San Cristóbal, Chiapas, about 80 miles from Arriaga as the crow flies. Mexico has a Holy Saturday tradition of burning Los Judas, papier-mâché dummies named after Judas, often crammed with fireworks and representing the ills and evils the community would like to purge. San Cristóbal hosts an annual Judas contest. This year the competition was brisk, with two effigies of George W. Bush (one as a rat, the other as a sea monster), two of Calderón, two of environmental pollution and global warming, and two of a grim-reaper-like figure representing abortion (Mexico City's decriminalization of which has appalled conservative Mexicans), among others.

Despite all these potent rivals, the winner was El Muro de la Vergüenza (the Wall of Shame), as Mexicans call the barrier the United States is erecting along the border. Less noticed, however, was an evocative sculpture showing a faceless figure with a club beating down a second faceless figure who was trying to clamber up onto a boxcar. "The plight of the Central American immigrant," said a simple label scrawled in chalk. We watched as they lit up the boxcar. The flames leaped up, the fireworks shot off, but as the fire died down again the crowd could see that the figures and the boxcar were still there. The celebrants tried twice more to relight the Judas, but it stubbornly refused to be consumed, and they finally gave up and moved on to the next one. For Mexico as for the United States, the treatment of migrants from the south will not be an easy Judas to burn.

RESOURCES

Isabel Vericat, "La otra frontera (México-Guatemala)," *La Jornada Semanal* (March 4, 2007); Casas del Migrante–Scalabrini, www.migrante.com.mx; *De Nadie*, www.lasamericas.org/films/Denadie.htm.

IMMIGRANTS AND THE LABOR MARKET: WHAT ARE "THE JOBS AMERICANS WON'T DO"?

BY ESTHER CERVANTES
Dollars & Sense, May/June 2006

Congress and the streets are abuzz with talk of immigration policy reform. Militias patrol the Mexican border under the aegis of national security, and the House decides that helping the undocumented should be a felony. Meanwhile, hundreds of thousands march for amnesty, and contractors tell newspapers that the undocumented are essential to their business. The president proposes a guest-worker program, which senators John McCain (R-Ariz.) and Ted Kennedy (D-Mass.) counter with a version of their own. The labor movement is divided on the issue of guest workers: SEIU backs the idea, while the AFL-CIO does not. It's clear that the economy is the elephant in the room, and it's time to take a good look at the familiar assertion: Undocumented workers do the jobs that Americans won't do.

It's a statement that raises many questions, such as: What are those jobs?

Among non-citizens, Latin Americans differ the most from U.S. citizens in their occupations. They have higher concentrations in production, construction and extraction, building and grounds maintenance, and food preparation and serving, as well as farming, fishing, and forestry. African noncitizens concentrate in health care support and technical occupations, personal care and service, and transportation. This has consequences for wages. In the employed civilian workforce, nearly two thirds of Latin American noncitizens—both documented and undocumented—find themselves in the occupational categories that are in the bottom half, ranked by pay. Compare that to 41.5% of Latinos who were born as U.S. citizens and 35.7% of U.S.-born whites.

The situation is even worse for undocumented workers; the Urban Institute estimates that two thirds earn less than twice the minimum wage, compared to one third of all workers. As a measure of just how low twice the minimum wage is, consider that if one member in a family of three earns twice the minimum wage at a full-time year-round job, the family still qualifies for many government programs for the poor, such as WIC and food stamps.

This gives us an answer to the question, Why won't Americans do those jobs? It's because the jobs don't pay well enough to live on, at least not if you mean to live and raise a family in the United States. But most undocumented

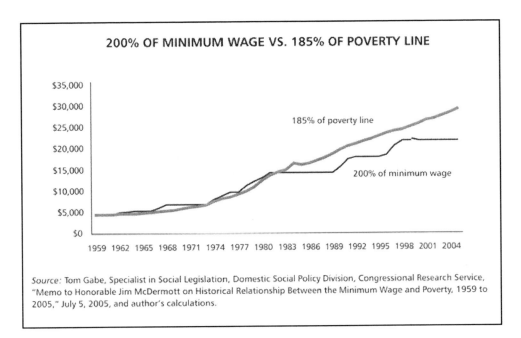

200% OF MINIMUM WAGE VS. 185% OF POVERTY LINE

Source: Tom Gabe, Specialist in Social Legislation, Domestic Social Policy Division, Congressional Research Service, "Memo to Honorable Jim McDermott on Historical Relationship Between the Minimum Wage and Poverty, 1959 to 2005," July 5, 2005, and author's calculations.

workers, especially the Latin Americans who make up about 75% of the undocumented population, don't intend to have an ordinary family life here. The Urban Institute estimates that 59% of the adult undocumented population are men, yielding a male-to-female ratio that would be considered a crisis in any permanent society.

The population pyramids show not only the gender imbalance among noncitizen Latin Americans but also that most of them are of working age, represented by the darker bars. (The population pyramid for the undocumented Latin American population would look much the same as the top right graph, since the Urban Institute's estimates imply that about 90% of noncitizen Latin Americans are undocumented.) The illustration on the following page shows the population pyramid for all Latinos (most of whom are citizens) in the United States, regardless of citizenship status. Perhaps a quarter of the children age 15 and under represented there are U.S. citizens with undocumented parents. The bottom right graph shows that a far greater proportion of noncitizen Latin American men are of working age than are their white, U.S.-born counterparts. According to the Urban Institute, undocumented Latin American men have a labor force participation rate of 96%, while according to the Bureau of Labor Statistics (BLS), the rate among white men is 76%.

Since it appears that most undocumented workers have one foot out the door, another good question presents itself: What can the jobs that Americans

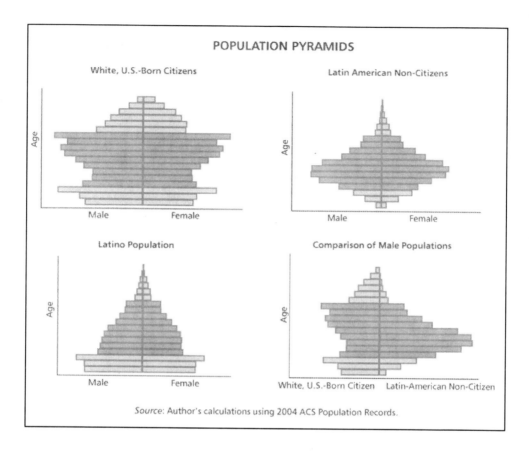

POPULATION PYRAMIDS

White, U.S.-Born Citizens

Latin American Non-Citizens

Latino Population

Comparison of Male Populations

Male   Female

Male   Female

Male   Female

White, U.S.-Born Citizen   Latin-American Non-Citizen

Source: Author's calculations using 2004 ACS Population Records.

won't do buy in undocumented workers' home countries?

According to Habitat for Humanity, it's a lot easier to build a "simple, decent" house on twice the U.S. minimum wage if the house is in Poland, Mexico, the Philippines, or Nigeria than in the United States.

And even near poverty wages in the United States make home ownership more attainable than the $2 or less per day on which 26.3% of Mexicans, 46.4% of Filipinos, and 90.8% of Nigerians live.

Undocumented workers take jobs at the low end of the U.S. wage scale, sometimes falling beneath the official minimum entirely. U.S. citizens won't do these jobs because they don't pay well enough to support a family in the United States. However, the extreme poverty of the undocumented population's home countries lends these low-paying jobs in the United States a certain appeal. Meanwhile, black and Latino U.S. citizens also cluster, though not as tightly, in low-wage occupations, bear more unemployment than whites, and suffer poverty without the undocumented worker's light at the end of the tunnel. How might we make this situation tenable?

Some critics of the various immigration reform proposals complain that policing employers to crack down on undocumented hires would be impractical and expensive. There is, however, an easier, less expensive, and time-tested alternative: unionization.

In this, so far it's the AFL-CIO that's leading the way. SEIU accepted guest worker proposals with the idea that regulating the flow of temporary workers would at least give immigrants the protection of health and safety laws and the right to switch jobs. But AFL-CIO President John Sweeney implied that this doesn't go far enough. "Guest worker programs are a bad idea and harm all workers," he wrote, by encouraging employers to turn good jobs into temporary ones and removing none of the current incentives to exploit foreigners willing to accept low wages and bad conditions. Now the AFL-CIO needs to take a cue from the IWW: "The working class knows no borders or races, but exists wherever workers are exploited for the benefit of capital." Whether as undocumented or guest workers, the poor of other countries will continue to pose problems for workers in more prosperous countries, unless they organize together to solve the problems of poverty, inequality, and exploitation—problems that know no borders.

OCCUPATION BY CITIZENSHIP STATUS & RACE

	Born Citizen			Noncitizen		
	White	Black	Latino	Europe	Africa	Lat. Am.
Mgt, Bus, Fin	15.1	9.5	9.9	15.5	10.3	4.2
Professional	8.4	4.5	5.7	13.2	9.2	2.6
Health Prac & Tech	5.0	3.7	3.2	3.7	7.1	0.7
Edu, Training, Library	7.0	5.9	5.8	7.6	5.2	1.7
Install, Maint, Repair	3.7	2.5	3.4	2.0	2.3	3.4
Const & Extraction	5.6	3.7	5.8	6.5	1.4	16.9
Community & Soc Svc	1.5	2.8	1.9	1.0	2.8	0.4
Protective Svcs	2.0	3.4	2.9	0.6	2.6	0.5
Offce & Admin	15.9	18.3	19.7	11.7	12.1	7.2
Production	6.4	8.9	6.7	7.6	6.0	15.8
Transportation	3.2	4.2	3.1	2.4	6.2	3.1

continued next page

	Born Citizen			Noncitizen		
	White	Black	Latino	Europe	Africa	Lat.Am.
Health Care Support	1.9	4.5	2.9	2.2	7.9	1.4
Sales	12.5	10.1	13.2	10.8	12.6	7.5
Bldg & Grounds Maint	3.0	6.5	4.5	5.0	3.9	14.8
Personal Care & Svc	3.1	4.4	3.8	3.9	5.9	3.2
Farm, Fish, Forest	0.7	0.4	0.7	0.3	0.1	5.2
Food Prep & Serving	4.9	6.5	6.6	6.0	4.5	11.4

Source: Author's calculations using 2004 American Community Survey Population Records (Census Bureau) and November 2004 National Occupational Employment and Wage Estimates (Bureau of Labor Statistics).

Note: Occupations ranked by descending median hourly wage. "Mgt, Bus, Fin" aggregates major Standard Occupational Classifications (SOCs, as defined by the Bureau of Labor Statistics) 11 and 13; "Professional" aggregates 15, 17, 19, 23, and 27; all others are major SOCs.

COST OF HOUSING

	Cost of House	Pct of 2x FT Annual Min Wage
United States	$50,000	233.4%
Poland	$30,500	142.4%
Nigeria	$7,500	35.0%
Mexico	$6,481	30.3%
Philippines	$2,290	10.7%

Source: Habitat for Humanity Annual Report FY2004, Worldwide Ministry; Congressional Research Service Memo to Honorable Jim McDermott on Historical Relationship Between the Minimum Wage and Poverty, 1959 to 2005; and author's calculations.

Note: These are the costs of sponsoring a Habitat house in these countries; actual building costs vary. Mexico, the Philippines, and Nigeria are the countries in their regions that send the most people to the United States. Poland holds that rank among Eastern European countries, though it is fourth in Europe as a whole.

SOURCES

Associated Press, "La reforma migratoria debe tomar en cuenta la economía," *El Planeta* (April 6–12, 2006); Elizabeth Auster, "Guest Worker Proposals Divide America's Unions," *The Cleveland Plain Dealer* (April 6, 2006); U.S. Census Bureau, *2004 American Community Survey Population Records*, available at factfinder.census.gov; U.S. Bureau of Labor Statistics, *National Occupational Employment and Wage Estimates* (November 2004), available at www.bls.gov; Jeffrey Passel, Randy Capps, and Michael Fix, "Undocumented Immigrants: Facts and Figures," Urban Institute Immigration Studies Program (January 12, 2004), available at www.urban.org; Tom Gabe, "Memo to Honorable Jim McDermott on Historical Relationship Between the Minimum Wage and Poverty, 1959 to 2005," Domestic Social Policy Division, Congressional Research Service (July 5, 2005), available at www.chn.org; Bureau of Labor Statistics, "Employment Situation," Table A-2 (April 7, 2006), available at www.bls.gov; Habitat for Humanity, Worldwide Ministry, *Annual Report FY2004*, available at www.habitat.org; United Nations Development Program, "Indicator 3: Human and Income Poverty: Developing Countries; Population Living Below $2 a Day (%)" (2003), available at hdr.undp.org; Mark Schoeff Jr., "Bill Likely to Put Pressure on Firms to Verify Worker Status," *Workforce Management* (April 11, 2006), available at www.workforce.com; Industrial Workers of the World, "May 1st—Defend the Rights of Immigrant Workers" (April 10, 2006), available at www.iww.org.

THE ANTI-IMMIGRATION MOVEMENT: FROM SHOVELS TO SUITS

BY SOLANA LARSEN
NACLA Report, May/June 2007

As millions of immigrants and their supporters took to the streets last year, the anti-immigration movement mobilized its own forces. The number of state and local anti-immigration groups in the United States has exploded, growing by 600% in the last two years. In 2005, there were fewer than 40 groups; today, there are more than 250.[1]

One fourth of the new groups are chapters of the Minutemen Civil Defense Corps (MCDC), the volunteer paramilitary group that patrols the U.S.-Mexico border, builds fences, and notes the license plate numbers of contractors who hire undocumented workers.[2] Its leader, Chris Simcox, has become a national icon, and locally, MCDC members are making their voices heard at protests, council meetings, and courthouses.

Although these armed vigilantes get most of the press, a national network of organizations working to end immigration has existed for decades. Today, 35 such groups, with a collective membership of between 600,000 and 750,000, work in research, advocacy, fundraising, and lobbying to influence state and federal policies.[3] Some of the most salient include the Federation for American Immigration Reform (FAIR), the Center for Immigration Studies (CIS), English First, and NumbersUSA.

Ten groups channeled $4.2 million into anti-immigration lobbying in 2005, and nine political action committees raised $3.4 million for campaigns in 2006. In Congress, the movement's growth is reflected in the Immigration Reform Caucus, which has grown from 16 members in 1999 to more than 90 today.

Not all anti-immigrant groups dedicate themselves solely or specifically to the immigration question. The movement is not unified in the traditional sense; groups promote different policy positions, and no umbrella organization unites them.

Despite their differences, they all advocate restricting legal immigration and deporting undocumented immigrants. These goals are also those of both the Minutemen and white supremacists, and this confluence of interests has made for a troubling alliance: The leadership of each of the major anti-immigrant organizations is linked in some way to hate groups.[4] (See chart at right.)

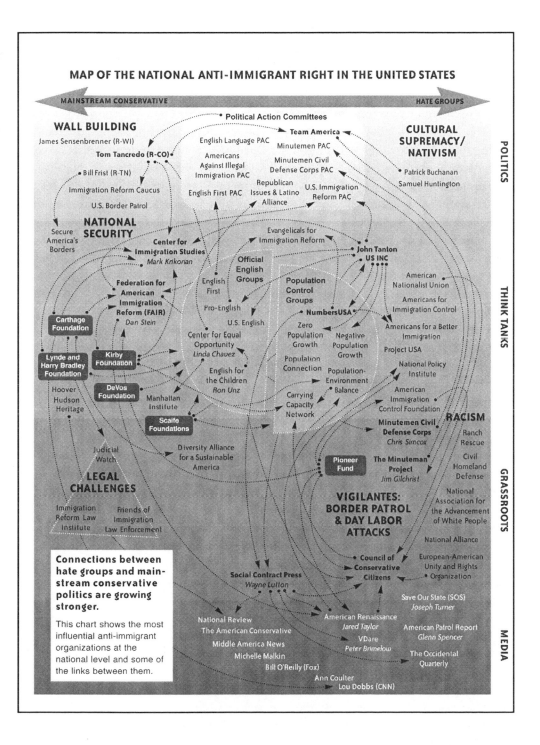

MAP OF THE NATIONAL ANTI-IMMIGRANT RIGHT IN THE UNITED STATES

MAINSTREAM CONSERVATIVE — HATE GROUPS

POLITICS

• Political Action Committees

WALL BUILDING
James Sensenbrenner (R-WI)
Tom Tancredo (R-CO)•
• Bill Frist (R-TN)
Immigration Reform Caucus
U.S. Border Patrol

English Language PAC
Americans
Against Illegal
Immigration PAC
English First PAC

► Team America ◄
Minutemen PAC
Minutemen Civil
Defense Corps PAC
Republican
Issues & Latino
Alliance
U.S. Immigration
Reform PAC

**CULTURAL
SUPREMACY/
NATIVISM**
• Patrick Buchanan
Samuel Huntington

Secure
America's
Borders

**NATIONAL
SECURITY**
**Center for
Immigration Studies**
Mark Krikorian

**Federation for
American
Immigration
Reform (FAIR)**
Dan Stein

**Carthage
Foundation**

**Lynde and
Harry Bradley
Foundation**

**Kirby
Foundation**

Hoover
Hudson
Heritage

**DeVos
Foundation**

Manhattan
Institute

**Scaife
Foundations**

Evangelicals for
Immigration Reform

**Official
English
Groups**
English
First

Pro-English

U.S. English

Center for Equal
Opportunity
Linda Chavez

English for
the Children
Ron Unz

**Population
Control
Groups**

► **NumbersUSA** ◄

Zero
Population
Growth
Population
Connection

Negative
Population
Growth
Population-
Environment
• Balance

Carrying
Capacity
Network

John Tanton
US INC
• • • •

American
Nationalist Union

Americans for
Immigration Control

Americans for a Better
Immigration

Project USA

National Policy
Institute

American
Immigration •
Control Foundation

THINK TANKS

RACISM

**Minutemen Civil
Defense Corps**
Chris Simcox

Ranch
Rescue

Judicial
Watch

**LEGAL
CHALLENGES**

Immigration
Reform Law
Institute

Friends of
Immigration
Law Enforcement

Diversity Alliance
for a Sustainable
America

**Pioneer
Fund**

The Minuteman
Project
Jim Gilchrist

**VIGILANTES:
BORDER PATROL
& DAY LABOR
ATTACKS**

Civil
Homeland
Defense

National
Association for
the Advancement
of White People

National Alliance

GRASSROOTS

**Connections between
hate groups and main-
stream conservative
politics are growing
stronger.**

This chart shows the most
influential anti-immigrant
organizations at the
national level and some of
the links between them.

Social Contract Press
Wayne Lutton

National Review
The American Conservative
Middle America News
Michelle Malkin
Bill O'Reilly (Fox)

American Renaissance
Jared Taylor
VDare
Peter Brimelow

Ann Coulter
► Lou Dobbs (CNN)

► Council of
► Conservative
► Citizens ◄

European-American
Unity and Rights
• Organization

Save Our State (SOS)
Joseph Turner

American Patrol Report
Glenn Spencer

The Occidental
Quarterly

MEDIA

There is more evidence for the connections between the U.S. anti-immigrant movement and organized extremists than there is room to explore in this article.

The Southern Poverty Law Center (SPLC) in Montgomery, Alabama; the Center for New Community (CNC) in Chicago; and the International Relations Center (IRC) in Silver City, New Mexico, compile most of this information, profiling the movement and its leaders and uncovering their links to each other and beyond.

Six anti-immigrant organizations focus on promoting the English language and campaigning against the translation of official documents. Another six deal with population control, arguing that immigration is environmentally and economically detrimental. A few wage legal battles against local government or employers of undocumented immigrants, and others focus on grassroots and vigilante action. Finally, there is the anti-immigrant media, which runs the gamut from fringe to mainstream and includes one book publisher; several magazines, websites, and blogs; and ubiquitous pundits like Pat Buchanan, Ann Coulter, Lou Dobbs, Michelle Malkin, and Bill O'Reilly.

At the far-right end of the spectrum, we find white nationalists, who think nonwhite immigrants threaten Euro-American culture. They include the Council of Conservative Citizens, founded in 1988 by members of the segregationist White Citizen's Council and of the National Alliance, which sells stickers and magnets on its websites that read, "Bring Our Troops Home and Put Them on the Mexican Border!"

"In the past decade, white supremacists have gone from bashing black people to bashing Hispanic people," says Heidi Beirich, the deputy director of the SPLC's Intelligence Project.

Also on the far right, street and border vigilantes, among them the MCDC and the Minuteman Project, barely conceal their hatred of undocumented immigrants and Latinos. (These two grassroots groups began as one in 2005 but quickly split and now continue their work separately.) Their members have been tied to hate groups and stand accused of using excessive force on the border.[5]

At the other end of the anti-immigration spectrum, mainstream think tanks like FAIR and CIS in Washington, D.C., put a respectable face on bigotry. Leaders of both organizations are called in as experts in Congress, they publish reports, and they tend to focus on the broad immigration debate in the media and in Washington. They frame their positions for a mainstream audience, but their records are not squeaky-clean.

FAIR, probably the most influential anti-immigration think tank, was co-founded in 1979 by John Tanton, a retired eye surgeon from Michigan who is linked to more than a dozen other large organizations. He came to the anti-immigration movement through his concern about population growth and the environment. He chaired the population committee of the Sierra Club in 1969, but when he couldn't persuade the group to take an anti-immigrant position, he joined Zero Population Growth, eventually becoming its president. After co-founding FAIR, he went on to establish U.S. English in 1982, CIS in 1985, Social Contract Press in 1990, ProEnglish in 1993, and most recently NumbersUSA in 1996.

Tanton's own views are not so hidden. In 1986 a memo he wrote—in which he wondered, "As Whites see their power and control over their lives declining, will they simply go quietly into the night? Or will there be an explosion?"—was leaked to the press, causing several people (including himself, Walter Cronkite, and Linda Chavez) to leave U.S. English.[6] From 1985 to 1994 Tanton accepted $1.3 million on behalf of FAIR from the Pioneer Fund, a formerly Nazi organization that finances research in eugenics and IQ differences between races.[7] Tanton also shares an office at Social Contract Press with Wayne Lutton, a writer who also sits on the board of the Council of Conservative Citizens and edits the anti-Semitic journal *The Occidental Quarterly*.

FAIR no longer receives money from the Pioneer Fund, but it has never offered to pay back its grants. Much of FAIR's research centers on demonstrating that undocumented immigrants are a menace to society; according to two of its recent studies, undocumented immigrants kill more people in traffic accidents and are far more prone to crime than U.S. citizens.[8]

"FAIR pretend in their literature and lobbying that they are making their case based on economic studies, environmental and social effects, when their conclusions are actually based on ideological elements," says Tom Barry of the International Relations Center.

A recent post on FAIR executive director Dan Stein's blog (www.steinreport.com), "Calif. Medical Authorities Concerned About Immigrant Blood Donors," attracted comments from people scared they would get parasitic diseases from undocumented immigrants. "Consider too the great increase in hepatitis A and B, drug resistant tuberculosis, and leprosy," says one reader. "Think about this the next time you go out to eat at a restaurant that hires illegals that sweat into your soup!"[9]

Although Stein cannot be held responsible for the discussions in his online forum, he showed a remarkable tolerance for white supremacism when, in 2004, he attended a biannual conference sponsored by *American Renaissance* magazine, which according to its website "promotes a variety of white racial positions" and is edited by Jared Taylor, a renowned white nationalist (he also sits on the board of *The Occidental Quarterly*).[10] That same year, Taylor's New Century Foundation received $20,000 from the Pioneer Fund, according to their tax filings. Last year's *American Renaissance* conference attracted such names as David Duke, former leader of the Ku Klux Klan; Dan Roodt, a South African writer who regrets the end of apartheid; and Nick Griffin, chairman of the racist British National Party.[11]

The Center for New Community's director, Devon Burghart, says every national anti-immigrant organization in the United States has ties to hate groups. "I can't think of one [that doesn't]," he says. He adds that CIS is the closest to the mainstream. "But even they were originally spun from FAIR," he says.

That may be the case, but the CIS's anti-immigrant bona fides are clear: In 2004, the group's annual media award went to Lou Dobbs. Congressman Tom Tancredo (R-Colo.)—Capitol Hill's most militant anti-immigrant representative, who has warned that immigrant terrorists "are coming here to kill you and kill me and our families"—gave a speech at the ceremony and presented Dobbs with the award.[12]

EXAGGERATED LINKS?

On the right, it's common to accuse the Southern Poverty Law Center and other groups of exaggerating these links to extremist groups. Peter Brimelow, author of *Alien Nation* and editor of the website VDare, has called it a "guilt-by-association conspiracy theory"; many have accused the SPLC of profiting from the connections they find.[13]

Heidi Beirich of the SPLC says this is a ridiculous accusation. "Not everybody involved is a racist," she adds, "but the kind of people we track don't like immigration because they don't want America to have a darker skin color."

Tom Barry, director of Right Web, says it's important to know what the links are, but warns it can be overdone. "The purpose is to understand who we are facing, not to label them all as nationalists," he says.

He emphasizes that the anti-immigration movement spans various groups and agendas, and that some groups are more extreme than others. Whatever their differences, however, they frequently form coalitions for short- and long-term campaigns. As FAIR's website puts it, "There are always people who support the right idea for the wrong reasons—but that doesn't make the idea itself wrong."[14]

This excuse rings hollow once you know a large part of the anti-immigration movement was created by a friend of white nationalists; that its leaders flirt with extremism; and that its organizations actively encourage the degradation of immigrants. Organizations like FAIR and others that operate in suits and ties rather than with shovels and guns provide a convenient cover for those who oppose immigration for "politically incorrect" reasons.

Thanks to the suits (and the media's reckless compliance), there is a much higher degree of comfort speaking of undocumented workers as though they were all violent criminals and casually discussing deportation as an option. Considering there may be up to 12 million undocumented immigrants living in the United States, many with U.S. spouses and children, those who call for mass deportation are ruthless in their denial of how many lives it would destroy.[15]

There is not much more forward thinking about how a loss of undocumented labor would affect the U.S. economy either. Activists have aggressively denounced "greedy" employers of day laborers, but their economic analysis is shallow and xenophobic—they simply blame undocumented immigrants for society's ills.

Yet it's an effective strategy. People across the country are donating thousands of dollars to protect themselves against what they perceive as a growing national threat, and their names and addresses have become a shared currency of the movement. The MCDC and others have made their mailing lists available through right-wing direct-mail companies like Response Unlimited. According to that company's records, many organizations, including FAIR, have rented the lists and used them for their own fundraising. The MCDC has also rented FAIR's.[16]

No one knows how much money the MCDC has raised or whether it has been spent appropriately, but *The Washington Times* speculates it may be millions.[17]

The amount of money a special-interest group spends on politics does not directly indicate the extent of its influence. But the millions of dollars being directed toward Washington, D.C., to support anti-immigrant advocacy, lobbying, and campaigns indicate the movement's ambitions.

Even deeper pockets are supporting the effort. Twelve large foundations—among them the Lynde and Harry Bradley Foundation, the Sarah Scaife Foundation, and the Carthage Foundation—fund the bulk of right-wing advocacy, policy, and training, according to the National Committee on Responsive Philanthropy.[18] According to their tax filings, they also fund FAIR, CIS, the pro-English organizations, population-control groups, and other anti-immigrant entities as part of their broader strategy.

Money, of course, drives electoral politics, and the fact that anti-immigrant activists are both receiving funds from national groups and organizing locally increases their influence. FAIR, for example, spent $500,000 on a ballot initiative in Arizona in 2004, according to *The American Prospect*, and Federal Election Commission records show that in 2006 the MCDC gave more than $200,000 to election campaigns in Arizona, Nevada, and Michigan.[19] And Team America—a political action committee founded by Tancredo and led by him and Bay Buchanan, sister of Patrick Buchanan—gave $5,000 last year to Minuteman Project leader Jim Gilchrist in support of his California congressional campaign.

With Tancredo having announced his bid for the 2008 presidential election, state elections like these could be significant for the movement. Anti-immigrant writers and activists are excited by this prospect; they know that even though Tancredo is unlikely to win, his campaign will push immigration higher on the political agenda.

Perhaps 2008 will be the year immigrants reclaim immigration reform as an issue of social and economic rights. But the scale and range of the anti-immigration movement should not be underestimated.

NOTES:

1. "Mapping the New Nativism," Center for New Community (January 11, 2007), downloaded from www. buildingdemocracy.org.
2. Ibid.
3. The Center for New Community reached this estimate by examining the mailing lists available for rent from these groups.
4. The FBI defines a hate group as an organization whose primary purpose is to promote animosity, hostility, and malice toward people belonging to a race, religion, disability, sexual orientation, or ethnic/national origin that differs from that of the organization's members. See www.umes.edu/police/CrimeDefs.html.
5. David Holthouse, "Arizona Showdown: High-powered Firearms, Militia Maneuvers and Racism at the Minuteman Project," *Intelligence Report* no. 118 (summer 2005), available at www.splcenter.org.
6. John Tanton, "Memo to WITAN IV Attendees From John Tanton," *Intelligence Report* no. 106 (summer 2002), available at www.splcenter.org.
7. Max Blumenthal, "White Noise," *The American Prospect* (August 31, 2004), available at www.prospect.org (Web only).
8. "Unlicensed to Kill," Federation for American Immigration Reform (September 2006), available at www.fairus.org; Federation for American Immigration Reform, "People Who Violate Immigration Laws Are More Likely to Violate Other Laws, Finds the FAIR" (March 8, 2007), available at www.fairus.org.
9. Dan Stein, "Calif. Medical Authorities Concerned About Immigrant Blood Donors," *The Dan Stein Report* (March 17, 2007), available at www.steinreport.com.
10. Ian Jobling, "Racial Heresies for the 21st Century," *American Renaissance* (April 2004), available at www.amren.com.
11. Michael Laris, "Promoting 'Preservation' of Whites in Suit and Tie," *The Washington Post* (February 26, 2006).
12. Max Blumenthal, "Republicanizing the Race Card," *The Nation* (March 23, 2006), www.thenation.com; Center for Immigration Studies, "2004 Eugene Katz Award for Excellence in the Coverage of Immigration," www.cis.org.
13. Peter Brimelow, "Is VDARE.COM 'White Nationalist'?" *VDare* (July 24, 2006), www.vdare.com; Ken Silverstein, "The Church of Morris Dees," *Harper's Magazine* (November 2000).
14. Federation for American Immigration Reform, "Answers to Tough Questions About Immigration" (March 15, 2007).
15. Pew Hispanic Center, "Size and Characteristics of the Unauthorized Migrant Population in the U.S." (March 2, 2006), pewhispanic.org.
16. Response Unlimited, www.responseunlimited.com.
17. Jerry Seper, "Minutemen Not Watching Over Funds," *The Washington Times* (July 20, 2006).
18. National Committee on Responsive Philanthropy, "The Strategic Philanthropy of Conservative Foundations: Moving a Public Policy Agenda" (1997), www.mediatransparency.org.
19. Ibid.

CHAPTER 7
NATURAL RESOURCES,
LAND, AND ENVIRONMENT

THE STRUGGLE FOR LATIN AMERICA'S WATER

BY MAUDE BARLOW AND TONY CLARKE
NACLA Report, July/August 2004

Latin America is blessed with an abundance of freshwater. The region contains four of the world's 25 largest rivers—the Amazon, Paraná, Orinoco, and Magdalena—and their combined run-off of 5,470 cubic miles almost equals the combined run-off of the other 21. Some of the world's large lakes are also located in Latin America, including Maracaibo in Venezuela, Titicaca in Peru and Bolivia, Poopó in Bolivia, and Buenos Aires, shared by Chile and Argentina. Twenty percent of global runoff—the renewable water source that constitutes our freshwater supply—comes from the Amazon Basin alone. With one fifth of the globe's water resources, Brazil on its own has more water than any other country.[1] The region as a whole has one of the highest per capita allocations of freshwater in the world—a little less than 110,500 cubic feet per person per year. Geography, pollution and social inequality, however, badly skew Latin Americans' access to water, and very few consume anything near their full personal allocation.

As a relatively parched country, Mexico has a miniscule potential supply of approximately 13,000 cubic feet per person. Natural desert is merging with a spreading human-induced desert over much of the Valley of Mexico, the country's cradle of pre-conquest civilization and present-day home of the nation's capital. Once called the "Venice of the New World" due to its being built atop a lake and intersected with canals, Mexico City is now sinking in on itself as it drains the last of its accessible aquifers from the lakebed below. This is a legacy of the conquering Spanish, who used slave labor to dismantle the more sustainable water systems of the original inhabitants.

In South America, human-induced salination is causing desertification in significant parts of Peru, Bolivia and northwestern Argentina. In total—factoring in the large natural deserts of Patagonia in southern Argentina and the Atacama in northern Chile—about 25% of Latin America is now arid or semi-arid. Most of the Caribbean is also freshwater deprived, since the islands are too small to have substantial rivers.[2]

Poor farming practices, unregulated industrialization, and urban poverty have massively and negatively affected Latin America's water resources. Booming, concentrated populations in Latin America's mega-cities are devouring and contaminating their water supplies, forcing officials to seek out increasingly distant sources. In most large cities, over 50% of the water supply is lost through infrastructure leakage. Some cities lose almost 90% through leaky pipes.[3] Mexico

City now depends on aquifers for 70% of its water and is mining these underground sources up to 80 times faster than they are naturally replenished.[4] Meanwhile, São Paulo is threatening residents with water rationing. The city is relying on sources farther and farther away, hiking the cost of delivery beyond many peoples' ability to pay for it.

Throughout the region, water basins and aquatic habitats are routine dumpsites for garbage, mining effluent, and industrial and agricultural waste. Pollution in the waterways along the U.S.-Mexico border is so bad that some refer to it as a "2,000-mile Love Canal," in reference to an upstate New York neighborhood that was declared a federal emergency in 1978 because of chemical contamination. The region's heaviest polluter is Brazil—the country with the most water. Brazil allows massive chemical and industrial pollution, including mercury dumping from its gold mining industry. Only parts of Eastern Europe and China exceed Brazil's levels of waterway contamination. Most of Latin America's wastewater still flows untreated back into its rivers, lakes and canals.

Rampant poverty is another factor. After years of structural adjustment imposed by the World Bank and International Monetary Fund, as a region, Latin America has the most inequitable income distribution in the world. Mirroring this is a pattern of tremendously unequal access to water. More than 130 million people have no safe drinking water in their homes, and only an estimated one out of every six persons enjoys adequate sanitation service.[5] The situation worsens as policies favoring industrial agriculture drive millions of subsistence farmers into the cities' overpopulated slums every year.

The destruction of water sources, combined with inequitable access, has left most Latin Americans "water poor." And millions live without access to clean water at all. While the region's available resources could provide each person with close to 110,500 cubic feet of water every year, the average resident has access to only 1,010 cubic feet per year. This compares to North America's annual average of 4,160 cubic feet and Europe's 2,255.[6]

An influx of private, for-profit corporations into the region over the last decade has exacerbated the problems of scarcity, urbanization, pollution, and inequitable access. Private water companies, determined to take advantage of Latin America's water crisis, are operating or planning to operate in most countries of the region, including Argentina, Bolivia, Brazil, Chile, Colombia, Dominican Republic, Ecuador, El Salvador, Honduras, Mexico, Nicaragua, Panama, Peru, and Uruguay.

Most of these companies are local subsidiaries of the three largest multinational water service companies—Suez and Vivendi of France, and RWE-Thames Water of Germany (the "Big-3"). A decade ago, the Big-3 serviced only 51 million people in just 12 countries. Together, the three now deliver water and wastewater services to almost 300 million customers in over 130 countries. Suez and Vivendi control over 70% of the existing water service market worldwide. Their revenues have kept pace with their growth. Vivendi, for example, earned over $12 billion in 2002 compared with just $5 billion a decade ago. All three are ranked among the wealthiest 100 corporations in the world with combined annual revenues in 2002 of almost $160 billion and an annual growth rate of 10%, outpacing many of the national economies in which they operate.[7]

Often, the World Bank and the Inter-American Development Bank (IDB) facilitate the aggressive entry of these companies into Latin American markets. Both Suez and Vivendi use their considerable clout among multilateral lenders to make private water delivery a "condition" for debt relief or new loans. According to Public Citizen, the IDB alone holds about $58 billion of debt in the region, giving it tremendous power to impose water privatization on desperate municipalities. The IDB's current projects have slated more than $1 billion in funding for privatized water and sanitation services. In fact, some of the largest IDB loans of the last decade went directly to transnational water companies for the operation of private water concessions in countries like Argentina, Bolivia, and Honduras.

Meanwhile, the World Bank has decided to triple its annual financing commitments to global private sector water projects. After a decade of lucrative assistance from the World Bank, the Big-3 are now demanding guaranteed financing to insulate themselves from foreign currency fluctuations before making any new investments in developing countries. At the same time, the major water privateers are facing mounting and fierce public opposition to their operations in many parts of Latin America. As in the rest of the world, the damaging effects of water privatization are well-documented: rate hikes, cut-offs to customers who can't pay, reduced water quality, huge profits for corporate investors, secret contracts, bribery, and corruption.

In the Maldonado province of Uruguay, water prices soared and supplies became contaminated when Uraqua, a subsidiary of the Spanish water company Aguas de Bilboa, received the concession to deliver water on a for-profit "full cost-recovery basis." Uruguayans successfully launched a binding national referendum, scheduled for October 2004, seeking the constitutional protection of water as a human right, a public good and outside the reach of for-profit companies.

In Puerto Rico, where Suez holds a 10-year, $4 billion contract to deliver water services, Solicitor General Carlos López decried the company's performance. López claims Suez has paid much attention to improving billing and fee collection, but has made "no improvement" in the delivery of potable water to consumers.

Arguably, the best-known reaction to water privatization occurred in Cochabamba, Bolivia, when the engineering giant Bechtel set up its subsidiary, Aguas del Tunari, in early 2000 and immediately raised the price of water beyond the reach of the vast majority of the population. Its contract even gave the company the right to charge people for the water they took from their own wells and to send collection agents to homes to charge for rainwater collected in cisterns on roofs. Consumers were hit with up to 200% rate increases as the company planned for annual profits of $58 million.[8] Public protests forced the government to reverse this privatization effort, but Bechtel is now suing Bolivia for $25 million in lost profits. Despite the fiasco in Cochabamba, the Bolivian government is still pursuing several other privatization schemes, including plans to export and sell bulk water to neighboring Chile for use in its mining industry. If last October's attempted exportation of gas through Chile is any indication, this plan is bound to provoke a negative response from the Bolivian public.

The nudge toward water privatization in Mexico provides yet another alarming example of how governments, the international financial institutions, and private water companies work in concert, with little regard for public well-being. The government of Mexico, along with others in the Global South, is laying the groundwork for the corporate takeover of the country's water system.

Back in the 1990s, a series of constitutional and legislative changes already started shifting water services to private hands in Mexico. In 1992, for example, the Salinas administration modified the Constitution to allow foreign-based corporations to obtain water contracts and concessions and introduced a new national water law permitting global corporations to invest in Mexico's water utilities. Later, as part of its national development agenda, the Zedillo government handed over responsibility for water and sewage services to municipal governments.

As a result, the past decade saw 20% of Mexico's water system privatized. The main corporate players have been the two leading French-based water giants, Suez and Vivendi, along with U.K.-based United Utilities and the Spanish company Agua de Barcelona. For these corporations, the prime targets for takeover have been water services in larger tourist areas and urban centers, leaving the smaller, less populated and less lucrative municipalities to governmental stewardship.

Mexican president Vicente Fox, a former Coca-Cola executive, has been even more aggressive in pursuing privatization. In the wake of September 11, his administration declared water a matter of national security. This allows the full powers of the state, including military operations and anti-terrorism measures, to be applied, if necessary, against anyone seen as opposing the government's plans for restructuring and privatizing the water sector.

Also in 2001, the Mexican government created the Program for the Modernization of Water Management Companies (PROMAGUA) to advance privatization. The World Bank and the federal government provided the $250 million needed to jumpstart the project.[9]

PROMAGUA coordinates the massive restructuring of Mexico's water systems by providing generous subsidies to projects and attracting private investment. It facilitates the corporate takeover of public water utilities by authorizing contracts or concessions—valid for periods ranging from five to 50 years—between local governments and private water companies, targeting urban centers with a population of 50,000 or more. By 2002, PROMAGUA had coordinated the signing of agreements with 28 of Mexico's 30 states, including 687 municipalities encompassing 70% of the country's urban population.

PROMAGUA established a national data bank to help foreign corporations decide where to invest in Mexico's water utilities. It achieved this with help from the World Environment Center (WEC), a New York–based nonprofit organization that promotes industry-government partnerships and is supported by some of the world's largest transnationals. The WEC works closely with PROMAGUA to obtain the information and intelligence required for this data bank. At the same time, PROMAGUA set up a center on the outskirts of Mexico City to train people for work in water systems. Co-sponsored by some 40 companies based in France, the center has prepared over 3,000 people for work in Mexico's revamped and privatized water system. Suez and Vivendi, of course, are among the most prominent and active supporters of PROMAGUA's training facility.

In addition to government funding, PROMAGUA receives hefty support from international financial institutions including the World Bank, the IDB, and the European Bank for Reconstruction and Development. In 2003, for example, the World Bank announced it would pump $5 billion into Mexico over the following two years. Although earmarked for a variety of infrastructure development projects, a considerable portion of the loan will fuel the corporate takeover of public water utilities through the Bank's International Finance Corporation.

Mexico City illustrates vividly what happens when for-profit corporations collude to carve-up public water utilities. In 1993, the government divided the city's water delivery system into four administrative quadrants. Suez and Vivendi each took control of one quadrant, while the U.K.-based companies United Utilities and Severn Trent captured the remaining two. The companies then proceeded to charge Mexico City residents different and, therefore, inequitable water rates. Furthermore, when the Democratic Revolutionary Party (PRD) assumed municipal office and called for a uniform water rate across the metropolitan area, the corporations initially protested. They later relented so as not to risk losing these valuable concessions.

Beyond unjustified billing rates, privatized water services in Mexico City and elsewhere in the country have brought countless other problems. Those residents who are unable to pay escalating water bills face frequent service cut-offs as well as long delays from company officials in dealing with their complaints. In 2001, for example, Vivendi increased its Mexico City rates by 60%, which led to payment defaults and, consequently, service cut-offs mostly affecting poor residents in that quadrant. Flooding has dramatically increased due to neglect of pipes and infrastructure. For the most part, the big water corporations have been unwilling to make substantial investments to improve water infrastructure, though they seem eager to pass on mounting debts to municipal governments.

All across Latin America, fierce resistance to this theft of public water is growing. In communities large and small, citizens are taking to the streets, organizing referenda and petitions, and fighting for their right to water. Latin American activists and academics are on the front line of the global water justice movement, speaking at international conferences, protesting World Bank policies and organizing for a binding UN Convention on the right to water.

On August 22, 2003, 47 grassroots organizations from 16 countries in the Americas met in San Salvador where they launched a new movement called RED VIDA. This inter-American network of water activists issued the San Salvador Statement for the Defense of and the Right to Water. Many of the member groups of this new network played pivotal roles at the World Water Forum in Kyoto, Japan in March 2003, where the World Bank and the big water companies tried unsuccessfully to sell their privatization "consensus" to the world. When the Big-3, the World Bank and their allies tried to convince the Forum participants in Kyoto to adopt "public-private partnerships" as the best model for the delivery of water services, civil society organizations and water activists from around the world formed an alliance to obstruct this agenda. Calling themselves "water warriors," alliance members went on to effectively challenge the predetermined "consensus" as it applied to nine other theme topics of the Forum. RED VIDA also played a prominent role in launching the Peoples' World Water Movement, which took place at a summit in New Delhi on the eve of the 2004 World Social Forum in Mumbai, India. RED VIDA members forged strong alliances with Indian groups that are also battling the invasion of private water companies.

For almost 20 years, the people of Latin America have been combating neoliberalism, with varying degrees of success. But the move to commodify their water for the benefit of faraway investors has injected new life into this effort. It is as if a line in the sand has been drawn. Because people cannot live without water, there is a distinctive urgency and tenacity to this struggle. Their demand for water democracy will not be silenced.

NOTES

1. Marq de Villiers, *Water* (Toronto: Stoddart Publishing, 1999).
2. Armando Chávez, "Latin America: Poor Distribution of Water and Even Worse Use," in *2004 Express*, available at www.barcelona2004.org, citing the Economic Commission for Latin America and Caribbean.
3. The World Resources Institute, the United Nations Environment Program, the United Nations Development Program, and the World Bank, *World Resources, 1998–99* (Oxford University Press, 1998).

4. Mario Osava, "Mega Cities Squander Water Resources," Inter Press Service (March 19, 2004), citing the Global Environment Outlook study by the United Nations.
5. Press release, Pan American Health Organization (October 3, 2002).
6. *World Resources, 1998-99*.
7. Center for Public Integrity, "The Water Barons" (2003), available at www.icij.org.
8. Maude Barlow and Tony Clarke, *Blue Gold: The Fight to Stop the Corporate Theft of the World's Water* (The New Press, 2002).
9. The following paragraphs on PROMAGUA in Mexico are based on research conducted by Alejandra Peña of the National Autonomous Univeristy of Mexico (UNAM) while on a study assignment at the Polaris Institute in Canada, 2003–04.

BLOOD ON THE PALMS: AFRO-COLOMBIANS FIGHT NEW PLANTATIONS

BY DAVID BACON
Dollars & Sense, July /August 2007

On September 7, 2006, paramilitary gunmen invaded the home of Juan de Dios García, a community leader in the Colombian city of Buenaventura. García escaped, but the gunmen shot and killed seven members of his family.

The paramilitaries, linked to the government of President Álvaro Uribe and to the country's wealthy landholding elite, wanted to stop García and other activists from the Proceso de Comunidades Negras (Process of Black Communities, or PCN), who have been trying to recover land on which Afro-Colombians have lived for five centuries. The PCN is a network of over 140 organizations among black Colombian communities.

García later told Radio Bemba, "When the *paras* [paramilitary soldiers] came looking for me, I could see they were using police and army vehicles. They operate with the direct and indirect participation of high government functionaries. So denouncing their crimes to the authorities actually puts you at an even greater risk."

South of Buenaventura along the Pacific, in the coastal lowlands of the department of Nariño, oil palm plantations are spreading through historically Afro-Colombian lands. The plantation owners' association, Fedepalma, plans to expand production to about 3,861 square miles, and the government has proposed that by 2020, more than 17 million acres will be used for export crops, including oil palms.

Helping planters reach their goal is the U.S. Agency for International Development (USAID). In what the agency describes as an effort to resettle right-wing paramilitary members who agree to be disarmed, USAID funds projects in which they are given land to cultivate. The land, however, is often located in historically Afro-Colombian areas.

On paper these resettlement projects may appear to be effective components of a national peace process. On the ground, however, what typically happens is that the paramilitaries take on the task of protecting the plantation owners' (and the government's) investment. And Afro-Colombian activists who get in the way pay a price in blood.

GROWING PLANTATIONS

In the 1960s, only about 44,000 acres were planted with the trees. By 2003 oil palm plantations occupied 464,000 acres—and closer to 300,000 counting fields planted but not yet producing. Colombia has become the largest palm oil producer in the Americas, and 35% of its product is already exported as fuel. Palm oil used to be used just for cooking. But the global effort to shift away from petroleum has created a new market for biofuels, and one of the world's major sources is the kernel of the oil palm.

Oil palm planters take advantage of the growing depopulation of the Afro-Colombian countryside caused by poverty, internal migration, and the civil war. But they also drive people off the land directly using armed guards and paramilitaries, who often seem to be the same people. "When the companies are buying land, if a farmer sells only part of what he owns, but not his house, he'll be burned out the next day," said Jorge Ibañez, an activist involved in land recovery, whose name has been changed to protect him from retaliation.

Ibañez organizes urban committees in Tumaco, a coastal city where many of the displaced Afro-Colombians in Nariño now live. Displaced people have traveled to the department capital, Pasto, to protest and demand services for the communities of shacks they've built on the edge of Tumaco's mangrove swamps. "But the government says the problem of displacement has been solved," Ibañez says, "even while those same displaced people are camping out in the plaza in front of the offices of the authorities, because they have no place to go."

Other community activists charge that coca production follows the palms. Raúl Álvarez explains that "we never consumed coca here, but now it's all over our schools and barrios." Residents accuse the newly arrived armed plantation guards of involvement in the traffic and suspect the planters themselves are its financial backers. The earliest and largest plantation owners have been the sugar barons of Cali, in the Valle de Cauca department, who for years have been suspected of involvement in the drug trade. Ibañez says the gunmen are "people who come here from other regions, go to work for these companies, and threaten people."

In Tumaco, among the shacks of the displaced, the network of armed guards runs loan sharking operations and pawnshops, keeping watch on community activity by monopolizing the tiny phone stores where residents go to make their calls.

"These people aren't a political force themselves," García says. "They're mercenaries. In an area like the Pacific coast, where the average income isn't even $500 a year, they offer $400 a month to join up. Even black and indigenous people get bought, and then they use one group to commit massacres against the other—blacks against indigenous, indigenous against black."

REGAINING LAND RIGHTS

In the face of the displacement and dispersal of their communities, Afro-Colombians have fought with the government for decades, trying to force recognition of their land rights. Those persistent efforts have produced important legal gains. As a result of Afro-Colombian and indigenous community pressure, the country's constitution, rewritten in 1991, finally validated their right to their historical territories. Law 70, passed in 1993, said these communities had to be consulted and had to give their approval prior to any new projects planned on their land. But having a law is one thing; enforcing it is another.

In Nariño's interior, displaced residents have joined forces with those still on the land. Together they've filed a series of legal challenges to regain title to land where their ancestors settled centuries ago. Francisco Hurtado, an Afro-Colombian leader who began the effort over a decade ago, was assassinated in 1998. Nevertheless, Afro-Colombians recovered their first collective territories in the department in 2005. Since the passage of Law 70, Afro-Colombians have gained title to 15 million acres of land. Recovery is still far from complete, however.

Tiny communities in the jungle, like Bajo Pusbi, still live in fear of the various armed groups who walk their dirt streets with impunity. And Palmeira, the largest of the Nariño planters, has ceded land planted in palms, but not the roads that lead to or through that land. As a result, the territory's inhabitants still earn their living by collecting wood. Most people can't read or write. Deep in the *selva*, or jungle, Bajo Pusbi has neither a school nor a clinic .

Uribe's response to this poverty is his plan to force Afro-Colombian communities to become the planters' junior partners, maintaining and harvesting the trees and turning over the product to the companies for refining. Further, he wants to take even more land for this monoculture. To support expanding palm oil production, conservative parties in the Colombian Congress—with encouragement from USAID—have promulgated new laws for forests, water, and other resources that require their commercial exploitation. If a community doesn't exploit the resources, it can lose title to its land.

At Fedepalma's 2006 congress in Villavicencio, Uribe told the growers' organization that he would "lock up the businessmen of Tumaco with our Afro-Colombian compatriots, and not let them out of the office until they've reached an agreement on the use of these lands." Leaders from the Community Councils of the Black Communities of Kurrulao condemned the idea in a letter to the president, claiming "it would bring with it great environmental, social, and cultural harm." They argue that more palm plantations would affect the ability to reproduce Afro-Colombian culture, and would replace one of the most biodiverse regions of the planet with monocrop cultivation.

"Afro-Colombian communities on the Pacific Coast," García told Radio Bemba, "use the land, and are the owners of what the land produces, but don't believe they own the land itself, which belongs to us all. We follow the concept of collective property. The fact that we've recovered some of our lands and now hold them in this way has infuriated powerful economic forces in our country, as well as transnational corporations."

The PCN was organized to push for land recovery and to address the extreme poverty Afro-Colombians suffer. Some of its leaders have traveled to Washington to denounce the project in meetings with U.S. Congress members, trying to convince them to vote no on the proposed U.S.-Colombia free trade agreement. That agreement would vastly expand palm oil production.

A HISTORY OF FORCED LABOR

Development projects like the palm oil plantations threaten more than just a group of families or a single town. They endanger the territorial basis for maintaining the unique Afro-Colombian culture and social structure, developed over nearly 500 years.

The first Spaniard landed at what would eventually become Colombia in 1500, finding a territory already inhabited by Carib and Chibchan people. Before the century was out, musket-bearing troops of the Spanish king had decimated these indigenous communities, forcing survivors away from the coast and deep into remote mountains. To replace their forced labor in plantations and mines, colonial administrators brought the first slaves from Africa. By 1521, a hundred years before slavery began in the Virginia colony, the first Africans had already started five centuries of labor in the Americas.

In Colombia, as in the U.S. South, Africans were not docile. They fled the plantations in huge numbers, traveling south and west to the Pacific coast and inland to the jungle-clad mountains of the interior. The runaways called their towns *palenques*. By the time Simón Bolívar and Francisco de Paula Santander raised the flag of liberation from Spain in 1810, African rage was so great that slaves and ex-slaves made up three of every five soldiers in the anti-colonial army.

Yet emancipation was delayed another 40 years until 1851, a decade before Lincoln's Emancipation Proclamation freed slaves in the United States. By then, the rural Afro-Colombian communities founded by escaped slaves were as old as the great cities of Bogotá and Cartagena.

POVERTY POLARIZED BY RACE

Today Colombia, a country of 44 million people, is the third largest in Latin

America and one of the most economically polarized. Its Department of National Planning estimates that 49.2% of the people live below the poverty line (the National University says 66%). In the countryside, 68% are officially impoverished. And within rural areas, poverty is not evenly distributed.

The Asociación de Afro-Colombiano Desplazados (the Association of Displaced Afro-Colombians) documents more than 10 million black Colombians living on the Pacific Coast, making up 90% of the coastal population. Even in interior departments like Valle de Cauca and northern Cauca, they are a majority. In Afro-Colombian communities 86% of basic needs go unsatisfied, including basic public services from sewers to running water, according to a report given to the 23rd International Congress of the Latin American Studies Association. Most white and mestizo communities, by contrast, have such services.

The country's health care system, damaged by budget cuts to fund the government's counterinsurgency war, covers 40% of white Colombians. Only 10% of black Colombians get health services, and a mere 3% of Afro-Colombian workers receive social security benefits. Black illiteracy is 45%; white illiteracy is 14%. Approximately 120 of every 1000 Afro-Colombian infants die in their first year, compared to 20 white babies. And at the other end of life, Afro-Colombians live 54 years on average; whites, 70 years.

And while non-black Colombians have an average annual income of $1,500, Afro-Colombian families make $500. Only 38% of Afro-Colombian young people go to high school, compared to 66% of non-black Colombians. Just 2% go on to the university.

Institutionalized inequality has been reinforced by decades of internal displacement. From 1940 to 1990, the urban share of Colombia's population grew from 31% to 77%. Afro-Colombians joined this internal migration in hopes of gaining a better standard of living. But those hopes were dashed—instead, they joined the ranks of the urban poor, living in the marginal areas of cities like Tumaco, Cali, Medellín and Bogotá. Currently, most Afro-Colombians are living in urban areas, according to Luis Gilberto Murillo Urrutia, the former governor of Choco state. "Afro-Colombians make up 36% to 40% of Colombia's people," he says, "although the government says it's only 26% (or about 11 million people). Only 25%, approximately 3 million people, are still based on the land."

MORE DISPLACEMENT EXPECTED

The Colombian government's current development program will depress that number even further. Afro-Colombian communities are in greater danger of disappearance and displacement than at any previous time in their history, thanks to huge new government-backed development projects, pushed by the United

States and international financial institutions.

Local communities do not control these large development projects. Palm oil refineries create dividends, but the only Colombians who benefit from them are a tiny handful of planters in Cali and Medellín. But the Colombian government, like many in the thrall of market-driven policies, sees foreign investment in these projects as the key to economic development, and thus revenue. It cuts the budget for public services needed by Afro-Colombian, indigenous, and other poor communities, while increasing military spending.

Plan Colombia, the U.S. military aid program, underwrites much of that growing military budget. Both Plan Colombia and a new free trade treaty, expected to be ratified by Congress this year, will lead to further displacement of rural Afro-Colombian and indigenous communities. Leaders who stand in the way of foreign investment projects will disappear or die.

PCN activists estimate that the proposed free trade agreement will force approximately 80,000 families working in agriculture off the land. They say this will be just the beginning, and point to the 1.3 million farmers displaced in Mexico under the North American Free Trade Agreement.

And while most displaced Colombians become internal migrants in the country's growing urban slums, that migratory stream will eventually cross borders into those wealthy countries whose policies have set it into motion. Since 2002, over 200,000 Colombians have arrived in the United States.

PRESERVING LAND AND CULTURE

García points out that Afro-Colombian communities are the historic guardians of the country's biodiversity. "The whole Pacific coast is made up of rich mangrove forests, to which we owe our subsistence," he explains. "Afro-Colombian and indigenous culture sees that territory as a place to live, and not as a potential source of economic wealth. But this is the basis for planning these megaprojects, so they are now using their private armies, the paramilitaries, and have assassinated thousands of our movement's leaders and displaced millions of people. That includes 1 million black Colombians who have had to leave the Pacific coast."

Afro-Colombian communities and their centuries-old culture have no place in the current megadevelopment plans. "They see black people as objects that have no value," García emphasizes. "Therefore sacrificing us, even to the extent of a holocaust, doesn't matter. That's the kind of racism to which we're subjected. We believe all acts against a people's culture should be considered crimes against human rights, because there is no human life without culture."

García and others warn that continued funding of Plan Colombia will produce more conflict and more displacement. The government often accuses the guerrillas of the Fuerzas Armadas Revolucionarias de Colombia (FARC) of committing massacres, and in fact uses their activity as a pretext for maintaining an extremely heavy military presence in the countryside. On the other hand, it says it has forced the paramilitaries to demobilize. "But at the same time they make these commitments in the U.S. and Europe, the paras are massacring people here," García told Radio Bemba. "The government asks for money for the peace process, but what happens on the ground is the opposite of peace."

The U.S. Congress has appropriated $21 million to aid the resettlement of paramilitaries. Local people say the same paras, with the same guns, are doing the same killing. High officials of the Uribe administration have been forced to resign because their links to the paramilitaries were exposed.

"The displacement of our communities isn't a consequence of conflict," García points out. "The conflict itself is being used to displace us, to make us flee our territories. Then the land is expropriated, because the state says it's no longer being used productively. We have no arms to fight this, but we will resist politically, because to give up our land is to give up our life."

MULTINATIONAL GOLD RUSH IN GUATEMALA

BY BENJAMIN WITTE
NACLA Report, July/August 2005

Somewhere amid the chaos that erupted January 11 along a stretch of the Pan-American Highway in Guatemala, a protester lost his life. The victim was later identified as Raúl Castro. He was 37.

With the exception of the man's name and age, information about what transpired that day in the northern province of Sololá is murky at best. Reports about how many police and soldiers the government dispatched vary from a couple of hundred to as many as 2,000. Nor is it clear who threw the first stone, fired the first shot or tossed the first Molotov cocktail. Simply put, the scene was pure chaos. Fires and exploded tear-gas canisters choked the air. The piercing sounds of gunfire, sirens, and manic shouting replaced what would have normally been the hum of highway traffic. Hundreds of police, soldiers, and campesino protesters scuffled half-blinded in the haze.

It's sad to say, but the death of a single person under violent circumstances doesn't usually constitute news in Guatemala, where murder and assassinations are rampant, even now, nine years after the official end of the country's 36-year civil war. And yet the story of Castro's death—presumably at the hands of government security forces—continues to arouse steady, albeit modest, public attention. There's something about that death, or more specifically, about the circumstances leading up to the conflict, that has set off persistent alarm—not only in Guatemala but also abroad.

Protests in Sololá actually began more than a month before Castro's murder. Starting in late November, demonstrators—campesinos (mostly of Mayan descent), local leaders, environmentalists, and Catholic Church–affiliated representatives—took up positions along the Panamericana highway. Their goal was to impede the transport of materials and equipment for a soon-to-be-operating gold and silver mine in neighboring San Marcos province, some 93 miles away. For 42 days they were successful, and then the government called in its troops.

The mine, known as the Marlin Project, is located near the towns of Sipacapa and San Miguel Ixtahuacán. It is owned and operated by a company called Montana Exploradora de Guatemala. The company is not, as its name would suggest, Guatemalan. Instead, Montana Exploradora is a subsidy of Glamis Gold, a company that is registered in Canada (it has a post office box in Vancouver) but maintains its headquarters in the United States.

Glamis Gold stands to make a fortune on the Marlin Project. Once in operation, the mine, which is spread over some 250,000 acres, is expected to yield about 250,000 ounces of gold and 3.6 million ounces of silver per year, output that will quickly make it the company's most profitable venture. Furthermore, of the company's various operations, the Marlin Project will be its least expensive to run, with an estimated cash cost of just $90 per ounce of gold, significantly lower than Glamis's overall cash-cost average of approximately $150 per ounce. Best of all, boasts the company on its website, "The project is fully permitted and enjoys strong local support, as well as backing by the Guatemalan Government and the World Bank." Well, at least some of that is true.

The World Bank threw its weight behind the project with its private-sector arm, the International Finance Corporation (IFC), which recently granted Glamis Gold a $45 million loan for the development of the Marlin Project. It's also clear that the Guatemalan government is fully supporting the project, as its willingness to send soldiers to aid the company suggests. Proponents of the project say Guatemala, one of the hemisphere's most impoverished countries, desperately needs this type of foreign direct investment. Foreign companies, they say, create jobs and boost government coffers by supplying tax revenue.

In fact, the government is so supportive of foreign mining ventures that in the last decade (since the signing of the 1996 peace accords), Guatemalan leaders have granted foreign companies more than 300 exploration requests and mining concessions. Many of those companies are Canadian.

Not surprisingly, Canada's ambassador to Guatemala, James Lambert, has thrown his active support behind the country's budding mining industry. In an article published last November in the Guatemalan daily *Prensa Libre*, Lambert penned a defiant defense of Canada and its mining companies as the Glamis controversy heated up.

"Is it possible," asked the ambassador, "for a country to be recognized as one of the most socially and environmentally responsible countries in the world, near the top of the list in the Environment Sustainability Index and, at the same time, be a major mining country, with a mining industry that contributes $41.1 billion to its economy?" And he answered his own question. "Yes," said Lambert, Canada is that responsible country, and its companies mine responsibly at home. There's no reason, therefore, why they wouldn't do the same in Guatemala.

But there is a reason, say opponents to the project. The ambassador's assurances aside, Glamis Gold and the other companies waiting in the wings are likely to cause tremendous social and environmental damage. Why? Because in Guatemala, with its weak, pro-investment government, tightly controlled media, and general atmosphere of repression, foreign companies can simply get away with it.

Despite Glamis Gold's insistence that its operations "enjoy strong local support," the list of people and organizations opposing the Marlin Project is growing. A poll conducted late last year by the survey company Vox Latina suggested that in Sipacapa and San Miguel Ixtahuacán more than 95% of local residents disapprove of the mining activity. Almost as many residents think metal mining will have a destructive influence on their towns, while only just under 9% are buying the line that the Marlin Project will bring wealth to the area. The poll, conducted in October 2004, involved 400 interviews with adults and has a 5% margin of error.

Backing the townspeople in opposing the mine are local church leaders, labor unions, numerous mayors from across the country, and several environmental groups. Álvaro Ramazzini, the archbishop of the diocese of San Marcos, has been a particularly outspoken critic of the project. In an open letter to Guatemalan president Óscar Berger last September, the archbishop wrote that the country's current laws provide an open invitation for potentially harmful mining practices. "A mining company will invest in countries where the laws governing mining constitute an open door. This is the case for Guatemala," he explained. Ramazzini's public stance against the project has earned him at least one death threat in recent months.

Nevertheless, the opposition has not been silenced. In early February, three weeks after the January confrontation, thousands of protesters in Sololá once again took to the streets, this time with the backing of 19 of the province's town mayors. Also, Archbishop Rodolfo Cardinal Quezada Toruño, the country's highest-ranked church leader, has sided with the opposition, as has the San Marcos–based union, the Movement of Catholic Workers (MTC).

It was through the MTC that Father Ernie Schibli of the Montreal NGO Social Justice Committee first learned about the mining controversy in Guatemala. This is not simply a Guatemalan problem say Schibli and other concerned Canadians. Glamis Gold, at least in name, is a Canadian company, as are several other mining companies with plans to operate in Guatemala. "The whole country's been mapped out," he says. And since the Canadian ambassador is actively backing these exploitative projects, says Schibli, people in Canada must direct opposition to their own government. "That's where Canadians have the most leverage," he explains.

Last November, Schibli went to Guatemala to investigate the situation in San Marcos firsthand. What he encountered confirmed the findings of the Vox Latina poll. The local, mostly Maya, residents simply don't support the project. "Despite what the mining company has to say, the broader community and the indigenous people of Guatemala as a whole have rejected their claims. They're firmly opposed to the mine," says the priest.

Meanwhile, says Schibli, in Canada, opposition "has snowballed." Canadian NGOs siding with Schibli's Social Justice Committee include the Canadian chapter of Friends of the Earth, the Toronto-based Rights Action, and the Atlantic

Regional Solidarity Network (ARSN) of Nova Scotia.

In March, ARSN sponsored a tour in eastern Canada called "Mining the Connections." One of the principal participants was José "Filóchofo" Chacón, a well-known political cartoonist who also works closely with Madre Selva, one of several Guatemalan environmental groups trying to bring attention to the mining issue.

According to the cartoonist, the risks posed by Glamis Gold and other foreign mining companies are not only environmental but also economic and social. Problem number one, says Chacón, is the measly 1% in royalty fees companies like Glamis are required to pay under Guatemala's flexible mining laws.

"One percent," he emphasizes, "for every $100 that the mining company takes in earnings, they leave 1% for the country. In other words, we're talking about a law that's shameful, a law that's defeatist, a law that belongs to governments that are willing to hand everything over. What's more, that 1% is divided in half. They leave 0.5% for the communities being affected. The other 0.5% goes to the state."

Undoubtedly, argues Chacón, communities such as Sipacapa and San Miguel Ixtahuacán are going to need every penny, because the Marlin Project will almost certainly result in environmental and health problems. One of the biggest effects of the mine will be increased competition for water. The average Guatemalan campesino, according to Madre Selva, uses roughly 30 liters of water per day. The Marlin Project, by its own estimates, will use 250,000 liters per hour, massive consumption that threatens to deprive local subsistence farmers of water they need to survive.

Pollution from the constant flow of trucks winding in and out of the mountainous region as well as from the oils and gases used to operate the mine's heavy machinery is a likely problem. Most alarming, however, is the vast amount of cyanide used by the mining process to extract gold and silver. Inevitably, say environmentalists, at least some of that cyanide will be absorbed by the environment and poison ground water, posing a long-term health risk to nearby residents.

Glamis Gold insists these concerns are blown way out of proportion. For one thing, it says, water competition need not be a concern, as the Marlin mine will only be using water pumped from its own 1,000-foot well. Nor should residents worry about cyanide poisoning. "The cyanide process," Glamis explains on its website, "is entirely contained in the process plant with redundant liners and safety systems." After all, boasts the company, in preparing the Marlin Project for operation, Glamis Gold dutifully conducted the requisite environmental impact study (EIS), and was subsequently granted approval by all the necessary parties. The EIS alone, says the company, should convince residents they have nothing to worry about. Or should it?

Colorado-based geologist Robert E. Moran, who's reviewed EIS's from all around the world, has carefully reviewed Glamis's impact study and isn't so sure the document offers anything in the way of assurances. Simply put, "the general quality [of the report] is poor," he says.

"Let me start by saying it's not the kind of report that would be acceptable in Canada and the U.S. It's too poorly written, too poorly organized. It lacks the basic information you need. There's not much data there." Moran says he's heard the 1,000-foot well promise before. "It's a pattern you see over and over with projects in developing countries." As far as potential cyanide pollution, it's the same story. "They all have redundant protection systems, but they almost all have leakages," says Moran. "It's oversimplified to say waste doesn't get released. If you leave out about 50% of the facts, then their statement is OK."

While in Canada, Chacón was able to meet with at least a few Canadian public officials, who made some sympathetic comments. Certainly, for those opposing the Marlin Project, some response is better than no response. However, the real power to influence the situation rests in the hands of the Guatemalan leaders themselves. Unfortunately, says Chacón, Berger's government simply won't listen.

"If the government of Óscar Berger were really democratic," he insists, "the first thing they'd do is pay attention to what the communities are saying. The mayors of many communities are getting together to say they don't want this. But the mining companies have a lot of economic power."

Guatemalans have seen gold prospectors before, starting with the first Spanish conquistadors who ventured into the country during the early part of the 16th century. They've also had a tumultuous past with North American companies that have set up shop and, like the United Fruit Company in the 1950s, haven't hesitated to use any means necessary in protecting their interests.

In the early 1950s, Guatemalans remember, then president Jacobo Arbenz instituted a number of "radical" measures, including a land reform plan that involved exercising the government's powers of eminent domain over uncultivated land owned by United Fruit. The government, said the president, was prepared to pay for the land fair-and-square, basing purchase prices on the company's own grossly undervalued land assessments. The plight of the well-connected U.S. company soon caught the attention of authorities in Washington, and in 1954 the CIA successfully executed an operation that resulted in Arbenz being ousted in a coup. In 1960 war broke out. The conflict didn't officially come to an end until 1996. By then, more than 200,000 people had been killed, most of them indigenous, murdered by government troops who forced their way into villages in the same highland regions that are now being prepped for exploitation by North American mining companies.

Taking all of that into consideration, it's easy to see why the specter of government troops, dispatched in the hundreds to break up a protest against Canadian and U.S.

mining interests, might arouse a sense of foreboding among villagers in highland Guatemala and among the people who empathize with their plight. Indeed, Raúl Castro's death, even in a country that continues to be as violent as Guatemala, is eerily disconcerting. "When we talk about the army," says Chacón, "we're talking about an army that's been accused of massacres. We're saying that now, during this time of peace, the army is returning once again to the communities. This produces a psychological impact."

In signing the 1996 peace accords, authorities in Guatemala agreed to abide by a number of international laws, including Convention 169 of the International Labor Organization (ILO). Among other things, this law states that indigenous peoples must be consulted and allowed ultimate say over any development plan that could affect them or the land on which they live.

"The peoples concerned," ILO-169 reads, "shall have the right to decide their own priorities for the process of development as it affects their lives, beliefs, institutions, and spiritual well-being and the lands they occupy or otherwise use, and to exercise control, to the extent possible, over their own economic, social, and cultural development."

Despite what Glamis Gold says on the matter, that consultation never took place. This is not, of course, the first time Guatemala's highland Maya have been shut out of national dialogues. But this refusal by the government and by companies such as Glamis Gold to inform, consult, and ultimately listen, breeds frustration. Without avenues to express their political voices, Guatemala's campesinos take to the streets—they protest, they block highways. And on January 11 and on countless other days in the country's tumultuous past, their mobilization has been met with heavy repression.

"Our concern is that democratic spaces, through dialogue, don't exist in Guatemala," says a wary Chacón. "In this very moment, every type of demonstration has been repressed brutally. Land seizures, by people trying to gain access to land in the country's interior, have been repressed in a bloody way. There is incredible violence in the city. Just last year they reported more than 500 murders of women. Within this context of violence, generated by different factors, you get the issue of mining. This is what scares us, that this is going to generate another period of violence like the one we've only just gotten out of."

A RARE HAPPY ENDING:
PIÑONES VERSUS THE DEVELOPERS

BY CÁNDIDA COTTO
NACLA Report, November/December 2007

As tourism continues to grow into one of the most profitable sectors of Puerto Rico's economy, many small communities have found themselves threatened by development companies. The small coastal village of Piñones, just outside the town of Loíza, has managed to defend itself from the designs of PFZ Properties, which belongs to a Puerto Rican developer named Joel Katz, an entrepreneur known to be close to the inner circles of the Partido Popular Democrático. "If there are still natural resources in Piñones, it's because of the community," says Milagros Quiñones, a local activist.

During the past decade, the community has waged a determined fight to stop PFZ from building a huge residential complex on its territory. Home to about 2,000 people, Piñones stretches across 10,000 acres near the tourist site of Isla Verde. It was settled in the early 19th century, when the lands the Spanish crown had ceded to the Order of Dominican Friars were gradually transformed into a refuge for free blacks and escaped slaves. With the passage of time, Piñones became one of Puerto Rico's traditional black communities and a bulwark against the dissolution of the country's Afro-Caribbean culture. Today, local families live in modest homes, making a living selling *comida típica* from kiosks along the beach.

The proposed development, to have been called Costa Serena, would have transformed Piñones into a gated community of at least 880 condo-hotel units, 42 residential units, 1,394 parking spaces, a casino, several tennis courts, a swimming pool, a beach club, six entrances with access control, and 52,818 square feet of commercial space. It would have represented the largest building complex in Puerto Rico, extending about a mile and a half along the coast of Vacía Talega. Not only would it have radically transformed the character of the community's natural and cultural environment, but it would have displaced its traditional inhabitants and effectively privatized the length of the coast it occupied.

The area is considered one of the most biologically diverse in Puerto Rico. Two lagoons, the island's largest mangrove, and a small peninsula called El Pescador are all part of the area's natural treasure. Mostly untouched, Piñones's 10,000 acres constitute a natural reservoir and dam against floods in the adjoining metropolitan area.

In 1996, after a lower court decision to allow a certain amount of development to take place, PFZ, apparently thinking nobody was paying attention, began the first excavations for the project. A community coalition succeeded in persuading a higher court to order PFZ to stop all activity until the company prepared and signed a declaration of environmental impact. By law, such a declaration must examine the environmental, social, and economic consequences of any large-scale investment project.

PFZ's inability to swiftly prepare such a declaration swayed public opinion against the project. It was only in November 2000, four years after PFZ broke ground on the project, that its declaration was released and the public found out just how massive the proposed complex would be. What's more, the courts determined that the 2000 declaration was insufficient to meet legal requirements, lacking information on the cumulative impacts of environmental disturbances. Opponents also questioned whether the project would do irreparable harm to the protected area of the Puerto Rican seashore, and whether the negative impacts of the plan's proposed widening of the only highway in the area from two to four lanes would be greater than the benefits.

PFZ was then ordered to prepare a new, updated declaration, which it completed in 2004. But the new document contained no updated maps of the area, leaving the impression that the company's analysis was still based on obsolete information and therefore on false premises. At a public hearing in April 2004, PFZ's chief engineer admitted that to construct the project, a lot of property would have to be expropriated, but "not by us," since it is the state planning board that does the expropriating.

In the discussion process, it also came out that the Costa Serena project was being developed within an area susceptible to flooding and severe storms. In July 2005, the secretary of the Department of Natural and Environmental Resources (DRNA) restated the danger to Costa Serena, noting that the development's location would force the state to evacuate residents every time there was a flood, endangering the lives of rescuers.

The role of Governor Aníbal Acevedo Vilá, elected in 2005, has been ambiguous, to say the least. This was made evident in November 2006, when the governor said in a meeting with the community that he did not know how the project's approval was progressing through the relevant agencies. Yet soon after the meeting, it was discovered that the Environmental Quality Board had already approved PFZ's final environmental declaration two weeks earlier, and that the governor knew about it before meeting with the Piñones community. It also became known that he had met informally with PFZ's Katz on several occasions in the governor's mansion.

Public planner José Rivera Santana, the former director of the Planning Division of the official Tourism Company, confirmed to the weekly paper *Claridad* that at least since April 2005, the heads of various agencies had all been pressured by the Executive Mansion to approve Costa Serena, making it very difficult to halt the project. Only Rivera Santana announced his opposition to the project, and he was relieved of his job shortly thereafter. Rivera Santana added that the government's backing of Costa Serena violated the procedures of the Environmental Public Policy Law with respect to the use of land, the protection of seashore areas, and the mandate to develop sustainable tourism.

While community groups prepared to relaunch the struggle against Costa Serena, Governor Acevedo surprised the country by announcing—just a few days after the Piñones meeting—that the project would not go forward and that the government would purchase the land from the Katz family. But the explanation for this was not very convincing, leaving people guessing about the real motives. The governor said he had run into Joel Katz "on a sidewalk in San Juan," and that the developer had told him he wanted to withdraw the project "for the good of Puerto Rico." Clearly, the governor wanted to convey the idea that Katz had acted in good faith.

This closeness between PFZ and the insular government goes all the way back to the company's origins in 1959, when its founder, a Cuban named Luis Puro (Katz's grandfather), arrived in Puerto Rico after fleeing the revolution. According to the historian Luis A. López Rojas in *La mafia en Puerto Rico: las caras ocultas del desarrollo* (San Juan, Puerto Rico: Isla Negra Editores, 2004), Puro linked up with the North American mafia, becoming the owner of various hotel-casinos in eastern Puerto Rico. While offering a historical analysis of the connection between the island's hotel and gambling industries and the colonial model of the Puerto Rican commonwealth, the author mentions Puro as one of the mafia figures who maintained close contacts with the era's government entities.

Today, the controversy has not ended. Why, it was asked, would the state buy land from PFZ that it considers to be in the public domain? The current expectation is that the Department of Natural and Environmental Resources will undertake a study of the area's land ownership and of the protected seashore's boundaries in order to truly confirm which lands belong to the Katz family and which are public. It would thereby determine how much, if anything, should be paid to the Katz family for the public lands.

In any case, environmentalists as well as community members still have reason to worry. Despite the governor's announced decision to halt the project, the Committee for Environmental Quality is still bringing the process before the courts, and the Planning Board considers the process "suspended" but not canceled. Environmentalists fear that both agencies are trying to leave the door open for other, similar projects.

In fact, five other projects are on the books, projects that, if carried through, would leave the citizens of Piñones strangers in their own land. These projects, in total, would build about 2,400 new tourist units, 575 residential villas, 130 cabanas, 300 residential apartments, and two golf courses that would be constructed on what is now 225 acres of mangrove. In Puerto Rico, as throughout the Americas, community and environmental well-being remain on the defensive.

But the fact that the Piñones community, together with environmentalists, has prevailed over a major developer provides an inspiration to other communities. While the end of this story has not yet been written, the Piñones coalition acted prudently, seeking help from the Environmental Law Clinic at the University of Puerto Rico; bringing public attention to the case by picketing the offices of PFZ Properties and the Puerto Rican government's Committee for Environmental Quality; and taking both entities to court.

There is no traditional coastal community that is not threatened by the plans of some developer. Besides Piñones, there has been a serious and intense public debate over the future of the "northeastern corridor," coastal lands between the towns of Luquillo and Fajardo. The privatization of beaches, environmental degradation, and the dislocation of centuries-old communities also threaten Humacao, Vega Baja, Dorado, Rincón, and Isabela, just to name a few.

The tourist industry remains profitable, powerful, and in line with officially held ideas about economic growth and development. More often than not it emerges victorious in its continuing struggles with the communities that stand in its way. But the struggle in Piñones has ended happily—at least for the time being.

CHAPTER 8
LATIN AMERICA AND
THE UNITED STATES

CLOSING THE "SEAMS": U.S. SECURITY POLICY IN THE AMERICAS

BY ADAM ISACSON
NACLA Report, May/June 2005

Looking around Latin America today, one could be reasonably encouraged by the regional security picture. Beyond Colombia and the remnants of Peru's Shining Path insurgency, there are no civil wars and relatively little organized political violence in the hemisphere. While social upheavals have occurred, they have most often been resolved constitutionally. The regional economy is no longer in a tailspin, and some countries are even seeing poverty rates decline. Elections generally regarded as free and fair are taking place, and left-of-center leaders are winning and even being allowed to govern.

The U.S. government, however, takes a much darker view. "Good progress has been made, but much work remains to better secure our region," Defense Secretary Donald Rumsfeld told a gathering of the hemisphere's defense ministers in Quito in November. "The new threats of the 21st century recognize no borders. Terrorists, drug traffickers, hostage takers, and criminal gangs form an anti-social combination that increasingly seeks to destabilize civil societies." In the spring of 2004, the Southern Command's General James Hill similarly warned Congress: "Terrorists throughout the Southern Command area of responsibility bomb, murder, kidnap, traffic drugs, transfer arms, launder money, and smuggle humans."

In its worldwide search for terrorists and other "new" transnational threats, Washington is once again encouraging Latin America and the Caribbean to arm, enlarge and reorient security forces to combat internal enemies. For the most part, this push is still incipient beyond Colombia, and some countries are resisting it. Nonetheless, the U.S. government's message for the next few years appears to be: The world changed after September 11, we all face borderless, stateless threats, and militaries must play an active role in helping governments administer their own territory.

There is little new about this. Over the past century, the region's militaries have needed little prodding to focus on perceived threats within their own borders. In a part of the world with few external threats—Latin American countries have fought relatively few wars against each other—armed forces have tended to look inward to find their reason for being.

In a region with the world's highest levels of economic inequality, the result is that militaries have historically made some citizens more secure than others, while too often targeting those working peacefully on behalf of the have-nots. During the past century, and especially during the Cold War, the definition of "internal enemy" came to include labor and campesino leaders, opposition politicians, human rights defenders, journalists, authors, and leftist intellectuals. Victims numbered in the thousands.

After the Cold War ended, many countries, vowing "never again," sought to diminish both the size and the role of their armed forces. The United States slowed this progress, however, by stepping in with a new internal role to guide its military aid to the region: the "war on drugs." Today, the "war on terror" provides a new and seemingly more urgent internal enemy.

Unless one is paying close attention to the hemisphere, the phrases "Latin America" and "war on terror" don't seem to go together. Images of the Guantánamo detention camp or perhaps of U.S. involvement in Colombia's conflict may come to mind. But the imperatives of the Bush administration's "global war" are beginning to manifest themselves through a still-incipient set of exercises, aid programs, policy initiatives, and proposed doctrinal shifts.

Colombia is beyond this incipiency. Counter-terrorism—really, counter-insurgency—is already the principal declared purpose of U.S. aid to Colombia. More than five years into Plan Colombia, with $4 billion appropriated (80% of it for Colombia's security forces), the U.S. government is carrying out a host of activities that would have been unthinkable back in 2000 when the Clinton administration promised that its new aid package would not cross the line between counternarcotics and counterinsurgency.

For two years now, a $100 million-plus program has sought to help the Colombian Army defend an oil pipeline partly owned by Los Angeles–based Occidental Petroleum. U.S. funds have paid for a Colombian army commando battalion charged with hunting down guerrilla leaders. U.S. personnel have helped set up special forces, mobile brigades, river-based marines, and other specialized units all over the country. The United States is also heavily supporting Plan Patriota (Patriot Plan), a massive, year-old military offensive in the guerrilla jungle strongholds of southern Colombia. This offensive requires significant logistical support, intelligence, and advising from U.S. military and private contractors, so the Southern Command asked Congress for, and was granted, a doubling (to 800) of the number of U.S. troops who may be in Colombia at a time. It also got a 50% increase in the U.S. citizen contractor presence (to 600).

Beyond Colombia, though, terrorists are rather scarce in Latin America, and terrorists who threaten U.S. citizens on U.S. soil are scarcer still. Possible exceptions may include some Hezbollah and Hamas fundraising activities; the potential presence of Al Qaeda–related cells in zones where criminality—particularly contraband smuggling—is already common, such as the triborder area shared by Argentina, Brazil, and Paraguay; or the chance that terrorists could enter the United States via routes used for illegal immigration. But for the most part, dealing with these phenomena has not required military skills as much as good police investigative work to root out clandestine networks.

Only four Latin American armed groups in two countries (Colombia's FARC and ELN guerrillas and the AUC paramilitaries, and Peru's Shining Path guerrillas) are on the State Department's list of foreign terrorist organizations. So to portray terrorism as a region-wide threat, from the Rio Grande to Tierra del Fuego, seems like a tough sell.

Nonetheless, the word "terrorism" appears as a justification for military aid in 16 of the Western Hemisphere country narratives in the State Department's 2005 congressional presentation document for foreign aid programs. For instance, this document tells us, "U.S. Anti-Terrorist Assistance programs brought Argentine officials to the United States for valuable counterterrorism briefings and training." The request for Bolivia "also includes equipment and training for the Bolivian Army's new Counterterrorism Unit." In the Dominican Republic, "FMF [Foreign Military Financing] will train Dominican forces capable of responding to terrorist threats."

When the terrorist threat inspires military aid in so many unlikely countries throughout the hemisphere, it is reasonable to wonder who exactly is being considered a "terrorist." Terrorism, after all, is a term that is easily abused and can easily come to mean both everything and nothing. If the definition of "terrorist" is not rigorously applied, the region's security forces may end up applying it far too broadly.

Are Bolivian coca growers who blockade roads terrorists? Coca-growing campesinos whose booby traps kill or maim eradication forces certainly deserve jail, but do they (as well as the union they belong to, the political party affiliated with it and allied labor and indigenous movements) really merit the terrorist label? Are Honduran peasants who stage road blockages to stop over-logging terrorists, as some in Honduras claim? Was the retired military officer who staged an abortive takeover of a rural Peruvian police station in late 2004 a terrorist, as the Peruvian government claims? Are Mapuches who damaged plantation property to press for land claims terrorists, as Chilean prosecutors have argued? When Colombian president Álvaro Uribe calls human rights groups "defenders of terrorism" in a speech before a military audience, is he engaging in rhetorical exaggeration or a veiled threat?

When employed so loosely, the term "terrorist" not only loses its usefulness as a way to describe some real threats, it risks becoming a pretext for action against internal opponents who do not even commit violence or work outside the system.

The term is politicized when it becomes part of the U.S. government's case against Latin American governments that have poor relations with Washington. Cuba, for instance, is one of seven countries on the State Department's list of "terrorist-sponsoring states," despite abundant evidence that it has long since abandoned any such practices.

As relations with Venezuela continue to sour, U.S. officials have hinted that President Hugo Chávez may have links to terrorist groups. "Venezuela is emerging as a potential hub of terrorism in the Western Hemisphere, providing assistance to Islamic radicals from the Middle East and other terrorists, say senior U.S. military and intelligence officials," claimed a 2003 story in *U.S. News & World Report*.[1] Bush administration representatives have increasingly sought to link Chávez to Colombian guerrillas; in January 2005, U.S. Ambassador to Colombia William Wood demanded "clarity" from Chávez regarding his relationship to the FARC.

The Bush administration, led by Secretary of State Condoleezza Rice, has characterized Chávez as a "negative force in the region," and has placed Venezuela near the top of its list of security threats in the Americas. But hints about terrorist linkages make up only part of the stated rationale. Despite the lofty rhetoric of Bush's inauguration speech, the administration has already blown much of its pro-democracy credibility in Venezuela. In blatant violation of the Democratic Charter of the Organization of American States, it rushed to recognize a government that briefly deposed Chávez during the April 2002 coup attempt. This has since made it difficult to express genuine concerns about some of the Venezuelan leader's autocratic tendencies.

Instead, U.S. officials have come up with a creative new label, "radical populism," to portray Chávez as a security threat. As General James Hill told Congress, "Traditional threats are now complemented by an emerging threat best described as radical populism. . . . Some leaders in the region are tapping into deep-seated frustrations . . . to reinforce their radical positions by inflaming anti-U.S. sentiment."

Chávez heads the administration's list of "radical populist" threats in the region. Evo Morales, the coca growers' union leader-turned-head of Bolivia's main opposition party and a presidential hopeful, also gets frequent mention. Elected leftists in other countries—Argentina, Brazil, Uruguay—do not yet appear to qualify, though the administration's attitude could change if these leaders should run afoul of U.S. interests.

When U.S. security planners come to define "radical populism" as a security threat, it is reasonable to be concerned that its containment or reversal could become a guiding goal for U.S. military assistance to Latin America. This concern is a serious one. If U.S. security assistance policy comes to regard national militaries as a counterbalance to elected populists, we run the very real danger of returning to a time when the region's armed forces assumed the extremely political role of deciding when civilian leaders had overstepped their constitutional bounds.

The spread of radical populism, Hill testified, is "overlaid upon states in the region that are generally marked by weak institutions and struggling economies. This resulting frailty of state control can lead to ungoverned or ill-governed spaces and people." Concern about "ungoverned spaces" recurs often in U.S. officials' discussions of hemispheric security threats. For U.S. security planners looking for the next terrorist threat, Latin America's many vast, neglected, and sparsely populated zones—strategically located jungles, navigable rivers, empty coastlines, busy but unmonitored borders—are viewed as places where "evildoers" can organize, recruit, raise funds, and plot attacks with little state interference. Terrorists and transnational criminals "often find shelter in border regions or areas beyond the effective reach of government," says Rumsfeld. "They watch, they probe, looking for areas of vulnerability, for weaknesses, and for seams in our collective security arrangements that they can try to exploit."

Bringing the rule of law and government services to historically neglected zones is not necessarily a military mission—unless, of course, dangerous armed groups are entrenched in these areas. However, the Bush administration is showing no interest in supporting the spread of non-military governance: The 2006 foreign aid request foresees a precipitous drop in economic aid to nearly all of the region, especially development assistance, and child survival and health programs.

Instead, the emphasis of U.S. security planners is on closing "seams" in security structures. Defense planners see terrorists potentially thriving in geographical gaps between countries or governed spaces, and in the functional gaps between the roles of militaries and the missions of police forces. Pentagon civilians call their proposed response "effective sovereignty," meaning that Latin American governments must effectively exercise sovereignty over their full national territory. They call for helping the region's security forces to operate in ungoverned spaces, encouraging a blurring of the "seam" between military and police roles.

"Effective sovereignty" has not yet led to an increase in military assistance to the region. Excluding Colombia, military and police aid levels have been rather flat at roughly $300 million to $350 million a year region-wide. The number of trainees from outside Colombia has also seen relatively moderate growth, from 8,797 in 2001 to 9,884 in 2003.

There are exceptions, however, which indicate where the effort to "fill the seams" has begun. Ecuador and Panama have received aid to beef up their security forces' presence along their shared borders with Colombia. The Southern Command's exercise program now includes "Panamax," a multinational exercise in which the region's militaries practice defending the Panama Canal from a terrorist attack. The 2006 aid request includes $5 million to launch "Enduring Friendship," an effort to increase maritime cooperation among the navies of the Caribbean. In the next few years, we can probably expect efforts to expand this program to the entire hemisphere.

Mexico may be seeing an increase in U.S. military and police assistance with a focus on anti-terror border control. According to State Department spokesman Richard Boucher, "In 2004, we sponsored over 100 training courses attended by more than 4,000 Mexican police officers and prosecutors, working on everything from criminal investigations, anti-corruption, border safety, forensics, kidnapping, hostage negotiations—there's a whole gamut of police techniques and police training."[2]

Meanwhile, the countries that offered soldiers for the Iraq war—El Salvador, Honduras, Nicaragua, and the Dominican Republic—are getting more aid and cooperation in return. This is especially the case with El Salvador, where Foreign Military Financing grants are expected to increase from $5 million in 2004 to $13 million in 2006.

Elsewhere in Central America, and in Mexico as well, U.S. defense planners have their eye on criminal gangs (a phenomenon that has been fed in part by massive deportations of Central American criminals from U.S. jails). While there is discussion in Washington of doing more to help the region's security forces to fight gangs, no concrete proposals—whether for military or police aid—have yet been adopted.

In its effort to expand "effective sovereignty," one of the largest obstacles the Bush administration faces is, in fact, self-imposed. The "American Servicemembers' Protection Act," passed in 2003, requires a cutoff of non-drug military aid for countries that are signatories to the new International Criminal Court and do not offer special immunity to U.S. military personnel on their soil. Currently, 12 militaries in the region, including such major aid recipients as Bolivia, Ecuador, and Peru, are getting no non-drug aid.

A more important obstacle to "effective sovereignty" is a lack of regional enthusiasm for the concept. This was evident in the November 2004 meeting of the hemisphere's defense ministers, at which Donald Rumsfeld's vague calls for "a new regional defense architecture" were largely rebuffed by governments who clearly do not share the Bush administration's perception of imminent threats rooted in ungoverned spaces, and who are unwilling to give police roles to their militaries. In a troubling development, reports from those present at the Quito summit indicate that the U.S. delegation resisted a push to include explicit references to human rights and international humanitarian law in the final declaration's discussion of anti-terrorism.

Anyone concerned about human rights, democracy, and healthy civil-military relations in the Americas must be extra-vigilant during this moment of

Washington's preoccupation with "seams," "ungoverned spaces" and "radical populists." Strategies and policy patterns begun now could become the blueprint for U.S. security relations with the hemisphere for some time to come. What's more, a renewed effort to mobilize militaries against an "internal enemy" risks a repeat of past policies that yielded such well-known tragic consequences.

The U.S. debate too often ignores the fact that the threats being envisioned rarely require a military response. Outside of Colombia and its border zones, armed movements have not emerged, and the terrorist threat to the United States cannot be described as immediate. There is still time to mobilize non-military resources to make "ungoverned spaces" inhospitable to terrorists. Democratic governance can be improved, and economic opportunity created by investment in civilian police forces, judges, courts, prosecutors, mayors and governors, roads, schools, clinics, energy, potable water, credit, land titling, technical assistance, and anti-poverty programs. Instead of changing the region's "security architecture," the U.S. government can make Latin America safer by helping to close the wide "seams" that persist between wealth and poverty, law and disorder, participation and isolation, and citizenship and neglect.

NOTES

1. Linda Robinson, "Terror Close to Home," *U.S. News & World Report* (October 6, 2003).
2. U.S. Department of State, "State Department Briefing" (January 27, 2005).

BEYOND THE LAST GASP: U.S. POLICY ON CUBA

BY PHILIP BRENNER AND MARGUERITE JIMENEZ
NACLA Report, January/February 2006

In the fall of 2005 the National Intelligence Council of the CIA added Cuba to its secret list of 25 allegedly unstable countries where U.S. intervention might be required.[1] This move followed Secretary of State Condoleezza Rice's appointment in July of Caleb McCarry as coordinator of the U.S. effort "to hasten the end of the dictatorship in Cuba."[2]

These recent measures and sharp rhetoric may be no more than the sort of mostly symbolic crumbs presidents have tossed to hardliners in the Cuban American community for at least a quarter-century—a little payback to a constituency that solidly backed both campaigns of President George W. Bush. But U.S. policy toward Cuba is rooted in geopolitical considerations well beyond merely satisfying a domestic constituency. Cuba has once again emerged as a foreign policy concern of U.S. national security managers, and they have turned to an old stratagem of containment and isolation to address the perceived problem.

At the start of the 1990s, with the disappearance of the Soviet Union and Cuban president Fidel Castro's announcement that his country would cease supporting armed struggle in the Third World, President George H.W. Bush began viewing Cuba as a domestic rather than an international problem and turned the policy reins over to Congress. There, virulent anti-Castro demagogues held sway, supported and often instigated by likeminded lobbyists and activists. The clout of this lobby in the legislature—and in the executive after the 2000 election—has been seen as the main source of a hostile U.S. policy.

More recently, however, U.S. policy toward Cuba has received declining support from the general public, younger Cuban Americans and U.S. companies eager to trade with the island. In fact, majorities in both the House and Senate have demonstrated they are no longer afraid to challenge the anti-Castro lobby and have voted to modify several components of the U.S. embargo. Commerce seems to be trumping anti-Communism as the interests of Midwestern farmers increasingly overshadow those of the Florida ideologues.[3]

From this perspective, anti-Castro hardliners in the Bush administration are faced with a "now or never" situation. The increasing stridency of U.S. policy reflects their desperation in making a last-ditch attempt to overthrow the revolutionary Cuban regime. It is the final gasp of a dying policy, because as the older generation of exiles fades away, the seemingly "irrational" U.S. policy would follow them to the grave.[4]

By late summer 2003, right-wing Cuban Americans were feeling betrayed. They had helped deliver Florida's electoral votes to George W. Bush and believed they had gotten too little in return—despite the appointments of anti-Castro activists to key posts in the State Department, the U.S. Agency for International Development (USAID), the Defense Department, and the National Security Council. The administration had also denounced the Cuban government rhetorically and backed resolutions condemning Cuba at the UN Commission on Human Rights; cut off semi-annual talks with Cuba on immigration; increased funding for dissident groups on the island; and directed the U.S. Interests Section in Havana to provoke the government's ire by openly supporting these groups.[5] But like Bill Clinton before him, Bush had waived Title III of the Helms-Burton Act, which allows U.S. nationals to sue over property nationalized by the Revolution, and his other moves seemed more symbolic than substantive. Faced with growing dissatisfaction in October 2003 from a small but aggressive segment of his electoral base, Bush offered this faction the promise of a major initiative against Cuba: the Commission for Assistance to a Free Cuba. He mandated the Commission "to identify ways to hasten the arrival of that day" when "Castro's regime is no more."[6]

The outline of the new policy became clearly evident in the "Report to the President" released in May 2004 by the Commission. The last five chapters of the 500-page report describe a post-Castro, U.S.-governed transition to a market democracy. As Wayne Smith, the former chief of the U.S. Interests Section, mockingly observed, the detailed plans lay out how the firm hand of the United States would guide Cuba's transition by "setting up the right kind of schools, making sure the trains run on time, and all such matters. We can be sure that contracts for Bechtel and Halliburton are already planned."[7]

Appropriately, few analysts examined these pie-in-the-sky ideas. Attention focused on the first chapter—"Hastening Cuba's Transition"—because it contained policy proposals endorsed by the president that would take effect immediately. These included: restrictions on family visits, so that Cuban Americans would be able to return to the island only once every three years and would be allowed to spend no more than $50 per day on lodging and food; restrictions on remittances, so that U.S. citizens would be permitted to send money only to immediate family members in Cuba; restrictions on educational travel, so that U.S. colleges and universities would be licensed only for programs lasting at least 10 weeks; increased funds for political opponents of the regime inside Cuba and for U.S.-based programs designed to support dissidents; and stepped-up propaganda efforts, using U.S. military aircraft to transmit Radio and TV Martí broadcasts to Cuba.[8]

The month after the report's release, the Treasury Department's Office of Foreign Assets Control (OFAC) issued sweeping regulations that flowed from the Commission's recommendations. The new rules quickly led to significant reductions in travel by Cuban Americans and by religious or humanitarian groups. More than 300 U.S. colleges and universities shut down their academic programs in Cuba.[9] Marazul Charters, one of the largest providers of licensed travel between the United States and Cuba, reports U.S. travelers to Cuba declined by 80% from 2003 to 2005.[10] Similarly, the number of religious or humanitarian groups traveling to the island has fallen in the past two years from 160 to 20, cutting humanitarian aid and assistance to Cuba by an estimated $6 million.[11] In addition, OFAC stepped up its enforcement of the travel ban. In all of 2004, it imposed 392 fines against individuals, but as of mid-October 2005, it had imposed 587 individual fines, already an increase of almost 50%.[12]

There is little doubt that the Treasury's May 2004 regulations and the tougher enforcement of previous rules have hurt Cuba, but the long-term significance of these measures is less clear. In the U.S. context, several observers have suggested that the draconian rules may ultimately contribute to the embargo's unraveling, because they anger younger Cuban Americans who want to travel more frequently to the island, as well as others who want to send remittances to aunts, uncles, and non-family members. The travel restrictions even prompted a group of exiles to form the Cuban American Commission for Family Rights, whose mission is "to preserve the integrity of the Cuban family and work to defeat those who want to divide it."

Interestingly, the negative reaction by the exile community came as no surprise to Bush administration officials, who were urged to pressure the commission not to recommend restrictions on travel or remittances by exiles. Joe Garcia, a former head and current board member of the Cuban American National Foundation, asserted that the president's action undermined the unity of the Cuban American community. "It divides our base," he said. "It's not in his political best interest to divide a community whose support for president Bush makes Crawford, Texas, look like enemy territory."[13] That a politically astute administration would risk fracturing this key constituency suggests that the policy aims transcended the president's domestic political considerations. This points to the restoration of an antagonistic policy toward Cuba, rather than its disappearance.

Congressional bipartisan approval for increasing trade with Cuba and limiting the enforcement mechanisms of the embargo suggests the Bush administration is running out of supporters for its tough Cuba policy. Yet major anti-embargo legislative initiatives were scuttled in 2003 by House Majority Leader Tom DeLay's (R-Texas) legislative machinations. When differing House and Senate versions of the Transportation-Treasury appropriations bill went to conference for reconciliation, each version contained an identical Cuba amendment preventing the use of Treasury funds to enforce Cuba travel restrictions or travel-related transactions. Typically, a conference committee does not even look at provisions in a bill on which both chambers have agreed. But after DeLay surreptitiously removed it during conference consideration, the amendment, which would have in effect lifted the travel ban, "disappeared into the Congressional ether," Republican senator Michael Enzi of Wyoming caustically commented. In 2005 DeLay killed a series of amendments that would have eased embargo restrictions related to educational travel, gifts, and family visits to Cuba.[14] But with DeLay's own future in question since his indictment by a Texas grand jury in October 2005, embargo supporters lost an effective inside strategist.

Meanwhile, with the steady growth of U.S. agricultural sales to Cuba since 2001, the administration found itself fending off another congressional offensive. In 2004 Cuba bought $401 million worth of U.S. agricultural products, up from $259 million in 2003. But from January to August 2005, U.S. food sales to Cuba dropped by 22% compared to the same period the year before.[15] The main cause for the drop was a February 2005 Treasury Department ruling requiring that Cuba pay for food shipments before they leave a U.S. port. Previously, Cuba had paid for agricultural goods after inspecting the shipment while in transit, or upon its arrival to the island. In an effort to force the Treasury Department to back down from its restriction, Democratic senator Max Baucus of Montana held up consideration of several Treasury Department nominations. He relented in July 2005 after the Treasury promised to modify the rule.[16]

Although the Bush administration lost this particular battle, the fight itself indicates the president is determined to press on aggressively against Cuba despite pressures from agricultural exporters. Moreover, the loss of DeLay was not a fatal blow to the administration's hostile Cuba policy, which now relies on Cuban American representative Lincoln Diaz-Balart (a Florida Republican, who gained a key leadership post on the House Rules Committee in January 2005) and on newly elected Republican senator Mel Martinez (also of Florida and the first Cuban American to hold a seat in the upper chamber).

Certainly some of the U.S. enmity toward Cuba is posturing, designed as in the past to appease hardline Cuban Americans, but the renewed emphasis in 2005 on promoting democracy in Cuba—essentially code words for regime change—go beyond the usual symbolic handouts to Miami extremists. The post of Cuba Transition Coordinator, a person whose sole responsibility in the State Department is to plan the overthrow of the Cuban government, remained empty for over a year after the Commission for Assistance to a Free Cuba recommended its creation. In announcing Caleb McCarry's appointment as Transition Coordinator, Secretary Rice strikingly described the position as "the keystone of our strategy" to "accelerate the demise of Castro's tyranny." A reliable conservative, McCarry was in charge of a USAID-funded, quasi-private "democracy" promotion program in

Guatemala in the late 1980s and later worked on the Republican staff of the House International Relations Committee.

McCarry's point man in Cuba is Michael Parmly, the new chief of the U.S. Interests Section, who replaced the abrasive and ineffectual James Cason last September. Parmly is a seasoned diplomat with significant experience in attempting to create market democracies in post-conflict situations. He served as the senior U.S. adviser involved in organizing the 2004 elections in Afghanistan and was charge d'affaires at the U.S. Embassy in Sarajevo, tasked with implementing the Dayton Accords. In naming a highly regarded professional with Parmly's background, the Bush administration indicated its serious commitment to challenging the legitimacy of the Cuban government and engineering a transition.

Parmly also has much more money at his disposal than his predecessor, thanks to a $59 million budget allocation earmarked for Cuban transition efforts. This is a whopping increase of $50 million from the year before. USAID doles out some of the money to the anti-Castro lobby in the United States, but significant amounts are spent inside Cuba, on programs designated to: "build solidarity with democratic activists"; "give voice to independent journalists"; "help develop independent Cuban nongovernmental organizations"; "[provide] direct outreach to the Cuban people."[17]

The Bush administration has tried to avoid interactions with Cuba that might be misinterpreted as a diminution of its hostility. For example, in the devastating aftermath of Hurricane Katrina, Castro offered the services of 1,100 Cuban doctors to the stricken areas, a number he soon raised to 1,586. Washington made no official reply to the offer. Even Senator Martinez decried the lengths to which the administration would go to demonstrate its hostility toward Cuba. "If we need doctors," he said, "and Cuba offers them and they provide good service, of course we should accept them, and we're grateful for that offer."[18]

From Cuba's perspective, the most egregious recent provocation has been the U.S. government's harboring of Luis Posada Carriles, a convicted international terrorist known to have been involved in the 1976 bombing of a civilian Cuban airliner that killed all 73 people on board.

In May 2005 he turned up in Miami, asking for political asylum. Bush seemed to be faced with the choice of angering Cuban Americans if he sent Posada to Venezuela, which had demanded the terrorist be extradited, or of vitiating his bold declarations on terrorism, such as his infamous dictum: "If you harbor a terrorist, if you aid a terrorist, if you hide terrorists, you're just as guilty as the terrorists."[19] The president chose to leave Posada dangling in limbo, languishing in a Texas jail until late September 2005, when a federal judge ruled that he could not be extradited to either Venezuela or Cuba, because both countries allegedly practice torture.

The explanation for Bush's behavior in this case may simply be that he bowed to the demands of those Cuban Americans who see Posada as a hero. But given how central the "war on terror" is to the President's overall foreign policy agenda, he stood to benefit much more from affirming his anti-terrorist credentials than from placating Cuban exiles. An alternative explanation is that by harboring Posada, the Bush administration sends a chilling message to Cuba, and perhaps Venezuela, that it would not rule out the use of terrorists in confronting the perceived threat these two countries pose, even at the risk of sacrificing the legitimacy of the war on terror.

Bush administration efforts to frame its Cuba policy in terms of U.S. national security strain its minimal credibility. Still, Cuba remains on the State Department's list of countries supporting terrorism, despite distortions in the evidence used to justify Cuba's inclusion. Mark Sullivan of the Congressional Research Service, for instance, observes that those who advocate that Cuba should stay on the list have succeeded in part by pointing "to the [Cuban] government's history of supporting terrorist acts and armed insurgencies in Latin America and Africa" during the Cold War.[20] Yet it is not an irrational Cold War legacy that propels Bush administration officials to consider Cuba a real threat. Daniel Fisk, now the National Security Adviser for the Western Hemisphere, clearly articulated the nature of the perceived threat at a congressional hearing in October 2005. Identifying the "strategically located Caribbean basin" as a "high priority for this administration," he warned of the growing influence of Cuba and Venezuela in the region:

Cuba employs diplomatic outreach, deploys medical personnel and services to Caribbean countries, and offers of scholarships and assistance to Caribbean students to study in Cuba. Likewise, Venezuela maintains an active diplomatic presence throughout the Caribbean basin and provides aid to several of the smaller islands. Most recently, Hugo Chávez launched Petrocaribe, a scheme to create a network of state-run oil enterprises to market Venezuelan oil. Venezuela's concept for Petrocaribe undermines the position of private sector companies in the region and advances his "Bolivarian alternative" trade and economic agenda.

Ultimately the threat is political, Fisk explains, because of "Cuban and Venezuelan attempts to drive a wedge between the U.S. and its Caribbean partners."[21] In effect, he is saying both endanger traditional U.S. dominance in the Western Hemisphere and are viewed as acting in tandem. Strikingly, Stephen McFarland, the U.S. Deputy Chief of Mission in Venezuela, simply switched positions in September with Kevin Whittaker, who had been head of the State Department's Cuba desk.

Ominously, Washington's establishment pundits have subtly embraced this security lens, which is fast becoming the standard way of describing Cuba and Venezuela. "Chávez is a man with a mission," Michael Shifter, vice president of the Inter-American Dialogue, said in a recent interview in reference to Venezuela's president. "He is intent on building a counterweight to U.S. influence in the Western Hemisphere." Similarly, Jackson Diehl, a *Washington Post* editorial writer, blithely asserted in a recent column that Chávez was the "political and ideological successor to Fidel Castro" moving forward in an "aggressive attempt to succeed where Castro failed in creating an anti-American alliance."[22]

Since Chávez was elected president in 1998, Venezuela and Cuba have entered into a series of economic agreements that provide both countries with resources each respectively lacks. Cuba receives 90,000 barrels of oil a day in exchange for sending thousands of doctors and teachers to work in Venezuela. In late 2004 Castro and Chávez signed an agreement they said formed the base of the Bolivarian Alternative for the Americas (ALBA), a proposed integration pact that seeks to include all Latin American and Caribbean countries as a counter-proposal to the U.S.-sponsored Free Trade Area of the Americas (FTAA). Despite the uncertain future of both agreements, the rise of left-of-center governments in South America giving Cuba unusual regard adds another reason for the administration to once again see Cuba as a foreign policy challenge.

Recent trade agreements between China and Cuba also fuel the Bush administration's wariness about Havana. President Hu Jintao's November 2004 visit to Cuba highlighted the importance his country seems to accord its new relationship with the island. Hu agreed to postpone the repayment of debt that Cuba incurred between 1990 and 1994, and said China would provide new credits for the purchase of 1 million television sets and hospital equipment. The Chinese also donated $9 million for airport X-ray equipment and cloth for school uniforms. Cuba secured an agreement in which it will send 4,000 tons of nickel per year to China through 2009 in return for a $500 million investment to finish the construction of a large nickel plant in the province of Holguín. The investment is projected to double the island's nickel production. Cuban trade with China is now 10% of the island's total international commerce, and it ranks China as Cuba's third largest trading partner behind Spain and Venezuela.[23]

The concern about China's relationship with Cuba is two-fold. First, China's investment reinforces Cuba's ability to withstand U.S. pressure, reducing the leverage exercised by the Bush administration. Second, the investments underscore a growing Chinese strategy in Latin America of securing long-term access to badly needed natural resources. In 2004, nearly half of China's foreign direct investment went to Latin America, whereas only 23% went to Asia. Similarly, China's bilateral trade with Latin American countries grew from $12.6 billion in 2001 to $26.8 billion in 2003.[24]

With these geopolitical considerations in mind, U.S. policy toward Cuba has in many ways reverted back to its Cold War aims. After the 1962 missile crisis, U.S. officials largely abandoned the goal of militarily subverting the regime, and focused instead on containing Cuba's influence in the Third World. Containment, with its components of subversion and destabilization, has once again emerged as the favored goal, not as an irrational vestige of the Cold War, but as a rational response to a perceived menace. The threat is not so great to warrant direct U.S. intervention, even if the United States had the military capacity to invade Cuba, which it does not. But by the administration's calculations, Cuba's renewed challenge to U.S. hemispheric dominance does warrant hostility—isolating it, denigrating it, and keeping it on edge so that it wastes resources on defenses against the possibility of a U.S. attack.

U.S. sanctions themselves are too insignificant to have a fatally destructive impact, as the recovery of the Cuban economy—particularly with the growing ties with countries like China and Venezuela—continues to show. Yet this does not suggest that sanctions are merely payback to Bush's conservative Florida supporters, and so would consequently disappear without Cuban American pressure. They serve a rational purpose within the hegemonic logic and unremitting confrontational stance that guides Bush administration policies, which in the Cuban case are rooted in a new assessment of "the Cuban threat."

NOTES

1. Guy Dinmore, "US Steps Up Planning for a Cuba Without Castro," *Financial Times* (November 1, 2005).
2. Announcement of Cuba Transition Coordinator Caleb McCarry, Bureau of Public Affairs, U.S. State Department (July 28, 2005).
3. William M. LeoGrande, "The United States and Cuba: Strained Engagement," in Morris Morley and Chris McGillion, eds., *Cuba, the United States, and the Post-Cold War World* (University Press of Florida, 2005).
4. Lissa Weinmann, "Washington's Irrational Cuba Policy," *World Policy Journal* (spring 2004): 23; "Election-Year Cuba Policy," *The New York Times* (June 27, 2004).
5. Alfredo Corchado, "Bush Favors Confrontational Approach to Castro, Cuba," *Dallas Morning News* (May 9, 2003); Philip Brenner, "Overcoming Asymmetry: Is a Normal US-Cuban Relationship Possible?" in H. Michael Erisman and John M. Kirk, eds., *Redefining Cuban Foreign Policy: The Impact of the "Special Period"* (University Press of Florida, 2006).
6. "President Bush Discusses Cuba Policy in Rose Garden Speech," Office of the Press Secretary, the White House (October 10, 2003).
7. Wayne S. Smith, "Cuba shaping up as Iraq II: Administration's Gaffes on Verge of Being Repeated in 'Transition,'" *The Atlanta Journal-Constitution* (May 27, 2004).
8. "Fact Sheet: Report of the Commission for Assistance to a Free Cuba," Office of the Press Secretary, the White House (May 6, 2004).
9. *Federal Register* 69, no. 115 (June 16, 2004), Department of the Treasury, Office of Foreign Assets Control, 31 CFR part 515, Cuban Assets Control Regulations; Joshua Karlin-Resnick, "Federal Rules to Cramp Study Abroad in Cuba," *Chronicle of Higher Education* (June 25, 2004): 41.
10. Bob Guild, staff member, Marazul Charters, personal communication with the authors (October 17, 2005).
11. Gary Marx, "Tougher U.S. Policy Curtails Aid to Cubans," *Chicago Tribune* (October 10, 2005).

12. Data compiled by the authors from "Civil Penalties Information," Office of Foreign Assets Control, U.S. Department of the Treasury. The average fine in 2005 was $1,157.
13. Susan Milligan, "New US Travel Restrictions Irk Some Anti-Castro Cubans: Administration Move Could Stir a Voter Backlash," *The Boston Globe* (July 4, 2004).
14. Wayne S. Smith, "Undemocratic Process," *The Nation* (March 15, 2004); Bob Cusack, "DeLay Swings Momentum Against Easing Cuba Limits," *The Hill* (July 6, 2005).
15. "Farm Products to Cuba Soar," *CQ Weekly Report* (May 30, 2005): 1424; U.S. Census Bureau, "Foreign Trade Statistics, Trade With Cuba: 2005" (October 13, 2005); U.S. Census Bureau, Foreign Trade Division, Data Dissemination Branch, Washington, D.C.
16. Edmund L. Andrews, "Senate Confirms 5 for Vacant Senior Posts at Treasury Dept.," *The New York Times* (July 30, 2005).
17. USAID, "FY 2005 Congressional Budget Justification: Cuba" (January 14, 2005).
18. Pablo Bachelet, "Martinez: Cuban Aid Should Be Welcomed," *The Miami Herald* (September 8, 2005).
19. See press release at www.whitehouse.gov.
20. Mark Sullivan, "Cuba: Issues for the 109th Congress," Congressional Research Service, Library of Congress, Report for Congress no. RL32730 (May 25, 2005): 25.
21. Daniel Fisk, "Statement Before the Subcommittee on the Western Hemisphere, House Committee on International Relations" (October 19, 2005).
22. Michael Shifter, "Dealing With Venezuela," *The Washington Post* (September 6, 2005); Jackson Diehl, "Buying Support in Latin America," *The Washington Post* (September 26, 2005).
23. Marc Frank, "Hu Extends Hand of Friendship to Forsaken Comrades of Cuba," *Financial Times* (November 24, 2004); Philip Peters, "Cuba's International Economic Strategy Pays Off," *Cuba Policy Report* (the Lexington Institute, February 2005).
24. R. Evan Ellis, *U.S. National Security Implications of Chinese Involvement in Latin America* (Strategic Studies Institute, U.S. Army War College, June 2005).

DEMOCRACY AND PLAN COLOMBIA

BY HÉCTOR MONDRAGÓN
NACLA Report, January/February, 2007

President George W. Bush has asked the American people to "be patient" so that Iraq can become like Colombia—so that the Iraqis can defeat terrorism and establish a stable democracy like the one Washington has nurtured in Colombia. I would like to comment on this nightmare.

Plan Colombia, a "pro-democracy" aid package provided by the United States to Colombia, was established in 1999. Its primary stated objective was to end drug trafficking in Colombia. Later on, it was discovered that the plan had the further objective of defeating the guerrilla movement, though that component of the plan was never acknowledged by Washington while Bill Clinton was in office. It was, however, made explicit in subsequent versions of the plan devised by George W. Bush's administration, which identified its principal objective as combating "narco-terrorism," thus conflating the drug war with the anti-guerrilla struggle. Furthermore, the Bush government has proposed that the plan combat any other threat to the security of the Colombian state, a proposal that has since been repeated in a State Department document. Obviously, these "other threats" to Colombian security do not refer to extraterrestrials, but to forces like the Chávez government in Venezuela and the indigenous mobilizations in Ecuador—forces that represent anti-neoliberal, anti-imperial changes in South America by way of democratic elections and popular mobilization.

Washington has now spent $4.7 billion on Plan Colombia, and if you include the expenditures of the U.S. Agency for International Development (USAID) in that total, it reaches $7.7 billion. But despite this investment, the U.S.-supported government of Álvaro Uribe has defeated neither the drug traffickers nor the guerrilla movement. To the contrary, the plan's only success has been to guarantee a majority to the parties that supported Uribe in the Congressional elections of March 2006, and to guarantee Uribe's own re-election last May.

When Uribe was first elected, his primary campaign promise had been to defeat the guerrillas, and to accomplish this, he instituted a one-time war tax. In his campaign for re-election, he proposed a second "one-time" war tax. The reality is that, far from being defeated, the guerrilla movement in Colombia is today much stronger than when Uribe began his presidency. The guerrillas had been hard hit in the last year of the Pastrana government and during Uribe's first year, in part thanks to U.S. technical assistance to the Colombian air force that allowed it to engage in effective anti-guerrilla bombing campaigns. The guerrillas had also suffered setbacks due to their own political and strategic errors, many of which negatively—and gravely—affected the civil population.

Nevertheless, the U.S. Southern Command and the Uribe government committed a huge military error known as Plan Patriota, which called for the Colombian armed forces to surround and annihilate the guerrillas in their interior strongholds. But these were locations the guerrillas knew well and where they enjoyed solid popular support, allowing them to soundly defeat the military. Today the guerrillas—especially the FARC—have gained political momentum after having launched an effective counter-offensive. Over the past year the Colombian military's losses in the civil war have considerably surpassed those of the U.S. military in Iraq. The departments of Putumayo and Caquetá have been paralyzed for well over six months, and in many areas of Colombia the army cannot guarantee anyone's safety. Yet despite failing to fulfill his main electoral promise, Uribe still managed to be re-elected. How was this possible? To paraphrase Bill Clinton: It was the economy, stupid.

Like many other areas in the world, Colombia is experiencing a post-Iraq-invasion economic boom. But Colombia's boom may be the least sustainable of them all. Stock exchange values have increased 1,100%, meaning prices have multiplied 11 times. This has not occurred anywhere else since the 1920s, simply because no other country would allow it. Any other national bank or federal reserve system would intervene to curb such inflation, knowing that such rapid unchecked increases in value—which are not the result of growth but of pure speculation—will eventually cause a terrible recession. In Colombia this has not only been allowed, but actually encouraged through specific economic measures. For example, the Colombian state buys its own treasury bonds. It takes the money from its left pocket and lends it to its right pocket, and whereas a moment ago it had only four dollars, it now has eight—four dollars plus a certificate proving it has borrowed another four! So Colombia receives billions of dollars from the United States as part of Plan Colombia, and the Colombian government then lends the money back to itself. It plays the same game with its public health and pension funds. What's going to happen when the government has to pay this money back?

But this doesn't explain the whole story of Colombia's spectacular growth. There is a much more important explanation: the agreement with the paramilitaries. Many have criticized this agreement, arguing that it amounts to an amnesty for crimes against humanity. But all of this discussion has obscured the economic essence of the agreement, which is to allow the legalization of billions of paramilitary narco-dollars. The paramilitaries finance not only their operations, but also their lifestyles with the country's largest drug-trafficking operations.

Since negotiations between Uribe and the paramilitaries began, billions of dollars and euros in drug profits have entered Colombia. Throughout 2003, 2004, and the beginning of 2005, moreover, the paramilitaries exported a huge quantity of the cocaine they had stockpiled, knowing that anything sold prior to the amnesty would be pardoned under the peace agreement. This is the true cause of the enormous wave of speculation—a sea of illicit funds entering Colombia. And like an emperor of ancient Rome, Uribe was able to provide the populace with "bread and circuses" prior to the presidential elections of May 2006. Was Washington aware of this? Of course it was.

What is the primary objective of Plan Colombia? Never before have drug traffickers had so much power in Colombia. Today they have penetrated the stock market, laundered their drug money in the form of treasury bonds and gained a foothold in the electoral process. And although those in Uribe's party who have been publicly identified as drug lords were purged, they created their own parallel pro-Uribe parties and have gotten themselves elected to Congress. This is not to say anything of those drug lords who have not been publicly identified and who remain on Uribe's party's lists.

In the past, drug traffickers financed electoral campaigns from the shadows, financing publicity and paying for hotels and travel. This was a relatively small-scale operation. Today, however, they openly finance entire electoral campaigns. The government's own statistics acknowledge that in 2005, $3 billion flowed through Colombia, with no record of how the money entered the country. No one planted money seeds and grew the $3 billion; this is just a portion of the billions of dollars and euros that the paramilitaries have laundered. Why does Washington, with its moral crusade, the war on drugs, permit this? Because Colombia serves as its base for attacking the democratic processes taking place in neighboring countries.

This is the reality of U.S. intervention in Colombia. Colombia is becoming an eternal battleground, in order to secure the country as a base of operations for controlling Ecuador, Venezuela, and possibly even Peru, Brazil, and Bolivia. They say, "Have patience with Colombia; we're heading to Venezuela and Ecuador! Be patient with Iraq; we're on our way to Iran."

In Colombia we are used to the fabrication of news that prevents us from seeing the reality that Uribe's government reaps a harvest of terror; of 60 years of violence; of the killing of 4,000 trade unionists; of the destruction of workers' rights; of the displacement of 3 million peasants from their land—and of transnational capital, which finds abundant cheap labor now that its trade unions have been violently destroyed.

In Colombia, however, there is also a democratic civil resistance that rejects the guerrillas' methods and that is often, in fact, victimized by the guerrillas. It proposes a different country—one not ruled by drug barons, where food is secure and where the social movements that have resisted decades of terror have the political weight they deserve. Before paramilitary narco-dollars arrived, this civil resistance was able to elect the mayor of Bogotá and defeat a referendum in which Uribe sought to change the constitution to nullify our democratic rights. It has organized general strikes in December 2002 and October 2004; massive indigenous marches called *mingas*; and a popular consultation against the free-trade agreement in indigenous regions, in which more than 86% of the population voted.

Every day those of us in social movements risk our lives to change Colombia so that our country will stop moving against the grain of the rest of Latin America. Every day we risk our lives so that Colombia can be united with Venezuela and Ecuador, with what the MST (Movimento dos Trabalhadores Rurais Sem Terra) is building in Brazil, with what the Uruguayans are doing, with what our people are doing these days in Los Angeles. The future of our country is in the balance.

ANOTHER SOA? A U.S. POLICE ACADEMY IN EL SALVADOR WORRIES CRITICS

BY WES ENZINNA
NACLA Report, March/April 2008

With a salt-and-pepper beard and darting, intelligent eyes, Benjamín Cuéllar explains how he has built a successful career as a human rights defender in El Salvador, where more than 40,000 political assassinations have taken place since 1977. We are sitting in his office at the Institute for Human Rights (IDHUCA) on the campus of the University of Central America, and he is telling me about the time he was almost kidnapped and murdered. "It was October 4, 1995," he begins, "and the sun had just gone down. Five men with guns came in a pickup truck." The harrowing tale ends, luckily, with Cuéllar's escape. Framed on the wall behind him are some of the awards the IDHUCA has won since Cuéllar became director of the organization in 1992: the French Medal for Human Rights, the Ignacio Ellacuria Human Rights Award, and the Washington Office on Latin America's 2007 Award for Human Rights.

But despite Cuéllar's work, many are questioning his legitimacy as a human rights defender because of his most recent endeavor: working as an instructor and human rights monitor for a new U.S.-run police-training school called the International Law Enforcement Academy, or ILEA, located in San Salvador. Classes at the school began July 25, 2005, and as of July 2007 the academy had graduated 791 students, mostly police officers, as well as prosecutors and judges. A quarter of classroom seats are reserved for Salvadorans, while the remaining students are drawn from other countries throughout Latin America.

The academy is part of a network of ILEAs created in 1995 under President Bill Clinton, who envisioned a series of U.S. schools "throughout the world to combat international drug trafficking, criminality, and terrorism through strengthened international cooperation." There are ILEAs in Budapest, Hungary; Bangkok, Thailand; Gaborone, Botswana; and Roswell, New Mexico. While the others have mostly been uncontroversial, the ILEA San Salvador has sparked outrage in both the United States and El Salvador, earning comparisons to the Western Hemisphere Institute for Security Cooperation, or WHINSEC, formerly known as the School of the Americas—the Fort Benning, Georgia, school for Latin American militaries that gained notoriety in the late 1990s for having trained some of the region's worst human rights abusers.

"The legacy of U.S. training of security forces at the School of the Americas and throughout Latin America is one of bloodshed, of torture, of the targeting of civilian populations, of *desaparecidos*," wrote SOA Watch founder Roy Bourgeois after Secretary of State Condoleezza Rice announced plans for the ILEA San Salvador at a June 2005 Organization of American States meeting in Miami. "Rice's recent announcement about plans for the creation of an international law enforcement academy in El Salvador should raise serious concerns for anyone who cares about human rights," he said.

And as recently as June, a member of the Committee in Solidarity With the People of El Salvador (CISPES) wrote, "The ILEA in El Salvador is functioning like another SOA, under a new name and in a new location."

Unlike the SOA, the ILEA is run jointly by the Salvadoran Ministry of Government and the U.S. State Department—though virtually all its instructors come from the United States, and most of the school's expenses are covered by U.S. tax dollars. By the end of 2007, the United States had spent at least $3.6 million on the academy, according to an estimate by ILEA director Hobart Henson. While the school is temporarily housed at the National Academy for Public Security in San Salvador, a permanent $4 million headquarters is under construction.

The school joins a slew of other police- and military-training facilities throughout Latin America run by U.S. agencies, among them the FBI, Customs Agency, and DEA, as well as training programs run by private U.S. security companies like DynCorp International. In 1999, the last year for which figures are available, Washington trained between 13,000 and 15,000 Latin American military and police personnel, according to the Center for International Policy.

U.S. and Salvadoran officials should not have been surprised with the opposition to the ILEA and the comparisons to the SOA. Before settling on El Salvador, the United States had hoped to establish an ILEA South in Costa Rica, but failed. "The story of what happened in Costa Rica," says Guadalupe Erazo of the Popular Social Bloc, a coalition of Salvadoran activists, "is instructive because it shows the undemocratic nature of the ILEA, and the [lack of] accountability to the public."

After a brief, aborted attempt to establish the school in Panama , U.S. officials chose Costa Rica to host the academy in 2002. An agreement with the Costa Rican government was signed, making the deal official, and the plan made headlines across the country. The agreement allowed for military topics to be taught and military personnel to participate in the school, and also gave immunity to U.S. officials. When this became public, a broad coalition of Costa Rican citizen, labor, and human rights groups demanded these clauses be removed from the agreement. The Costa Rican government ultimately adopted the public's demands in its negotiations.

The United States, however, refused to meet these conditions, and as Kathryn Tarker of the Council on Hemispheric Affairs put it, "Washington decided to 'pick up the marbles and go home' rather than offer concessions to transparency and anti-military safeguards."

Hoping to avoid the problems encountered in Costa Rica, the U.S. and Salvadoran governments worked quietly to establish the ILEA in San Salvador. In fact, at the time of Rice's June 2005 announcement at the OAS—the first time the school had been mentioned publicly—U.S. officials were already planning for classes to begin. Little more than a month after Rice's announcement, 36 students from Colombia, the Dominican Republic, and El Salvador began a course titled "Organized Crime and Human Rights" at the Comalapa air force base on the outskirts of San Salvador. Yet it wasn't until almost two months later, on September 20, that then U.S. ambassador H. Douglas Barclay and Salvadoran minister of governance Rene Figueroa signed an agreement officially establishing the school.

In the months prior to September, public debate about the ILEA was scant. Members of the U.S. Congress were not briefed about the academy, nor was the main opposition party in El Salvador, the Farabundo Martí National Liberation Front (FMLN). But once the news media reported that the two countries had signed an official agreement in September, activists in El Salvador demanded to see the text of the document. Protesting their exclusion, a coalition of Salvadoran activists, including the Sinti Techan Citizens Network, demanded that President Antonio Saca make the agreement public and develop an open debate, consulting "all social sectors of the country before submitting it to the Legislative Assembly."

This never happened. While FMLN senators denounced the school in the assembly and made a last-ditch effort to prevent the agreement from being ratified, their bile-filled rants, rather than critical arguments, did little to convince anyone. "We cannot support them coming in to deform the minds of our police, prosecutors and judges," FMLN deputy Salvador Arias later said. Ultimately, the FMLN failed to mobilize the country's social movements, and much of the public remained in the dark on the details of what was at stake. On November 30, 2005, the National Assembly ratified the ILEA agreement, with 48 out of 88 members voting in favor.

In the end, the United States achieved what it couldn't in Panama or Costa Rica: The ILEA was official, and the ratified agreement making it so allowed for no mechanism of transparency or civilian oversight, included no agreement excluding military personnel or topics, and left the door open for a later clause that would give U.S. personnel immunity from prosecution.

STILL NO TRANSPARENCY

While Salvadoran activists struggled to obtain more information about the ILEA in the months leading up to the Legislative Assembly vote, there was someone—

outside of powerful police and political circles—who knew all about what the school was up to: Cuéllar. "During this crucial time, Cuéllar did not share key information with his supposed allies," says Erazo. For this reason, many in the anti-ILEA camp distrust him and believe he is implicated in the school's secrecy.

In May 2005, Cuéllar and the IDHUCA were invited to discuss the ILEA at the U.S. Embassy with officials from the Department of Homeland Security and the FBI. IDHUCA was asked to participate in the ILEA by giving a course on human rights, based on similar courses they had given to police in the past. After researching the other ILEAs worldwide, Cuéllar signed on. (Cuéllar says he suggested to U.S. officials that they invite other Salvadoran human rights organizations to participate in the ILEA. These groups, including FESPAD, Las Dignas, and CENTA, could not be reached for comment or to confirm this claim.)

For its participation, the IDHUCA would be paid $500 for two days of human rights courses during every six-week "core program." Cuéllar and his colleagues would have no power to change the curriculum or to participate in organizational decisions, though they would be able to review everything taught at the school, attend any class, and speak with any instructor.

Many of El Salvador's most prominent activists came out strongly against Cuéllar's participation. "Cuéllar is being fooled," says labor leader Wilfredo Berrios. "It's a shame because his presence at the school gives some people the impression that it is promoting and safeguarding human rights. I don't know whether to laugh or to cry."

Cuéllar dismisses his critics as unrealistic. "The school is here, and that's a fact— are we supposed to cry over spilled milk? You have to protect human rights with concrete plans, not screams," he says. He also believes it is better to be on the inside monitoring the school, because you have to be "inside to have any influence."

"We don't know what the future holds," he adds, "but for now, from our perspective, the school appears to simply offer technical training—it offers some of the resources we need."

ILEA officials say their exclusive goal is to teach police, prosecutors, and judges in improved law enforcement techniques focusing primarily on drug and gang crime. Cuéllar insists he has seen all the course materials and can verify this. But no one besides Cuéllar can be sure what the school is up to because its curriculum is private (except for course titles, which are available online), as are the names of all its students and graduates.

Many observers are troubled by this secrecy, considering how some School of the Americas atrocities came to light: with *Washington Post* reporter Dana Priest's discovery, in September 1996, of SOA torture training manuals, and later with Roy Bourgeois's acquisition of a previously classified list of SOA graduates, many of whom were recognized as leaders of death squads and notorious counterinsurgency groups. U.S. organizations like SOA Watch and CISPES, as well as the Popular Social Bloc and Sinti Techan, have demanded that the school make public its course materials and the names of its graduates. In a March 2007 visit to the school, ILEA officials promised to send course materials to leaders of a CISPES and SOA Watch delegation. The materials never arrived, and to date the ILEA has not made public any information on its courses or graduates.

"You can't track the graduates of the ILEA in Salvador or their own country [in the case of non-Salvadoran students]," says Erazo. "So how are we supposed to monitor the school? We wouldn't even know if an ILEA grad had been involved in something, or if the ILEA was teaching objectionable topics." Course titles like "A Police Executive's Role in Combating Terrorism" further worry critics about what is being taught at the school.

Presented with these concerns, the ILEA's top official, Hobart Henson, who spent 24 years with the Indiana State Police before coming to El Salvador, assures me, "This isn't the SOA. We're not teaching torture or water boarding or anything like that. I wouldn't be involved in something I didn't feel good about." When I ask to see course materials, Henson equivocates, at first saying he doesn't have them in the office, then that it is school policy not to give them out. I also ask if I can speak with an ILEA graduate, and Henson says at first that the ILEA does not release the names of its graduates because some end up working as undercover agents. But when I repeat my request to speak with a graduate later in the interview, Henson asks Program Manager Juan Carlos Ibbott to make some phone calls.

The next day, I am speaking with Francisco Gómez, a midlevel officer in the National Civilian Police (PNC), who attended the "Law Enforcement Management Development Program" in early 2007. Gómez tells me his experience was a positive one and explains that it focused on technical matters like gathering evidence and crime-scene investigation, with a lesser focus on counter-terrorism ("This isn't a problem in El Salvador," he says, "but I suppose it could be"). He promises to get me the course materials and syllabi from his ILEA program. Nine months and many e-mails later, I haven't received anything.

A Freedom of Information Act request for ILEA course materials, filed in October, was denied.

CONTINUING POLICE ABUSE

ILEA critics point out not only the school's lack of transparency, but also the record of abuse already established by the PNC, which most of the school's Salvadoran students are drawn from. With about 16,000 officers, the PNC is El Salvador's largest police force. Its establishment in 1992 after the end of the Salvadoran civil war was seen by many as a step in the right direction, since it incorporated elements from the country's various political factions. As a Human Rights Watch report explains: "The formation of a professional, apolitical police force was generally seen as the most transcendent potential contribution of the historic 1992 peace accords." However, the PNC did not make good on its initial promise. "The most disturbing indication of setbacks in the establishment of this new force, the National Civilian Police," the report continues, "came with the news . . . of the involvement of a PNC agent in the 1993 assassination of FMLN leader Francisco Velis."

Abuses attributed to the PNC have continued since then. A September article by Raúl Gutiérrez for the Inter Press Service titled "Death Squads Still Operating in El Salvador" details numerous instances of murder committed by PNC agents since 1993, including a "social cleansing" death squad called Black Shadow, allegedly responsible for a spate of killings in 1994 and 1995.

In 2006, a little more than a year after the ILEA graduated its first class, three unknown men carrying large guns burst into the home of Carlos and Wilfredo Sánchez in the department of Sonsonate. The pair of brothers, both members of the Mara Salvatrucha gang, were pulled from their beds. As the Sánchez family looked on, the intruders beat the gang members, dragged them into the street, and shot them to death. Moments earlier, they had done the same to another Mara Salvatrucha member down the street.

A June 2006 report published by the Salvadoran government's human rights ombudswoman, Beatrice de Carrillo, identifies the gunmen in the Sánchez case as PNC officers. It details this and other PNC abuses, including the case of Abimilet Ramírez, who after being picked up by PNC officers was thrown down a well and later murdered. Another report by the Archbishop's Legal Aid and Human Rights Defense Office (Tutela Legal) provides evidence for 10 murders allegedly committed by PNC officers during 2006. One of the victims was, according to the report, tortured to death; one involved a nine-year-old boy shot to death; and eight of the murders resembled "death squad executions." The report also notes patterns of attempted "social cleansing," as well as strong evidence of political motivations behind several of the murders.

De Carrillo's report also notes that between 2001 and 2006, 40% of abuse complaints submitted to her office concerned the PNC.

Despite the evidence of abuse, U.S. officials deny that the PNC has done anything wrong. Lisa Sullivan, an SOA Watch member who visited the ILEA as part of the March 2007 delegation, confronted U.S. Embassy officials with the evidence of PNC abuse detailed in the Salvadoran government's human rights report. She says they showed "complete disdain" for the ombudswoman and said her reports were "illegitimate sources of information" and that there was no evidence to support her claims. Charles Glazer, the U.S. ambassador to El Salvador, would not go on record to comment about PNC abuse, but he did ask that I provide him with the human rights reports, which I did, offering to translate key passages for him. Neither Glazer nor his press attachés responded.

For his part, Cuéllar does not deny PNC abuse and says the ILEA will nonetheless improve and reform the police force. "In the way that [the ILEA] will develop the technical skills of police officers . . . many victims [of human rights crimes] will see results, and we will be able to denounce their victimizers with more clarity and objectivity," Cuéllar says.

This, however, contradicts the official U.S. line: Officials, including Hobart Henson, have said El Salvador was chosen to host the school in the first place because of the PNC's supposedly exemplary record. Ombudswoman de Carrillo believes that rather than reforming the PNC, the ILEA will only make it more "professional and elegant in its use of violence."

SAFEGUARDING FREE TRADE

The ILEA has arrived in El Salvador in a context of decades-long turmoil. The country is still struggling to overcome the legacies of a civil war that ended 16 years ago, one in which 75,000 people were killed. Although the formal conflict ended, violence continues to rage. In 2005, a typical year, an average 15 people a day were murdered in El Salvador. Youth, faced with few opportunities for political representation or economic advancement, have turned in startling numbers to gangs—one police estimate puts the number at 25,000 gang members nationwide—that mirror the most reactionary elements of the Salvadoran state in their level of ultra-violence.

Since the war's end, the country has become intensely polarized, with political assassinations continuing at a frightening pace. The violence and lack of economic opportunity continue to drive many into exile, and today remittances, primarily from the United States, account for an astounding 16% of the country's GDP. Moreover, the environment for civil liberties is one of the worst in the hemisphere. The result of so many years of formal and informal civil war has led to a striking loss of faith among Salvadorans in the political institutions of their country: In a 2007 Latinobarómetro poll, only 38% of Salvadorans said democracy is preferable to all other political systems.

The Salvadoran government has responded to the gang violence with zero tolerance, or *mano dura* ("iron fist"), policing. Mano dura policies have swept Central America in the 21st century, frequently combining military troops with police units to patrol crime-plagued areas. The first anti-gang mano dura law introduced in El Salvador, in July 2003, allowed police to use tattoos on a suspect's body as evidence of gang membership. A November 2006 report by the Washington

Office on Latin America points out that "in the year after [this] first *mano dura* law was enacted in El Salvador . . . 19,275 people were detained by the police on the charge of belonging to a gang. In a striking illustration of what happens when police are allowed to carry out detentions based on such arbitrary criteria, 91% of those detained were released without charge due to lack of evidence."

But the ILEA may have another goal besides training police to crack down on alleged gang members. The PNC has played an active role in a larger crackdown against civil liberties spearheaded by President Saca and his ARENA party, aimed at curbing both crime and social protest. Various government policies, especially free trade agreements like CAFTA, have been highly contentious, and Saca's administration has gone to significant lengths to ensure that they succeed— including passing an anti-terror law in September 2006, modeled on the USA Patriot Act, that has been used to arrest everyone from anti-water-privatization activists in Suchitoto to San Salvador's CD and DVD vendors who violated CAFTA's intellectual property rights stipulations. Charges against the vendors have been dropped, but the 13 people arrested in Suchitoto will begin trial this February, and could face up to 65 years in prison. The judge presiding over this case, Ana Lucila Fuentes de Paz, was installed as the head of a new court created by the September 2006 anti-terrorism legislation—not long after she completed her training at the ILEA.

An authoritarian government supported by a corrupt police force in El Salvador can help safeguard U.S. economic interests in the country. As much of Latin America turns away from extreme free-market policies, El Salvador remains one of Washington's key allies against the "pink tide" sweeping the region. El Salvador is, in many ways, one of the most important frontiers of Washington's unquestioned economic influence, governed by a president who cited a desire to please the United States as a prime reason for why he supported CAFTA.

That ILEA officials and the Saca administration share similar economic interests is confirmed by a report I obtained titled the "Law Enforcement Training Needs Assessment for the Latin American Region." This report, written in February 2005, is the founding document of the ILEA San Salvador, and was prepared by criminal justice expert Anthony Pate and the law-and-order think thank Police Executive Research Forum. (The president of this think tank is John Timoney, who has spearheaded mano dura law enforcement models in the United States; as the head of the Philadelphia and Miami police, respectively, he gained national notoriety for his jackbooted treatment of anti-free-trade protesters in the two cities, resulting in hundreds of injuries and several lawsuits.)

The "Needs Assessment" report establishes as one of the ILEA's priorities— alongside drug trafficking, arms trafficking, and kidnapping—"intellectual property rights." The raid on the bootleg vendors accused under the anti-terrorism law occurred less than a year after the ILEA opened its doors, and labor leader Berrios believes it is likely that ILEA graduates participated in the raid. He also speculates that pressure from the United States to enforce CAFTA's regulations could have prompted the raids in the first place.

While it may not be the school's primary function, promoting free trade and protecting U.S. economic interests is certainly part of the school. Henson acknowledges this much when he says, "A by-product of the school is to protect free trade and foreign investment." The State Department also notes that one of the ILEA's goals is to "enhance the functioning of free markets through improved legislation and law enforcement."

STAVING OFF CRITICISM

Cuéllar likes to tell a story to illustrate why he is involved with the ILEA. The Casquerilla brothers, aged 29 and 12, were eating breakfast one morning when several men entered their San Salvador home, which is also a small restaurant. When the men pulled out guns, the younger brother fled, and as he ran, the men shot him in the back. After the shooters left, the police arrived, and while they secured the house and restaurant, the boy, who had survived the shooting, bled to death. The police then told the women who had witnessed the shooting to leave.

"Beyond the fact of letting the child die," Cuéllar says with bewilderment, "they lost the principal witness [the boy] because of incompetence, and they let the women, who saw the shooters, leave without giving testimony and without getting their names or telephone numbers. This was five years ago, and his mother is a wreck. How can I look her in the face and deny her this opportunity to better train the police?"

But for all its pragmatism, Cuéllar's belief that the school will reform the PNC seems misguided. When U.S. officials categorically deny that the PNC is or has ever been involved in any abuses, it seems a contradiction to believe that they will reform them, or any other police force. Beatrice de Carrillo suggests that an earnest attempt to reform the PNC would take place at the Salvadoran National Police Academy, which is accountable to the Legislative Assembly, not the U.S. State Department.

And if Cuéllar's presence at the school might reassure some observers, trusting one man or organization is hardly a sound strategy to protect human rights. After all, in spite of the sacrifices he has made and the criticism he has received, it doesn't appear as if Cuéllar has challenged the secrecy that reigns supreme at the ILEA. The contradictions of Cuéllar's position are best illustrated by the way in which he is often compelled to defend the ILEA during our interview, frequently referring to the professionalism that the academy can offer El Salvador's police and skirting the issue of PNC abuse. This is something he should not have to do as human rights monitor of the organization, and something it is hard to imagine him doing at any time before in his career: defending the police and the U.S. government. Another contradiction is the ambiguity of Cuéllar's jurisdiction at the school—for instance, ILEA director Henson does not refer to Cuéllar as a human rights monitor, but rather as an "instructor of human rights courses."

Considering this, it seems Washington is benefiting much more from its relationship with Cuéllar than the other way around, and his presence at the school causes as many problems as it solves. As Lesley Gill, an anthropologist at American University and author of the book *School of the Americas: Military Training and Political Violence in the Americas*, explains, "The use of human rights discourses–in U.S. military and police training is something that started with the SOA. After the SOA was criticized for promoting violence and torture, they started to include a human rights course in their curriculum, and to use human rights language to describe what they were doing." She continues, "This human rights talk is more aimed at an outside, domestic audience—at the school's potential critics—than it is indicative of any effort by the U.S. to reform the military or police forces they are involved with. It is designed to stave off criticism. It seems to me that this is what they are doing [at the ILEA] by bringing on board someone like Cuéllar."

The ILEA continues holding classes, training hundreds of PNC officers as well as police from countries like the Dominican Republic, Colombia, and others throughout the hemisphere. As U.S. officials work to build the school's new headquarters in San Salvador and to expand the police academy's presence throughout the Americas, Cuéllar himself finally acknowledges the potential for abuse at the school.

"Contrary to what critics claim, the ILEA is not another SOA," Cuéllar says. "But it could become one."

Research assistance: Adam Evans.

CONTRIBUTORS

Florence E. Babb is professor of anthropology and women's studies at the University of Iowa. She is the author of *After Revolution: Mapping Gender and Cultural Politics in Neoliberal Nicaragua* (University of Texas, 2001).

David Bacon is a journalist and photographer covering labor, immigration, and the impact of the global economy on workers

Ricky Baldwin is a labor and anti-war activist and organizer whose articles have appeared in *Dollars & Sense, Z Magazine, Extra!, In These Times, Labor Notes,* and elsewhere.

Maude Barlow is chair of the Council of Canadians. Her book with Tony Clark, *Blue Gold: The Fight to Stop Corporate Theft of the World's Water* (The New Press, 2003) is now available in Spanish, *Oro azul: Las multinacionales y el robo organizado de agua en el mundo* (Barcelona: Ediciones Paidós Ibérica, 2004).

Hope Bastian is a freelance writer and popular educator for Witness for Peace. She currently lives in Mexico.

Betsy Bowman is on the editorial collective of *Grassroots Economic Organizing*. She is among the co-founders of the bilingual Center for Global Justice in San Miguel de Allende, Mexico, where she serves as a research associate.

Philip Brenner is a professor of international relations and director of the Interdisciplinary Council on Latin America at American University.

Aldo Caliari is coordinator of the Rethinking Bretton Woods Project at the Center of Concern (www.coc.org).

Esther Cervantes is a former member of the Dollars & Sense collective and a graduate of the LBJ School of Public Affairs.

Tony Clarke is the director of the Polaris Institute. His book with Maude Barlow, *Blue Gold: The Fight to Stop Corporate Theft of the World's Water* (The New Press, 2003) is now available in Spanish, *Oro azul: Las multinacionales y el robo organizado de agua en el mundo* (Barcelona: Ediciones Paidós Ibérica, 2004).

Cándida Cotto is a reporter for *Claridad* (www.claridadpuertorico.com). She teaches part-time at the University of Puerto Rico, Carolina.

James Cypher teaches economics at California State University, Fresno. In 2003 he was visiting research professor at the Facultad Latinoamericana de Ciencias Sociales (FLACSO-Chile). He is a *Dollars & Sense* associate and co-author of *The Process of Economic Development*, 2nd edition (Routledge, 2004).

Wes Enzinna is a graduate student in Latin American studies at the University of California–Berkeley. His articles have appeared in *The Nation* and other magazines, and on CBSNews.com.

Michael González-Cruz is Professor of Sociology and Director of the Centro de Investigación Social Aplicada (CISA) at the University of Puerto Rico, Mayagüez.

Gretchen Gordon is a research associates with the Cochabamba-based Democracy Center. She is a contributor to the book *Dignity and Defiance: Stories From Bolivia's Challenge to Globalization* (www.democracyctr.org).

Bret Gustafson teaches anthropology at Washington University in St. Louis. He is the author of *New Languages of the State: Indigenous Resurgence and the Politics of Knowledge in Bolivia* (Duke University Press, forthcoming).

Forrest Hylton is a Ph.D. candidate in history at New York University and author of *Evil Hour in Colombia* (Verso, 2006).

Adam Isacson has worked since 1995 at the Center for International Policy, an independent research and advocacy organization in Washington, D.C. He coordinates a program that monitors security and U.S. military assistance to Latin America and the Caribbean.

Marguerite Jimenez is a doctoral student in the School of Public Affairs at American University, and is co-editor, with Philip Brenner, John M. Kirk, and William M. Leogrande of *A Contemporary Cuba Reader: Reinventing the Revolution* (Rowman & Littlefield, 2008).

Karen Kampwirth is professor of political science at Knox College. She is the author of *Feminism and the Legacy of Revolution: Nicaragua, El Salvador, Chiapas* (Ohio University Press, 2004).

Marie Kennedy is professor emerita of Community Planning at the College of Public and Community Service, University of Massachusetts, Boston. She was a Fulbright Scholar at the Colegio de Tlaxcala in Mexico, and is on the board of Grassroots International.

Solana Larsen is an editor for openDemocracy.net in New York. She is also the founder and president of the Danish–Puerto Rican Society.

Gladys Lechini is professor of international relations at the National University of Rosario, Argentina. She is the author of *Argentina y Africa en el espejo de Brasil* (CLACSO, 2006).

Aaron Luoma is a research associates with the Cochabamba-based Democracy Center. He is a contributor to the book *Dignity and Defiance: Stories From Bolivia's Challenge to Globalization* (www.democracyctr.org).

Deidre McFadyen worked as editor of *NACLA Report* from 1991 to 1996 and now serves on NACLA's board of directors. She is an editor and writer at the United Federation of Teachers, in New York City.

Brian Meeks is professor of social and political change and director of the Centre for Caribbean Thought at the University of the West Indies, Mona, Jamaica. His books include *Caribbean Revolutions and Revolutionary Theory: An Assessment of Cuba, Nicaragua and Grenada* (Macmillan Caribbean, 1993) and *Narratives of Resistance: Jamaica, Trinidad, the Caribbean* (University of the West Indies Press, 2001).

Karin Monasterios P. is a sociologist and, until recently, a women's studies professor at the Universidad Mayor de San Andrés, in La Paz, Bolivia. She is now an adviser on indigenous and gender issues to the Morales government.

Héctor Mondragón has been a human rights worker in Colombia for 35 years, working closely with homeless shelters, labor organizations, human rights and church groups, and a number of indigenous groups. Trained as an economist, he has worked as an adviser to the Indian National Organization of Colombia and the Peasant National Council.

Pedro Monreal is a research economist at the Center for International Economic Research (CIEI) at the University of Havana.

Alejandro Reuss is a historian and economist, and writes on contemporary Latin America and global economic issues.

Karen Robert teaches Latin American and world history at St. Thomas University in New Brunswick, Canada, and is currently researching the social history of the automobile in Argentina.

Fred Rosen is NACLA's senior analyst. He divides his time between Mexico and New York.

Katherine Sciacchitano is a former labor lawyer and organizer. She currently teaches at the National Labor College in Silver Spring, Maryland.

Richard Stahler-Sholk is an associate professor of political science at Eastern Michigan University. He has served as a human rights observer in Chiapas on numerous occasions since 1994.

Bob Stone is on the editorial collective of *Grassroots Economic Organizing*. He is among the co-founders of the bilingual Center for Global Justice in San Miguel de Allende, Mexico, where he serves as a research associate.

Chris Tilly is professor of Regional Economic and Social Development at the University of Massachusetts Lowell and a member of the *Dollars & Sense* collective. He has worked in Latin America solidarity movements for many years.

Harry E. Vanden is a professor of political science and international studies at the University of South Florida, Tampa. He has published some 30 scholarly articles and six books, including *Politics of Latin America: The Power Game* (Oxford University Press, 2002).

Matías Vernengo is assistant professor of economics at the University of Utah, Salt Lake City.

Benjamin Witte is a Santiago-based freelance journalist. He is a former editor of *The Santiago Times* and a former reporter for *The Tico Times*.

Printed in the United States
206759BV00002B/103-261/P